No Rules

No Rules

A Memoir

SHARON DUKETT

SHE WRITES PRESS

Published 2020
Printed in the United States of America
ISBN: 978-1-63152-856-9
ISBN: 978-1-63152-857-6
Library of Congress Control Number: 2019918529

For information, address:
She Writes Press
1569 Solano Ave #546
Berkeley, CA 94707

She Writes Press is a division of SparkPoint Studio, LLC.

Interior design by Tabitha Lahr

All company and/or product names may be trade names, logos, trademarks, and/or registered trademarks and are the property of their respective owners.

Names and identifying characteristics have been changed to protect the privacy of certain individuals.

Women in Sexist Society by Vivian Gornick, copyright © 1971. Reprinted by permission of Basic Books, an imprint of Perseus Books, LLC, a subsidiary of Hachette Book Group, Inc.

For my sister—
Her support gave me my freedom.

Chapter 1

January 1971
South Windsor, Connecticut

I slipped the floor-length dress I'd sewn from a purple Indian-print bedspread over my head and pulled it down to cover the two pairs of long pants, three sweaters, and four pairs of underwear I'd put on moments before—then realized how huge my waist looked. If I didn't wear my coat to cover these clothes, my mother would realize something was wrong. I yanked my dress sleeves over all my other sleeves. If anything showed, I'd be screwed.

While stuffing a pair of jeans and my fake suede jacket with a peace sign on the shoulder into a paper bag, I scanned the closet for my sandals. I'd need sandals in Southern California. I was certain it would be hot there, even in January.

With my meager belongings stashed for my journey, I took a last brief look at my room—the room in which I'd spent twelve of my sixteen years living in—and wondered how I could abandon all my things: the FM radio that my parents had given me for Christmas three weeks earlier, the guitar I had begged for when I was twelve, my notebooks full of poetry I'd written over the last four years. Above my twin-size bed was a poster I'd made with magic markers the previous spring, flowers and peace signs forming a border around large decorative letters that read, "War is Not Healthy for Children and Other Living Things."

"Don't get hung up on it," I coached myself. "It's only stuff."

I crammed my arms into the sleeves of my brown corduroy winter coat and could barely bend them. Grabbing the paper bag and my schoolbooks, I dashed toward the kitchen, knowing my mother was waiting there to say good-bye before I left for school. I took a deep breath.

"You're wearing your new dress." She sounded suspicious; I avoided eye contact. "I didn't realize you had finished making it."

"Yeah, I finished it last night. I'm late for the bus. I have to go." I dove past her.

"What's in that bag?"

"Gym clothes," I shot back without turning around.

"It's awful big for gym clothes."

"I've got to run, okay? Bye."

I bolted out the side door and let it shut behind me, not looking back to see my mother for what might have been the last time in my life. But I couldn't think about that. If I did, I couldn't leave, and I had to leave. This was my only opportunity.

I knew she was standing by the door, following me with her eyes, that worried frown cemented on her lined, sad face.

While closing the chain link gate behind me at the end of our driveway, I recalled the dreams I'd had throughout my childhood where I tried to escape through this gate. I was always running with legs of lead that made me move in slow motion, trying desperately to run faster as long arms reached out to drag me back. I never knew what I was running from in those dreams, but I always awoke before escaping. I couldn't let that happen now.

Dirty snow lined the road, remnants of yesterday's storm. I snickered at it. *Sunny California, here I come*, I thought. *Only one last ride on the school bus.* My heart raced, making me almost dizzy.

❄❄❄❄

The warning bell rang, signaling that homeroom was about to begin. I scanned the nearby students walking through the hall, looking for friends with cars. I needed to find someone willing to skip out of school after they took attendance in homeroom and drive me to Hartford, twenty minutes away.

I spotted Dixie and suffered a moment of guilt knowing all the money from the profits of the underground newspaper we'd worked on together were stuffed in my coat pocket. Dixie had written the last issue's cover story on a Black Studies group at our school, typed the mimeograph sheets, and endured insults from our journalism teacher right alongside me. It was my creation, though, I rationalized, stuffing down my guilt. All that mattered now was that Dixie was a junior, a grade ahead of me, and had friends with driver's licenses.

I cornered her near the wall and spoke quietly. "Dixie, I need a ride to Hartford right away. I did it. I'm leaving home today and going to California with my sister. I can't live like this anymore, hiding my whole life from my parents."

Her eyes grew wide, reminding me of Liza Minelli, that same elfish dark hair framing her face. "Oh my God! Far out! How are you going to get there?"

"Anne bought a car yesterday for fifty dollars, even though she can't drive. Eddie's going to drive it." I balanced my oversize paper bag and books awkwardly in my arms; I hadn't made it to my locker yet.

Dixie cocked her head to the side and frowned. "I thought

you and Eddie broke up when that chick from California moved in with him."

"We did." I nodded. "It's a long story. I can't tell you now because I have to get out of here or they'll leave without me. Anne wouldn't, but I can't trust Eddie and he's driving. He tried to get her to move to Boston yesterday, but I convinced her to go to California instead, like we were planning to do in the spring."

"What a shit! Your own sister?" Dixie glanced around. "Don't worry. I can help you. Meet me in the girls' lav by the cafeteria right after homeroom."

"Thanks, Dixie. I'll never forget this." I turned to hurry off before the bell rang.

"Think of me when you're sitting under a palm tree smoking a joint," she called out, and I turned and smiled back at her before darting away.

❮❮❯❯

I didn't know the two friends of Dixie's who drove me to the city, but I had seen them around school. I followed them to the student parking lot, not turning around to avoid looking suspicious. Once in the car, I watched out the rear window for anyone who might have noticed us. My jaw ached from clenching it all morning. I wished I still prayed, so I could pray that I made it to Hartford before Eddie and Anne took off. Nine o'clock was his deadline, and it was eight thirty-five. Luckily, Dixie's friend was a fast driver.

I tried to focus on the future. Everything after today would be perfect, that much I knew. Without my parents telling me what to do, my problems would be over. If it weren't for them, Eddie would still love me, and we'd still be together. They were ruining my life, just like they'd ruined Anne's when she was my age, and I couldn't stand it anymore. I was screaming inside to break free.

Minutes before the deadline, we reached the apartment building where Anne lived with her coworker.

I hopped out, bag of clothes in hand. "Thanks for the ride, you guys. Say good-bye to Dixie for me."

The driver raised two fingers into the peace sign. "Watch out for The Man, and stay cool."

I took the stairs to the second floor two at a time and banged on the door. When Anne opened it, she already had her coat on.

"You made it!" She smiled and threw her arms around me, her blue eyes a bit teary, her long brown hair falling against my face. She was my big sister, and even though I had almost caught up to her, she was still taller than me. She whispered close to my face, "Eddie didn't want to wait. He kept trying to get me to leave without you."

Her words caused a dull pain in my chest as I looked past her into the room where Eddie was pacing, his hands buried in the pockets of his navy-blue pea coat. I ached at the sight of the familiar brown corduroy bell-bottoms flapping over his square-toed Dingo boots, the way he lurched when he walked, obviously impatient. He glanced at me from the corner of his eye as though afraid to look straight at me, his dark, chin-length hair obscuring much of his face. He pulled at his mustache self-consciously.

"Let's hit the fucking road," he growled, turning to grab his bag.

"I'm so glad you made it," Anne said out loud, looking into my eyes, her mouth quivering. "There's no way I was going without you."

"That's cool for you chicks," Eddie snapped. "You get caught, the cops send you home to mommy and daddy, but my ass is in the slammer. This is crossing state lines with a minor. It's a felony. Anne, you're cool, you're twenty-one, but Sharon, you're nothing but jailbait. I don't know how I got talked into this."

Even after telling myself I was over Eddie, it stung to hear him speak to me this way. After all, he had been my lover, my first and only. How could he act like that had never happened?

Once outside, we threw our belongings into the backseat of our new ride, a white '59 Dodge Coronet with winged taillights pointing backwards like a jet airplane's. Anne sat up front with Eddie and I climbed into the back. It was painful seeing Eddie and Anne sitting together as a couple.

Snow began to fall as we reached Interstate 84 west, and the windows started to fog. I wondered when my mother would figure out I had left. I guessed probably not until I didn't come home from school, although with her suspicious nature, it could be sooner. My father would be home from work at four o'clock. She would be hysterical by then.

I blocked that image out, forcing myself to think about California and not my parents. Everything was happening so fast, but I knew I had to escape; otherwise, I would drown in their misery.

Chapter 2

1960s
South Windsor, Connecticut

"I wasn't always like this." My mother gulped down tears, her eyes red from crying. She looked at me, then away, the white Mallen streak of her hair falling forward onto her face. She felt around and pushed it back into her hair grip as she looked down at me. At seven, I had seen her cry too many times already, and it always caused me pain.

"I was carefree and happy," she continued through tears. "I ran everywhere. I used to laugh all the time."

She took my father's shirt from the clothesline, folded it, and placed it in the wicker basket next to me.

I knew I should be helping her, but I hated going into the basement with her and sorting laundry. It was boring, and there seemed to be no end to it. She almost never asked me or Anne for help, so I didn't think of helping her until I heard her crying.

"Mother always told me, when you have daughters of your own, they will help you. I had to do everything." Her crying stopped and she was starting to sound angry. This was a familiar story that she told often. "I had to take care of my baby brother all by myself when I was twelve and Mother had a nervous breakdown. I had to stay home from school, cook for Father, change and wash the diapers, clean the house. No one even thanked me."

It was as though she wasn't talking to me anymore, but instead to an invisible person. I took the towel she handed me and folded it as she continued, "Mother said, don't worry, when you grow up your daughter will help you." She turned and looked at me in anger. "But you two don't help me at all. I had to do everything then, and I have to do everything now. When will it be my turn?"

"I would help you if you asked." I avoided her eyes, feeling ashamed.

Her voice grew louder. "I shouldn't have to ask. You can see I need help. Someday, when you get married and have children, you will have to do this, so you need to know how."

I got a bad feeling inside when she said this, thinking how awful that future sounded. Would I cry all the time too?

It wasn't so bad when Anne and I did jobs together. Then we could talk. But Mummy got mad when we talked. She would complain that we were so busy talking, we weren't getting the work done.

Mummy handed me a blouse of mine from the clothesline and threw the clothespins into the bag she had made from fabric scraps to hold them. I started to fold the blouse in half.

"Not like that. You'll put a crease down the middle and it will be harder to iron." She grabbed it from my hands. "Never mind, I will do it myself. You just make more work for me. Take this other basket with the ones I folded already upstairs and put it in the living room. And don't let those clothes tip over."

I grabbed the two handles on each end of the wicker laundry basket and headed upstairs, glad to have an excuse to leave.

❖❖❖❖

The only time my mother seemed happy was when she played the piano. Chopin was her favorite composer. Playing his music, she transported herself back to England—where, I was certain, she longed to be, studying piano as she had before the war.

I was still seven when the piano became part of our lives. My parents spent weeks dragging us from one store to the next, searching for one they could afford. My mother insisted she could find more ways to save money to have one, but I couldn't imagine how. Already she made all our clothes, saved green stamps to buy furnishings, and grocery shopped with a paper and pencil in hand, adding the prices of her purchases to ensure there was enough money in her purse before she got to the register. She even made my father's boxer shorts and our winter coats, and knit our hats and mittens. When the ice cream truck drove down our street and the other kids ran out to greet him, I knew better than to ask for any. There was no money for such frivolities.

My father reminded us often that we were not poor, however.

"We have a roof over our head and food on the table. There are a lot of people in the world who don't," he told us while we were all eating dinner together one night. "In London during the war, I would see families living in the subway and I would give them the care packages my mother sent. They needed those things a lot more than I did. We are very lucky, having what we do."

I knew my father had grown up in a poor neighborhood of immigrants in Lawrence, Massachusetts, where his parents had worked all their lives in the woolen mills, speaking only Lithuanian. My father had worked there too before Pearl Harbor was bombed and he was drafted.

He was proud of owning his own house, a dream his VA loan and his job assembling jet engines at Pratt and Whitney Aircraft had made possible. He hated unions, as he blamed them for causing the mills to close and move out of Lawrence. So when the union at Pratt and Whitney went on strike, he'd risked being injured by crossing the picket lines to work. As a result, he'd earned enough money during the strike for a down payment on the house. Then he'd quit smoking two packs of Camel cigarettes a day so he could afford the mortgage.

The day the piano arrived, I sat beside my mother as she dug out her sheet music from a cracked, worn, brown leather bag that she kept in her steamer trunk with other mysterious treasures from her former life. I was always intrigued by what lay hidden under the trunk's heavy lid with its clunky, metal buckles.

"Why is this picture of a boat on here?" I asked her, pointing to the partially missing sticker of the bow of a large ship plastered to the side of the trunk. Although I knew the answer from other times I had asked, I loved to hear her repeat the story of her journey to America.

"That's the ship I came over on from England, the Holland America Line. It was a Dutch ship, see the windmill behind it? They pasted it on the trunk so they would load it on the correct ship. I had to ride out three miles in a tender with my trunk. That made me seasick for the whole six days of sailing."

"How come you had to ride so far to get on the ship?"

"It was just after the war, and the British weren't letting Dutch ships land yet. It was difficult getting any ship at all. The only reason I got on that ship was because I was getting married to your father, and he was an American soldier. Otherwise, I would have had to wait longer."

I knew about The War. My parents talked about it often, and even at seven I was keenly aware of the importance it held in my parents' lives. It had killed Mummy's oldest brother, the uncle I would never know, the person she'd loved most in her youth. And it had brought my parents together on a train full of troops as they were both returning to their bases, my mother in the British Signal Corps, my father in the American Army Aircorps. They were two people from different worlds who had nothing in common and would never have met otherwise.

After the piano arrived, music filled our house: soft, gentle music; sentimental, romantic music; music that spoke of starry nights and green pastures; music that evoked English gardens and Irish eyes; music that caused my mother to sing instead of cry, and occasionally to sing and cry.

I enjoyed sitting nearby and listening to her play. Once, when she was taking a break after singing one of them, she told me, "When I was in the army, the only piano available was in the local pub. I would play songs and all the soldiers would gather around and sing. We had a lovely time, all of us. We could forget about the war for a while. It was great fun."

Another time, she was playing a difficult Chopin piece and was getting frustrated, replaying the same section over and over, until she finally stopped, looking defeated. "All I ever wanted to be was a concert pianist, but my piano teacher told me I wasn't strong enough," she said. She turned her hands to look at them as she spoke. "He said a woman's hands aren't big enough, which is why there are no women concert pianists." She looked at her hands a moment longer before rising from the piano stool. "Besides, I wanted to get married and have a family, and

I couldn't do that if I was a concert pianist, after all," she said, looking into my eyes.

Anne was twelve then, and my mother offered to teach her to play, but she declined. I didn't get it. Playing the piano looked like fun. I begged her to teach me, even though I was only seven.

"Sharon, come here!" she called, beckoning me to the piano, one afternoon. "I have a new book of songs for nursery rhymes."

She opened the cover, pulled out a cardboard foldout, and placed it behind two sets of piano keys, right in the middle of the keyboard. The foldout had different colors that aligned with each piano key, and they had letters on them, A through G.

I turned the page to the first song and was surprised that the musical notes were in all different colors too. In my mother's music books, they were all black.

"Each of these colors on the keys corresponds to the color of the musical note on the page. When the note is yellow, you hit the key next to yellow, and when the note is orange, you hit the key next to orange."

She arranged my fingers over the keys, then put her hands over mine and showed me how to move them. Easy!

Within a few days, I could play the songs in the book by myself. And best of all, I could do something that Anne couldn't, so I was pretty sure Mummy loved me best.

The nursery rhymes got boring after a while. I wanted to play the real music with the black notes like she did. When she decided I was ready, she bought another book where the music was easier at the beginning and got harder as you continued. Over time I progressed through the music, but as it got harder, I practiced less and was less interested in playing.

❖❖❖❖

When I was nine, the Beatles appeared on the *Ed Sullivan Show*. After that they were all I cared about, the same as Anne, who was fourteen. The Beatles didn't play the piano. As a result, I announced I was not going to play the piano either, which made my mother cry again. I thought Anne was so cool, and I wanted her to think I was too. She knew all the neat fashions, hit songs, and trendy dances.

That summer, when the Beach Boys became popular, Anne and I fantasized we were surfer girls with boys dropping at our feet. We pretended we lived on a beach in California where we hung around with surfer boys as we lounged on chairs in the backyard and listened to the transistor radio she'd bought with babysitting money. We put on sunglasses and pretended to be sunbathing, though we were actually sitting in the shade so our pale skin wouldn't get burned.

This was our secret; we knew we were too old to be playing pretend, but it sure beat real life.

Throughout our childhood, my mother insisted on raising us both as though we were living in England. American children, she told us, were too loud, rude, and impolite, and she would not have us "behaving like the hooligans" in our neighborhood.

Our neighborhood was full of inexpensive ranch houses in a development carved out of a tobacco field. The neighbors' children played hopscotch, baseball, and tag in the road, which ended nearby in a cul-de-sac. They circled their bikes and red wagons into groups and congregated until after dark during the summer. But Anne and I were forbidden to play in the road, or with most of the neighborhood children. I had to play hopscotch on my driveway and play in my own yard, unless I was formally invited to someone's house.

On balmy summer nights with my window open, I listened to the other kids laughing and screeching to one another outside and, consumed with longing to be out there with them, cried into my pillow.

Anne's high school reality was quite different from our fantasies. My mother made her wear ankle socks instead of the stockings other girls wore. She was not allowed to wear makeup, and only wore homemade clothes. In winter, my mother made her wear red rubber boots that fit over her shoes, which she removed on the school bus and hid under the seat until the ride home. Already she was the brunt of taunting and private jokes.

At home, she screamed, cried, and argued with my parents, begging for more freedom, nicer clothes, or lipstick, while I watched. *They will not do this to me when I am her age*, I thought to myself, seething. *When I am a teenager, I will have a life, whether my parents let me or not*. But how exactly that would happen, I had no idea.

At school, I made a few friends from other neighborhoods, but because of our rapidly growing town, our neighborhood was frequently redistricted into different schools. That meant leaving behind my new friends and having to start over.

Toward the end of fourth grade, I finally made a friend who lived nearby. Mary Ann came from a large family and her house was always full of children. I was allowed to go to her house when I was invited. When summer came that year, she invited me to play in her pool. I couldn't swim, but it wasn't that deep. Kids could stand in it. And maybe I would even learn how to swim! My heart pounded with excitement as I headed home to tell my mother the good news.

"I don't want you going in her pool," Mummy replied, her voice full of worries. "Too many children play in there. They may not wash, and they may even pee in there. I don't want you getting sick."

I stood immobilized; my summer fun gone in a flash. None of this had ever occurred to me, but I assumed my mother knew best. I wondered how all those other children could be swimming in there and still be alive.

I never went to Mary Ann's house again, as that summer her friends became the ones willing to join her in the pool.

What my mother knew was fear—a creeping, pervasive kind of fear that reaches out of the dark edges of your soul in ways I didn't understand. When the airport near us began having night flights, planes occasionally flew over our house on a landing approach, low enough so we could hear the engines roaring overhead. I was startled from my sleep one night when I heard her screaming from her bed. I ran to my parents' room and found Mummy sitting up with wide, terrified eyes, my father holding her closely.

"She thought it was the Germans," he explained. "She thought it was a bombing raid and she hadn't heard the air raid signal."

I climbed up next to them and hugged her too. When she came out of her daze, she seemed embarrassed. "Those darn planes, they scared me. I'm sorry I woke you." She cuddled me in her arms, reassuring me that everything was all right, before rising to take me back to my room and tuck me into bed.

There was more fear in her than I could ever understand. I did understand, however, that she needed to protect me and the people she loved because she knew how little it took to lose the most important people in your life.

🍀 Chapter 3

1968–1969
South Windsor, Connecticut

It was election season in the fall of 1968. Richard Nixon was running for president of the United States against Hubert Humphrey, while at Timothy Edwards Middle School, Joe was running for class president against Lenny.

Lenny was good looking, popular, a below-average student but an athlete. All the girls were in love with him. Joe was smart, funny, outspoken, wore glasses, and struggled with bad skin. He had plenty of ideas about how to improve our school. His popularity was limited to the nerdy kids in honors classes. He also sat in front of me in my eighth-grade current events class.

Our current events class was in charge of running the school election so we could learn about the election process. I joined the voting day committee, as did Joe. We appointed ourselves as roving officials, a role that allowed us to wander the halls while talking and laughing together.

At the end of the day, Joe asked for my phone number and I gladly gave it to him. He lost the election to Lenny, but later that night, when he called me, he said he didn't care anymore, and I knew he meant "because of you."

A few weeks later, we were going steady.

Like Joe, I was in all honors classes and getting A's and B's, except in math. Joe was applying to go to East Catholic High School, a school with a strong academic program where most of the students went on to college. Many others in my honors classes were applying also, and I wanted to be one of them.

"We can't afford to send you to East Catholic," my mother replied when I asked about attending. She put aside the shirt she was mending and looked me in the eye. "Besides, they're all going to college, and we can't afford to send you to college. And you'll never get a scholarship. You have to get straight A's to get a scholarship and you have a C in math."

"But maybe I could work my way through college," I pushed on, hoping to find a better answer. I had heard of students doing this.

My mother frowned and gave me a doubtful look. "It's too hard to work your way through college. You would never make it." She picked up her mending and continued sewing the frayed seam without looking at me. "Besides, girls don't need to go to college. I've told you that before. They only go there to find husbands, and you don't need to go to college to do that."

Her voice had that tone to it that said there would be no arguing with her. She cut the short piece of thread off with scissors, then threaded a new, longer piece through the needle to continue the repair.

"If you learn how to type and take shorthand, you can get a good job as a secretary. I could never do shorthand fast enough, but you could learn, just like Anne did. There is always a demand for secretaries. I don't know why Anne doesn't get a job doing shorthand. She could do better at work."

Mum had a book of shorthand from a business school she had attended in London. It was full of squiggly lines that were supposed to be words or even whole sentences that a secretary would write while the boss was dictating, so that she could type everything out in full at a later time. I could not imagine how anyone could memorize that nonsense. I thought about Anne in her job as a clerk typist at The Travelers Insurance Company. She was bored. She spent her evenings and weekends at home with my parents, having no more fun than she did in high school. After she paid her room and board to my parents to help with expenses, she had just enough money to buy clothes and records and put a few dollars in the bank. What was the point?

"What if I don't want to be a secretary?" I argued. "What if I want to do something else? I could be a writer! I had that poem published in the *Hartford Courant*, and I even got fan mail!"

My mother stopped sewing again and sighed, her left hand forming a fist on the armchair, her face twisted with frustration. I could feel as much as hear the impatience in her voice as she said, "If you want to have a career, you can't get married and have a family. You can't do both. You have to choose." She nodded her head for emphasis. "And if you aren't going to get married, then you shouldn't be thinking about boys!" She glared at me now. "There is no point in dating if you're going to be a career girl. It's a lonely life, if that's what you want."

My father, who'd been sitting in the room seeming not to pay attention to our conversation, folded his newspaper and looked at us. He rubbed his brow and shook his bald head. "I'm fifty-seven now and I'll be forced to retire at sixty-five, before you could finish college. We won't be able to support you. You'll need to have a job. Even if you could pay for college, what would you live on?"

My mother, no longer looking at me, talked to my father as

though I wasn't there. "I've always said it was a good thing we had girls, because I have no idea how we would have paid for boys to go to college. You know how I always wanted boys because they're much easier. My brothers never caused my parents any trouble at all, not like these two."

My father said nothing in response, just returned to reading the *Hartford Times*. I stormed out of the living room, entered my tiny bedroom, and slammed the door behind me, wanting to scream. I had homework to do, but I didn't care. No one asked to see my homework anyway, since my parents admitted they didn't understand it. My father had dropped out of school at sixteen to work in the mill, and my mother had taken nothing but piano lessons after fifteen, since any higher education was not required in England.

What was the point of getting good grades in honors classes if I was going nowhere? Even my C in math was for an advanced-level algebra class. Maybe I would have an A if I were taking eighth-grade math!

I sat on my bed, picked up a magazine a friend had given me, and started reading a short story called "Baby Hip." It was about a teenage girl who leaves home to live in Greenwich Village and become a hippie.

❧ ❧ ❧ ❧

It was Christmas Eve. I had the day off from school, but Anne was in bed with the flu. It was boring without her to talk to. I stared at the beige rotary phone sitting on the old maple wood cabinet next to the kitchen table, wishing Joe would call. Normally we talked on the phone every day, but I knew he was busy with his family.

When the phone finally rang, I grabbed it. "Hello?"

"Hi," my father's voice said softly. "It's Dad."

"Oh, hi." I was disappointed. I lowered my voice so Mum wouldn't overhear. "I found out what to get Mum for Christmas."

I knew he'd been too tired to shop and hadn't been feeling well. He thought he was getting the flu, but if he called in sick, he wouldn't get paid for the Christmas holiday. He was determined to make it through the workday.

"Not now," he interrupted in a hoarse voice. "Tell your mother I have the flu, and I'm coming home. I have to go to medical to get a pass first."

Three hours later he still wasn't home, and he only worked twenty minutes away. When the phone rang again, Mum answered it and listened silently for a long while.

"Is there anything I can do?" she finally asked. "Should I go to the hospital?"

She listened again.

"Okay. I'll wait for the doctor to call."

My mother slowly replaced the receiver on its cradle, then turned toward me. Her eyes were watery, and her mouth was quivering.

"That was Medical at Pratt and Whitney. They said he doesn't have the flu, he's having a heart attack." She gulped before continuing. "They took him to Manchester Hospital in an ambulance. I have to wait for the doctor there to call me. She said it may be awhile and I should wait here." She stared at me.

I stared back at her, stunned. Then I felt tears pour from my eyes, and my mother started to cry too. I walked over to where she was standing and put my arms around her, feeling her warm, soft body shake. She reached her arms around me too and we stood together, sobbing.

I couldn't believe this was happening. It was Christmas Eve; we should all be sitting by the tree together. If I didn't think too hard, I could pretend my father was still at work, as he always was during the day, and not in an ambulance racing along for his life.

Hours passed. Anne was still sleeping, and Mum didn't want to wake her since she was sick. It grew dark as the two of us sat together in the kitchen, discussing how this could have happened and what would have happened if he had come home instead of going to Medical. We would not have known to call an ambulance.

Anne finally awoke and staggered into the kitchen. When Mum told her what had happened, she started crying along with us, but we kept our distance from her, not wanting to catch her flu. The hospital called once to tell us they were admitting my father, and that the doctor would call back with more details later. We waited. The evening lingered on. Anne finally grew too feverish to stay awake and crawled back to bed with more aspirin. Mum realized we hadn't eaten and made a bologna sandwich for us to split; we both nibbled on our halves, but my mouth didn't seem capable of chewing. After a while, my mother sent me to bed, saying she would wake me as soon as she knew anything.

I couldn't sleep. I lay in bed, thinking of all the sleepless Christmas Eves I had spent trying to hear reindeer hoofs on the roof or imagining the gifts that would be under my tree in the morning. It all seemed stupid now. How could I have ever thought that mattered? I tried to imagine life without my father. I prayed the *Our Father*, several *Hail Marys*, and the *Our Father* again. I offered deals to God, promising never to want anything for Christmas again, just as long as he let my father stay alive. I clung to the clear blue rosary beads I had recently received for my Catholic Confirmation, hoping God could hear me better that way.

Much later, I heard the phone ring. I listened to my mother's calm voice from my bed. When she finished, her footsteps approached my room, and I held my breath. She left my bedroom light off, so only the light from the hallway came in as she opened the door. The springs of my bed squeaked as she sat on its edge.

She reached out and stroked my hair away from my face. "Your father's alive, but he's in intensive care. Apparently, his heart stopped for two minutes and they used electric paddles to restart it, but he's out of danger now." Her voice choked out the words. "The priest was there and gave him last rites."

Last rites! They had thought he was going to die! My mother and I wept and held each other, then she suggested we say a prayer together. We folded our hands and said another *Our Father*. It made me think of when I was little, and we knelt by my bed as we said my bedtime prayers together. I remembered the two of us praying: *Now I lay me down to sleep. I pray the Lord my soul to keep. If I should die before I wake, I pray the Lord my soul to take.*

Please don't take my father's soul tonight, I prayed silently that night. *Please keep him alive.*

❖ ❖ ❖ ❖

Christmas morning, we didn't open our presents. We stayed out of the living room and didn't look at our tree. Anne was still sick, so Mum and I went to the hospital to see my father without her.

I'd never been in a hospital. The receptionist gave my mother directions to the intensive care unit, and we wound our way through the halls and took the elevator up three floors. The nurse there informed us we could each go in alone for five minutes and we couldn't get close to him.

I waited outside the room while my mother went in first. Then it was my turn.

The room was full of tubes and machines that were attached to a frail old man who I realized, with a jolt, was my father. He lay in the bed, his eyes straining to open, unable to speak because of the tube down his throat. I knew I should speak, but would he even hear me? He scared me, this ghostly shadow of my father whose breath I could hear long and slow, in and out, in and out. I took his hand and was surprised at how cold it was. He gave me a weak squeeze. I knew I mustn't cry. That would make him feel worse, wouldn't it?

"I love you, Dad. Get better soon."

His breath went in and out faster and I heard the beep, beep, beep of the heart monitor accelerating.

The nurse walked over to my side. "Time to go now, dear. He needs his sleep."

⋘⋙

The presents stayed under the tree until my father came home three weeks later. Each day, Mum and I—and later Anne, when she was well—went to the hospital to visit him as he gradually improved.

I was miserable during school vacation. I grew depressed, bitter, and angry. I needed a reason for this, so I blamed my father's job. I believed if he didn't have to work so hard, standing and lifting all day in the heat, cold, and noise of the plant, this would never have happened.

When Joe called, I didn't want to talk to him. What did he know about this? His father worked in an office where he sat at a desk. He didn't have to see his father come home in dirty work clothes with slivers of sheet metal clinging to them. I couldn't talk to Joe about what I was feeling, because I was sure people like his family looked down on people like my family. I hated Joe because he could afford to go to East Catholic, and to college. He would never know how it felt to be trapped in a lifetime of scrimping and saving, having nothing, wanting everything, and knowing the future offered nothing better.

When I went back to school in January, I gave Joe his bubble gum machine ring back and told him I didn't want to go steady anymore.

A few months later, we had to enroll in our high school classes. I refused to take math, which wasn't required at the time. My parents agreed that algebra was useless, said they didn't see the point in learning it.

I enrolled in art, typing, and home economics. I made sure I didn't take any honors classes. My parents thought I was making good choices in deciding to learn practical skills. I hoped the school would place me in classes with kids like me—kids who didn't care about college.

Chapter 4

August 1970
Connecticut

"Sharon, look!" Anne alerted me in a loud whisper as we started crossing Main Street in downtown Hartford. "Check out these guys."

Two men with long, dark hair, mustaches, and bell-bottom jeans, one in a tie-dyed T-shirt, the other in a plain white T-shirt with WOODSTOCK FESTIVAL written across the top and a picture of a dove sitting on a guitar handle below it, were crossing the other way. They were several yards away, but they looked straight at us.

I was feeling bold on this August Saturday, a few days before my sophomore year of high school was due to begin. Anne had just turned twenty-one; I wouldn't be sixteen until November. We'd taken the bus to downtown Hartford for the day—"to go shopping" is what we'd told our parents, but our real goal was to look for excitement. I was wearing my new woven headband, and around my neck were several strands of beads I'd strung together. Anne wore large, round, rose-colored sunglasses.

"Keep staring," Anne encouraged me as the two of us continued across the busy downtown road.

Instead of turning away, we looked straight at them as they passed, and their eyes stayed latched onto ours. Finally, we spun forward, giggling wildly to each other over our brazen behavior. As we reached the sidewalk, I glanced back to see if they were still watching us.

"They turned around!" I gasped. "They're following us!"

"Really?" Anne's eyes went wide with surprise, and her cheeks flushed pink. "Walk slow," she muttered through clenched teeth.

We calmed our pace to a nervous crawl, unsure of how close they were. They caught up with little effort and, after a moment's hesitating, one of them spoke.

"Where you chicks heading?" Woodstock T-shirt asked. "Going to the park?"

"No, we're on our way to have lunch," Anne answered.

There was a small restaurant in Hartford that had become a ritual for us to dine at ever since Anne started working and she could treat me. We both looked forward to it.

"You don't want to go to lunch. Let's take a walk to the park, see what's happening."

"Actually, we do want to go to lunch," Anne said. "In fact, we're here now." We'd arrived at the restaurant, a small breakfast and lunch spot with prices Anne could afford. "Do you want to join us?"

I heard the nervous excitement in her voice.

"Yeah, I guess we could get a cup of coffee," Woodstock T-shirt replied. He held the door open for us while we walked into the dinette.

We settled into a booth for four, Anne and me on one side and the two of them on the other, next to a silver jukebox on the wall. I was sitting across from the one in the tie-dyed T-shirt, who had thin hair to his shoulders, no smile, and droopy eyes that made me wonder if he'd recently woken up. Anne and I took the menus from the metal stand on the table while the guy across from Anne did all the talking.

I was awestruck over the presence of these real hippies, particularly the one across from Anne. He had long, thick, chin-length dark hair, dark brown eyes, and an olive complexion. He had a dimple in his chin and a thick mustache. Italian, I thought. I hoped he couldn't tell how young I was. Anne often told me I could pass for seventeen.

"So what's your names?" he asked. "I'm Eddie. This is Gene." Gene nodded in our direction.

"I'm Anne, and this is my sister, Sharon."

"Sisters, huh? All right." He nudged Gene, who pulled out a pack of cigarettes and offered each of us one.

We declined.

"Gimme one of those," Eddie said, taking one from the pack. They both lit them from Gene's lighter, then turned their attention back to us.

"Did you go to Woodstock?" Anne nodded toward Eddie's T-shirt.

"Sure. It was far fucking out. Hey, you chicks seen the Woodstock movie yet?" Eddie smoothed down the ends of his mustache with his thumb and index finger, almost hiding the tiny dimples to the side of his facial hair. His devilish smile sent strange shivers through me.

"No, but we have the album," Anne told him. "We've been playing it nonstop since June."

"You ought to go see it. It's playing right up the road at Cinerama. They got quadraphonic stereo and a huge wide screen. No other movie theater like it." Eddie flicked the ashes of his cigarette into the ashtray on the table, then turned his face upward and blew smoke through his lips.

The waitress arrived to take our order.

"Just coffee for me," Eddie told her.

She gave him a disdainful look. "There's a three-dollar minimum at lunch time. If you don't want to eat, you'll have to leave."

Eddie and Gene looked at each other and, shaking their heads, rose to leave. "This place sucks. Let's get out of here. See you chicks around, okay?"

"Okay," Anne replied. I was disappointed that they couldn't stay.

We ordered club sandwiches and Cokes, then burst into a flood of conversation once we were alone.

"Oh my God!" Anne blurted out. "Do you think Eddie liked me?"

"Yeah," I said, "he kept looking at you the whole time. He was really cute. Maybe we should have left with them."

"We'll walk around after lunch. Maybe we can run into them again."

I wished I was old enough for Eddie to like me but knew he probably thought I was a kid. Anne put a quarter in the jukebox at our table and "Mama Told Me Not to Come" by Three Dog Night began to play.

We didn't run into Eddie and Gene after lunch, and although we talked about Eddie for days after, I never expected to see him again.

❧ ❧ ❧ ❧

Two months later, in mid-October, a political rally was held in downtown Hartford at which Senator McCarthy was to speak in support of Joseph Duffy, a peace candidate running for Senate in

Connecticut. Although McCarthy had been defeated in the democratic presidential primary in 1968, he was still actively outspoken
against the Vietnam War and remained a huge draw. The event
would take place during lunch hour on a Thursday, and any student
at South Windsor High with parental permission was allowed to
leave school to attend.

After I swore to my mother that practically the whole school
was going, and that I could ride the city bus downtown, she wrote
me a permission slip. I forged two more for my friends Carolyn
and Joanne, and Anne and I made arrangements to meet when
she was on her lunch break.

Carolyn, Joanne, and I arrived downtown early. We were
walking around when I recognized the hippie walking toward
us as Eddie. A few days prior, Anne had reported spotting him
downtown for the first time since that chance encounter two
months earlier.

"Bring him with you when you meet me at lunch," she had
joked that morning, and we'd both laughed over that daydream.
Now the daydream approached as I rapidly filled in my friends.

"Carolyn, that's him! The guy I told you about. He is so far out!"

"He's cute," Carolyn acknowledged. "Do you think he
remembers you? You should talk to him."

As he approached, I scanned his face—that same familiar
face I had memorized in the restaurant—for signs of recognition.
He wasn't much taller than me. His hands were buried deep in
the pockets of his unbuttoned navy pea coat, and his wide-wale
corduroy bell-bottoms swayed with each step.

He slowed to a stop as we grew near. "Any of you chicks have
a light?" He smiled as he placed an unlit cigarette between his lips.

"I think I do," Carolyn answered, smiling back. I could tell
she liked his attention as she searched the contents of her fringed

tote bag. She produced a book of matches and lit one; he cupped his hands around hers to block the wind.

"Is your name Eddie?" I asked, already knowing the answer.

"Yeah, where do I know you from?" He turned his eyes toward me as he raised his head to exhale smoke into the air above him.

I was elated to think he might remember me.

"My sister and I met you last summer, on our way to eat right over there at that restaurant." I nodded in the direction of the building, which sat just a block away. "Do you remember?"

"Oh yeah, I remember that." He smiled at me as though this meant we were old friends, and I was thrilled all his attention had shifted to me. "Where are you chicks going? You skipping school?"

"We're walking around until the rally starts on the plaza," I explained.

"Mind if I come with you?"

"Sure," I agreed, giddy with excitement, wondering if I could convince him to stick around long enough to meet Anne with me at lunch. *She will die*, I thought to myself as we rounded the corner to Union Place.

We stopped first in a dimly lit head shop cluttered with clothing racks of flag print shirts and flowering bell bottoms, wall posters illuminated by neon black lights, and drug paraphernalia. Eddie monopolized the conversation, telling me how he had recently returned from Florida, where he'd jammed with the Allman Brothers, and had been at Columbia University during the student strike two years earlier. I was impressed by how much he had done.

As we all walked back toward the rally, he surprised me by reaching over to hold my hand, an action I felt was warranted: it would keep me from flying up into the clouds. When Eddie wasn't looking, Carolyn winked at me, and then she and Joanne started walking ahead of us.

I explained to Eddie about meeting my sister for lunch, and he agreed to wait for her with me. When we reached the building where Anne worked, Carolyn and Joanne promised to meet me at the city bus stop at two thirty, in time to get back for the school bus ride home, and left for the rally.

We leaned against the wall of the Travelers Insurance Company, watching the clean-cut men and women leaving the building for their lunch break. Some looked over at us and grimaced. I loved it. *Let them eat their hearts out, wishing they were free like us,* I thought. Eddie put his arm around my shoulders and leaned in close to my ear, making small talk.

After about ten minutes, Anne came out through the doorway. When she spotted us—Eddie's arm around me and his face near mine—her face froze in a look of shock.

"Look who I ran into," I announced, gloating in my accomplishment of capturing the prize. "He wants to come with us to the rally."

"Sure," she answered, not looking at me or Eddie as she led the way to the plaza. I had expected her to be excited but instead I could see she was hurt, and I regretted gloating.

Anne had never considered me a threat with guys she was interested in. It had not occurred to either of us that I was old enough to be one, as my sixteenth birthday was still two weeks away. Eddie's interest in me was unexpected, and I felt as though I had advanced several years forward, to the age I wanted to be.

The crowd was elbow to elbow on the plaza when we arrived, and the three of us squeezed through to get closer. I could hear a speech over the sound system, followed by cheers and applause, but I wasn't following the event. Only Eddie's hand in mine had my attention. My stomach fluttered. What waited for me in the future? Where would this lead? And how would I ever convince my parents to let me see him again? For I knew with absolute certainty I would see him again. Nothing they could do would stop me.

When Anne's lunchtime was over, she barely said good-bye before turning to hurry back to work. I could tell she was upset. Eddie suggested we walk to the park instead of being squeezed by the mob of onlookers, and I let him pull me through the crowd, oblivious to the people we passed.

The mid-afternoon sun had taken the autumn crispness out of the air. Striking blue skies and wispy clouds offset the gold, yellow, and red leaves filling the trees of the park; the green grass had been raked clean by city workers. Bushnell Park was small enough that you could see most of it from one end to the next. There was no privacy to be had, so I felt safe there with this guy I barely knew.

He stopped by an area of grass that was thick and dry and pulled me down to sit with him. Then he wrapped me in his arms and kissed me, leaning me back into the grass.

My eyes darted around to see if anyone was watching. I was filled with apprehension, worried I was in over my head. We were in broad daylight, but his assertiveness scared me. I knew free love was an integral part of the hippie lifestyle, same as smoking pot. I was torn between enjoying his kisses and worrying about where this was leading.

Finally, I pulled away and sat up to check my watch. It was two twenty. I was going to miss the bus if I didn't leave immediately.

"Don't worry about it," Eddie reassured me. "I can drive you back to school."

"But my friends are supposed to meet me, they'll be wondering what happened."

"They know you're with me. They'll figure you're having a good time and didn't make it. Don't be so uptight. You worry too much. Enjoy yourself, have fun."

I knew he was right. I did worry, just like my mother. And how much fun did I ever have? Hippies didn't worry, they lived for the moment, and I wanted to be that way too.

"Okay, I'll stay a little longer, as long as you promise to give me a ride to school by three o'clock."

"I told you I would, didn't I? You can trust me."

And I did. I trusted him at that moment and for the next three months we spent together. I trusted him when he called me each day and we talked late into the night, when he asked me to be his steady chick and told me he loved me. I trusted him when he took me to his apartment, and I gave him my virginity. I trusted him until the day he stopped calling and I learned two girls from California had moved in with him and his roommate.

But on that October day in the park, all that was still to come. On that day, we walked to his car through fallen leaves that filled the sidewalks. I loved hearing the swish, swish, swish of our feet kicking through them, and the feel of Eddie's arm around my waist, holding me close. I loved watching his heavy leather boots step in time with my shoes, thinking how right they looked next to each other and how magical a day this was.

Chapter 5

January 1971
Venice, California

Anne, Eddie, and I arrived in downtown Los Angeles as the light was disappearing from the late-afternoon sky. We were on our way to the YWCA; I had called ahead to inquire if Anne and I could get a cheap room there.

"I hate fucking LA," Eddie grumbled as he steered across five lanes of freeway traffic and made a quick right off the exit.

"Careful with Anne's car," I wanted to shout, but then I thought, *Why bother?* Although she'd paid for the car and everything else on this five-day trip, since neither she nor I had a driver's license, we needed Eddie to get here. In exchange, he was keeping the car. I held the directions I had scribbled in a phone booth at a gas station earlier, glad I would only need to listen to Eddie's rambling for a short time longer.

"I don't know why you chicks want to stay here. Look at this smog, you can't even see the sky, this is fucking gross. I wouldn't stay in this shit hole. You chicks should come to Bakersfield. Why use all your money in this fucking place when you got somewhere to stay there for free?" He glanced sideways at me in the passenger's seat, then into the rearview mirror at Anne. "How come no one's talking? I mean, what the fuck! I drive you all the way out here and this is the thanks I get?"

Not like you did it for free, I argued silently. Anne and I were both fed up with listening to him. Eddie had a former girlfriend in Bakersfield and had been trying to convince us to join him, but our plan had always been Southern California; we wanted to be near the ocean.

The YWCA appeared as we drove off the exit. Eddie jerked the car over to the curb, oblivious to the honking traffic. Jumping out, he rushed to the trunk, pulled out our belongings, and dumped them beside us on the sidewalk.

"You're making a mistake staying here. But what the fuck, can't tell you chicks nothing. See you around."

He hurried back into the driver's seat and inched away through the traffic. I waited for sorrow to set in, but all I could feel was indifference. This trip had taught me more about Eddie than I had learned in the three months we'd spent together as a couple. My parents had managed to limit my time with him, but all that had done was make me like him more. I suppose they were trying to save my virginity, but there is always time for sex, no matter how little time there is. They should have let me spend every minute of every day with him, so I got to know him better. That would have ended it.

❖ ❖ ❖ ❖

Anne and I shared a dormitory style room with four other women that night and were given a copy of the New Testament.

In the morning, we rode a bus to the end of the line, where Venice Boulevard stops, then walked onto the beach for our first view of the Pacific Ocean.

"There it is," I said, reverence in my voice. "We're here."

That January afternoon, the air was cooler at the beach, so I slipped my arms into my jacket and buttoned it against the breeze. We strolled along Ocean Front Walk, a wide, straight walkway separating the beach from the city. In the distance, someone rode a bicycle toward us; on our right, a lean, bearded man accompanied by his golden retriever walked by, nodding a greeting in our direction.

We sauntered south, awed by the newness of the landscape: palm trees planted at intervals in the sand, low one- and two-story stucco buildings facing out to sea, some with high walls and wrought iron railings. I kept thinking, *This is really happening. This is California, just like in the movies!*

The bicycle we had been watching approach inched by, and its rider greeted us. When we answered his hello, he spun the bike around and pedaled along beside us.

"I've never seen you two out here before. You new to Venice?" He was wearing a red bandana as a headband. Under the bandana, he had long, sleek, black hair. His Fu Manchu mustache gave his grin a slightly sinister appearance. He was tall and fashionably hippie thin in his faded bell-bottom jeans with a few patches of colorful fabric sewn over the worn spots and heavy, leather sandals. I later discovered his tan skin and high cheekbones were the result of his Cherokee descent.

"Yeah, we just got here," Anne replied. "Someone told us this is where all the hippies live, so we're checking it out."

"This is *The Place*, all right. Where're you from?"

"Connecticut. We just got to California yesterday."

"My name's Ed. What's yours?"

"Oh no," we both said in unison. "Not another Ed!"

"Hey!" Ed said indignantly, applying the brakes on his bike. He stepped off the pedals. "Ed is a good name. Just because you know some asshole named Ed, you can't condemn us all. I'm a nice guy. You should get to know me."

We introduced ourselves and he continued riding his bike as we walked, asking us questions, occasionally circling us like we were prey he was cornering and stalking. He made me nervous.

"Want to get stoned?" he finally asked. "I live just a couple of blocks from here."

Anne and I exchanged uncertain glances, searching for a clue from each other. The offer was tempting. I knew she was as eager as I was to try some California grass.

He let out a low chuckle, apparently amused by our hesitation. "Hey, you don't need to be afraid of me, I don't bite." He laughed again, then added, "Not unless you want me too."

Finally, Anne agreed. I wondered what we were getting into, my stomach churning.

❦ ❦ ❦ ❦

Ed lived in a yellow one-floor stucco house on the corner of two canals. Bushes were falling over onto the sidewalk, leaving little room to move between them and the water.

We entered his living room, where a huge American flag with a peace sign in place of the stars hung across one wall; on another was a psychedelic poster of a couple sitting in a tantric sex embrace, facing each other, arms and legs encircling one another. Peter Max posters of each of the Beatles hung in rainbow hues along the side wall. I was awestruck.

As we walked across the room, my feet sank into the wall-to-wall carpeting. It felt like I was walking on pillows; I wondered what was underneath.

Ed switched on the stereo, then the TV, leaving it silent. The first guitar riffs of Jimmy Hendrix's *Electric Ladyland* blasted as colorful electrical streaks pulsed through an attached globe in time to the music.

Ed motioned for us to sit on his faux couch—padding a few inches thick that encircled the room, including a back rest leaned against the wall that was covered in matching fabric. Looking up, I saw an Indian bedspread hung harem style from the ceiling, obscuring a yellow light bulb.

Ed sat cross-legged across from us and laid out several joints. He lit the first one and took a hit before passing it to Anne, and then me.

"So tell me what brought you here," he said.

We took turns telling him our story, including how I was sixteen and had run away from home and that our parents had no idea where we were.

Ed offered us Red Mountain wine out of the bottle to wash down the smoke, which made me choke a bit. I had never had wine before; it burned my throat with its heat and tartness. He laughed at my reaction and listened to our tale with a delighted expression on his face.

"Listen, you two," he said when we were done. "I need to fill you in on a few do's and don'ts if you're going to be staying here in Venice, and you are going to both have to learn quickly." He gave me a stern look. "First, don't tell anyone you are sixteen. From now on you are eighteen. Learn your birthday, learn a new name, forget the real one, it doesn't exist anymore. Sixteen is too young for a lot of the things that go on around here."

I told him I wasn't that innocent.

He laughed. "You've never lived in Venice before. Most of the parties I go to, I wouldn't dream of bringing you to. You have no idea of what goes on around here. Are you both on the pill?"

I was shocked at this personal question, but he asked it so matter-of-factly that I felt obligated to provide an answer, a muttered no that was barely audible while I blushed. Anne had gone through the routine in Connecticut of borrowing an engagement ring and lying to a doctor that she was getting married so she could legally get a prescription. I'd had no such opportunity, nor the money, to perform the necessary charade.

"Well," Ed said, "get down to the free clinic right away. It opens every weekday at four o'clock over on Venice Boulevard— it's next to the police station. They give you pills free. Remember, you're eighteen. They don't check. You can always get an abortion now in California if you need one, but I've heard it's not a fun thing to go through, so make sure you don't have any sex until you get them."

His bluntness surprised me. I had never heard a man speak so openly about stuff like this.

Ed reached into his pocket and pulled out a small metal box. He opened it to display some dried herbs that looked like pot.

"Here, smell this stuff," he ordered, passing the box under our noses. It had a sickly, perfumed scent. "If you're ever at a party and you smell this, don't smoke it, unless you want to get really fucked up. It's this new stuff called Angel Dust, just started going around here. I'm sure they don't have it back in Hicksville, Connecticut yet. Somebody gave me a hit of this stuff and I damn near passed out. And I've done more than a few drugs in my day!"

Anne and I exchanged anxious looks with each other while Ed continued his intro-to-Venice narrative.

"Listen, I've lived here for a long time, and I'm not going anywhere." He lit another joint and passed it to me. "But I see these guys come and go all the time in this town. They don't give a shit about you, so don't let them take advantage of you. I'm going to see you every day walking down the street. If you need anything, come see me. I'll take care of you. I know you're probably thinking who the hell is this guy, but I'm very up front about who I am. I don't bullshit anyone. Why bother?" He shrugged his shoulders and looked from Anne to me and back again.

I was fascinated by this man, so different from anyone I had ever met. But, of course, I had never lived in California before. Ed was just the beginning.

"And hey, if you chicks want to make some money, I'll sell you some mescaline for fifty cents a hit. You can turn around and sell them for two dollars each."

Anne told him thanks, then inquired where we might find a place to stay that night—we planned to look for an apartment in the morning.

"You can stay here if you want. I have a big bed." He winked. "But not until after midnight, 'cause I have company until then." He stood. "Or you could try the Other Side Coffee House out on Ocean Front Walk. Keep walking the direction you were going when we met, you'll come to it. Good people run it. They could probably help you out."

I staggered to my feet, nearly falling over on the pillow-floor. Anne looked stoned; she giggled as Ed walked between us to the door, his arms around us both.

"Make sure you come back and visit, okay? Good luck!" He leaned over and kissed me on the lips quickly then turned and kissed Anne. He was smiling as we wandered out the door.

 **Chapter 6**

January 1971
Venice, California

The morning after we arrived in Venice, getting our own apartment was our top priority. We had walked nearly the length of Pacific Avenue searching for an affordable place in a half-decent building with two young men from Texas we'd met over breakfast. Bob and John had offered to drive us downtown to fetch our belongings from the YWCA once we found a place, and I was enjoying their company; they had a relentless sense of humor that kept Anne and me laughing throughout the tedious search.

We entered yet another building and buzzed the superintendent. She had a vacant apartment for $90 a month—Anne could afford that. While we waited for her to return with the key, Bob sat on the stairs that led to the second floor and stared into my eyes as I conversed with John. I'd never understood the attraction to blue eyes until this moment. What was it about Bob's? Was it his almost smile that told me he was flirting, or those magnetic eyes that were reaching right into my soul? I wanted to turn away. I knew I was returning his gaze for far too long to pretend innocence. John was my typical type, chin-length dark hair and dark eyes. Bob, on the other hand, had curly, light brown hair just long enough to suggest a budding afro, a beard that was still trying to fill in, and a dimple in each cheek.

I shifted away from Bob's stare, self-conscious, but he continued to focus on me as he spoke, as though the world began and ended with my face. By the time the superintendent returned, something in my stomach—I later came to know it as longing—cascaded through me every time I looked at him. The feeling grew more intense as the day wore on.

Anne and I agreed to take the one-room furnished studio with a tiny kitchenette and an old-fashioned bathroom containing a claw-foot tub and no shower. A small, unvented heater gave off a strong odor of gas in the room, and there was only one twin bed, but we loved it. Our very own apartment! We'd fantasized about this since we'd pretended to live by a California beach when I was nine!

Bob and John helped us separate the mattress from the box spring to make a bed each for Anne and me. As Anne was paying the rent, I claimed the box spring, where my jacket would serve as a pillow and my coat as a blanket.

When it was time for the ride to retrieve our belongings, I was surprised to discover that Bob's car was a two-seater Triumph Spitfire convertible.

"We can do this," he assured us, noticing the dubious looks on our faces when we saw the tiny car. "It's been done before. It helps to take the top off. How 'bout we leave it in the apartment? That'll make room for your stuff."

We agreed. He and John started unsnapping the canvas hood from the red sports car and folding it accordion style, but the storage area behind the seats was still full.

"We'll have to take our stuff out, too," Bob said. "Otherwise, I dunno if y'all's will fit."

Bob opened the trunk and heaved out a box of canned goods, while John pulled coats and bags from behind the seats and handed them to Anne and me. Within a few minutes, our apartment was cluttered with their belongings. We paused to smoke a joint together, sitting cross-legged on the floor in the apartment, leaning against boxes and jackets, having a few more laughs before the ride.

Finally, giggling from the effects of the pot, we maneuvered our way into the car's small space. Bob climbed first into the driver's seat, and John slid into the seat on the passenger's side. The two of them half lifted me over John, and I positioned myself partially on both seats, Bob's jacket padding the emergency brake, my shoulders bending inward as I squeezed between Bob and John. Anne nearly fell face first into John's lap as she climbed into the car, and the four of us collapsed in a laughing fit.

It was a warm, sunny day, and I enjoyed the wind hitting my face as I rode above the line of the windshield back into the city. I had to cross my legs so Bob could shift, but the top of his hand still rubbed the outside of my thigh each time he did, regardless of how much room I tried to make. Occasionally I glanced sideways at his handsome face a few inches away, feeling the warmth of his arm pressed solidly against mine.

Once at the YWCA, we loaded our belongings into the trunk. We had to tie one suitcase to the luggage rack to make it all fit. On the ride back, a motorcycle passed us and the driver gave us a peace sign, then a tractor-trailer truck double honked its approval; we joked that passing vehicles must think we drove all the way from Texas like this.

≪ ≪ ≫ ≫

By evening, I'd lost track of the number of joints we'd smoked, and my face hurt from laughing. We strolled along Venice beach, then climbed onto the rock jetty near our new place to watch our first sunset over the ocean.

Back at the apartment, we threw together a dinner for the four of us with the canned goods from the guys' car, cooking in an old frying pan that had been left in the apartment.

"Tomorrow we have to go to the Salvation Army store and get cooking utensils, plates, and stuff," Anne said as we scraped up the last bits of food from the frying pan with our plastic spoons. "But right now, I've got wicked munchies. Let's go see what they've got at the Liquor and Deli on the corner. There's one right near Ed's house."

"Who's Ed?" John asked.

"This guy we met yesterday on Ocean Front Walk. He's got tons of drugs. He offered to sell us mescaline for fifty cents a hit."

"Wow." Bob perked up immediately. "What do y'all say we drop mescaline and head to Malibu tonight? God, it's such a beautiful night, I can't imagine a better time and place to trip. Y'all up for it?" Raising an eyebrow, he looked directly at me.

Hearing that Bob wanted to continue this dreamy day made me warm all over. My mescaline trips in Hartford had been interesting, but the prospect of tripping under the stars at Malibu beach with this exciting new guy sounded like pure fantasy. I couldn't imagine a better time and place myself.

"That'd be far out," I replied. "I'm up for it. Ed said come over anytime, so I guess we could go now."

I loved that Bob enjoyed discovering California as much as I did. They'd been in Bakersfield for a few weeks but had only arrived in LA the day before.

Anne, John, Bob, and I stopped at the Liquor and Deli for Twinkies along the way to Ed's house, stuffing them into our mouths like starving children. Bob wiped a bit of Twinkie cream from my check.

I could hear Ed's stereo blasting as we approached, even though his lights were barely visible. While Anne knocked, I imagined his warm welcome. Instead, he peered through the crack of the door, scowling, before opening it to let us in.

Ed shut the door behind us and motioned for us to sit on the floor. The couch area was already occupied by several stoned people; one couple groped each other in the corner. I waited for Ed to crack a smile, but it didn't come.

"This is John and Bob," Anne introduced them as we sat. "They helped us move today. We got a place on Pacific Avenue. We wanted to get some mescaline to trip tonight."

Ed's scowl grew fiercer, bordering on anger. I wondered what could be wrong. He looked from Bob to John.

"You guys got any pot?" he demanded.

"Yeah, sure." Bob looked confused.

"Well, bring it out, let's smoke it."

Bob pulled a joint from his pocket with a worried look on his face. He lit it and passed it to Ed, who took a good, long hit before passing it on. Without another word, he rose, beckoning to Anne and me to follow, and led us into the kitchen.

Spinning around to face us, he launched into an attack. "Now listen and listen good, because I'm only going to tell you this once. Don't ever, *ever*, bring anyone over here again! You two are welcome anytime, but there are narcs everywhere, and you don't know who these guys are. You chicks don't know your way around here, and I'm not about to get busted because of your stupidity."

I felt frightened by the hard anger in his face.

"They're definitely not narcs," I assured him, worrying about what might happen next. "We've been smoking with them all day.

And they're not even from around here. They have a car with Texas license plates and everything. They're really far out, I swear."

I recognized the way Ed was looking at me now, as though my naiveté was showing. The anger began to disappear from his voice, replaced by sarcasm.

"Listen, sweetie, I'm glad you're enjoying yourself, but I'm going to look out for my ass, because no one else is going to. I can't let a little innocent sixteen-year-old get me busted, however sweet you may be. That's why I asked to smoke their pot. Narcs aren't allowed to smoke when they're working, it's one way of flushing them out. If they didn't bring pot, none of you would still be here right now."

He paused, watching us closely to see if we were getting the message. I began to relax as I heard a touch of softness finally come from his mouth.

"And remember what I told you about these transient guys, okay? Have a good time, but don't go getting attached. I've seen this happen too many times. And by the way, I offered to sell you mescaline so you could sell it and make money, not go turning all your friends on."

He shook his head like a distraught parent, wondering what to do with these naughty children before him. Anne responded to his calmed tone by asking for what we had come for.

"Can we still get some mescaline? Maybe ten hits?"

He shifted his eyes from her to me and back again a few times, a smirk on his face.

"This is highway robbery, you know. I'm not even breaking even at this price." He walked out the back door and returned with a brown paper bag. He pulled a plastic baggie from his kitchen drawer, counted out ten white gelatin capsules and placed them inside it, then handed it to Anne.

When she passed him the five-dollar bill, he held onto her hand with both of his.

"This is a favor, so you owe me one now. Remember that." He leaned over and gave her a quick kiss on the lips. "Next time, come alone."

He was smiling at last, a satisfied smile that made me slightly uncomfortable. Tossing his head back to fling his long black hair away from his face, he slid both hands into the front pockets of his jeans, then leaned toward me and whispered in my ear, "You too," then kissed me briefly as well.

He straightened and looked at us both. "You chicks have a good time, okay? This is a nice, mild trip, nothing scary, so enjoy the ride. And by the way, I'm having a party tomorrow night. Why don't you come by?"

Flattered by the invitation, we agreed, then headed back to the living room to leave. As I turned to say good-bye, I saw him leaning against the doorway watching us, one hand running his fingers through his hair to brush it from his face, his mustache framing a wicked grin. I wondered what the mescaline would really cost.

❖ ❖ ❖ ❖

By the time the mescaline was taking effect, the four of us were once again packed together in the car, defying the design intentions of Triumph engineers. As we rode along Highway 1 under the stars, I buttoned my winter coat tightly against the cold wind that blasted over the windshield.

When we arrived at Malibu Beach, we descended the stairs along a sand cliff to reach the ocean—a location from my adolescent dreams. I wondered on this whimsical evening if this was indeed my life now, or if I would roll over in a moment and find myself back in my room, alone in my bed.

The mescaline was mild, as Ed had promised. No hallucinations, just a heightening of the senses and a feeling of joy and abandonment. I sat in the sand for a while, watching the white foam of the incoming waves rise before breaking near shore and then gradually thinning out before me, turning from a deep whoosh into a high-pitched hissing.

"Want a hit?" Bob asked from behind me, jolting me from my hypnotic state. I stood and turned to face him, staring into those haunting eyes lit by moonlight and mescaline. My fingertips lingered near his as he slipped the joint between them. I raised it to my lips and inhaled deeply, holding his gaze now that drugs were giving me courage. I slipped the joint back to him as John approached.

"Hey Bogart, how 'bout passing that joint over here?"

Bob handed it to John without looking at him, then John moved away.

Unencumbered, Bob wrapped his arms around my waist and pulled me close to him, exploring my eyes with his for an extravagantly long moment. I reached my arms over his shoulders, resting them on the wide sheepskin collar of his suede jacket. I feared I would collapse in a heap of desire if he didn't kiss me soon. When his lips at last touched mine, I understood passion for the first time, a sensation so consuming I would have failed to notice the devil's own fire if it had been burning at my feet. My existence consisted only of his warm, silky mouth exploring mine, the gentle pressure of his strong arms as he pressed his body against me, our thick coats keeping a teasing barrier between us.

A strong ocean wind blew my long hair across his face, and he gently scooped it away, running his fingers through it to hold it in place. I let my fingers wander through his thick curls, eager to explore the newness of him, to finally give in to the impulses I had felt all day.

I had daydreamed and imagined that kissing could be magic, and this moment proved it. Could anything be more perfect? Caution meant nothing to me. I wanted to indulge myself in its glorious spontaneity, follow where it led me, into new realms. Bob sparked sensations in me I'd never known existed before this moment.

We made love for the first time in our new apartment, with the early-morning light coming through the window. Neither of us had slept all night as we squeezed together on the twin box spring, oblivious to the jabbing spring ends. Anne and John had quietly fallen asleep on the other mattress hours earlier, in a tacit agreement of friendship only. I had spent hours pretending to resist Bob, never wanting to for a minute, conflicted over this vast confusion of emotions. Sex with Eddie had been dutiful and dull, a routine I went through with the belief it was part of being "in love." Now, for the first time, I experienced desire, propelled by the incredible joy I felt being in Bob's company for nearly twenty-four hours, the best of my life. I thought maybe I should be waiting, but also sensed this was no ordinary moment. Some people waited their whole lives for someone who could make them feel this way, I was certain. I was a free person now. I could follow my feelings wherever they took me. I could worry about tomorrow, tomorrow.

 **Chapter 7**

February 1971
Venice, California

You do your thing, I do my thing.
I am not in this world to live up to your expectations,
and you are not in this world to live up to mine.
But if by chance we find each other, it's beautiful . . .

These words (a quote from Frederick Salomon Perls's Gestalt prayer, I would later learn), were on a poster in our apartment, along with two hands reaching out to one another, not quite touching. I pretended I agreed with this attitude about relationships, because wasn't that how I was supposed to feel? Inwardly, though, I thought it sad that two people weren't supposed to touch—that they could hover in each other's presence but never completely connect.

In the three weeks since I'd met Bob, I hadn't managed to get used to his random arrivals and departures. I knew I had no claim to him. My heart soared when he walked in the door from wherever he might have been and filled with despair when he drove away two or three days later.

Bob had been back from his latest escapade for one day, and we were awake on the single box spring we shared. It was nearly morning, and the only light in the room came from streetlights. He had woken me with his insistent caresses while I groaned and brushed him away, begging for more sleep.

Suddenly, a strange vibration shook the floor, startling us both. Bob sprang to his knees and jerked open the window blind, but it crashed down on him and he was thrown back to the bed. The room was swaying, like we were sailing over ocean swells in a great storm without a solid piece of ground beneath us. It was as though the walls and floor were stretching and heaving in opposing directions; hairbrushes and bottles jiggled across the dresser top, and cabinet doors banged open and shut in the kitchen.

Instinctively I cried out to God, begging him not to let me die, terrified that this was my final moment on earth. It didn't matter that only weeks before I had pronounced myself an atheist. The God of my Catholic childhood exploded from my subconscious. My thoughts flooded with visions from pictures I had seen of the earthquake that had struck Peru months earlier—how buildings had collapsed and tens of thousands had died—and I wondered if I would be a faceless statistic in tomorrow's world news. My mind screamed at the unfairness of the possibility. From the next bed I heard Anne wail, "Oh my God! Oh my God!"

The whole event took less than a minute. Once the room stilled, Bob and I threw open the window above the bed. I expected to see wide cracks in the ground with buildings tumbling in, but the street looked surprisingly unchanged, except for the absence of lights. There was an eerie silence punctuated only by a distant hissing and snapping of raw electricity.

Bob fumbled around on the table next to our bed for Anne's transistor radio and switched it on, scanning first the FM, then the AM radio bands. Silence. Had Los Angeles been destroyed beyond our street? Anne came over to my bed and sat near me, gripping her own arms into a hug, her eyes wide and teary.

"Can y'all find a candle?" Bob fiddled with the dial. "I'll keep trying to get a station. Isn't there supposed to be an emergency broadcast or something? It's all dead air!"

He located a voice as we felt a second tremor, a tiny one in comparison, but long enough to renew our fear. The announcer spoke in a soothing tone.

After a few minutes, I sensed a group exhale, and then we all began talking rapidly.

"I thought that was it, I really did," Anne said. "But it doesn't look like anything happened except the power went off."

"Wow," Bob said. "I have been through hurricanes and even tornadoes in Texas, but they're nothing like this. What the hell can you do? You can't outrun the damn thing!"

"I was sure I didn't believe in God," I told them. "Now I don't know. When you feel this close to death, it makes you wonder."

We rattled on at each other until we succumbed to the laughter that follows fear, nervous giggling that shook through us like a small tremor.

"You know what?" Bob interrupted, jumping up. "There's only one thing to do: get stoned! I'll bet Jack's up. Let's go see."

Jack lived downstairs from us in a basement apartment. After Bob's first absence, he had returned to Venice without John, and Jack was his new buddy.

"I'm going to try to sleep," Anne told us. "Maybe I'll come down later."

When Bob and I reached Jack's apartment, he and his roommate Bill were already smoking.

"Hey, man. Come on in, have a toke." Jack stood in the doorway holding a joint, his tailored shirt unbuttoned and hanging loosely over stovepipe pants that were two inches too short. Jack had returned from Vietnam and been discharged from the Marines a few months before we met him. He looked like a civilian of an outdated era, without a single pair of bell-bottoms in his wardrobe. His straight blond hair was beginning to grow, but not enough to fit in.

With the radio for our centerpiece, we settled around the room on the pillows and chairs in the studio apartment. Jack crouched on his mattress, leaning against the wall with his knees to his chin, chain-smoking cigarettes. His stance—his elbows resting on his knees, one arm dangling in front of his legs, the lit end of the cigarette cupped inside his hand—was appropriate for spending long hours in fox holes, hiding burning butts from enemy eyes.

Jack was the first Vietnam veteran I'd met, and the Vietnam he spoke of didn't sound like what I'd heard about on the evening news. Any time we got together, the conversation would turn to his experiences there. Even today, as we discussed the earthquake and what we could do while the power was out, Jack brought it up.

"Over in 'Nam, we had our ways of entertaining ourselves. My buddy and I, we'd smoke a few bones and then slip out over the hill and light grenades, fling 'em into the hootches. Man, you should see those things burn. Looked like the goddamn Fourth of July."

"Were there people in there?" I was horrified.

"Just gooks. They're all trying to kill you while you're sleeping, we were getting them first." He broke into a cackle, amused at the look on my face.

"But how do you know there weren't children in there?"

"The kids are more dangerous than the grownups. They'll walk right up to you like they're trying to sell you cigarettes, and next thing you know, out pops a grenade. That's in the villages, though, not in Saigon." He relaxed and his expression changed, turning to a knowing smile. "I gotta admit, I had a terrific girl living with me in Saigon. I really miss her. 'Nam is a great place, except for the war. A guy like me can live pretty good. What the hell do I have here?" He motioned across the room at the small studio. "If you're tough, and you know your way around the streets, there's nothing you can't have there."

"I guess that's cool," Bob said. "Never heard anyone tell it like that."

Music had returned to the transistor radio, and Elton John's love song, "This Is Your Song," played. Bob sat across the room, watching me, and began singing along to the words as if he was singing them to me. His eyes looked full of emotion, telling me things I longed to hear him speak. *Is he telling me he loves me with these lyrics?* I wondered. But I knew this moment would pass and tonight, or another night, he'd be gone again, leaving me to pine in his absence. "Don't be good, be happy!" he liked to say on his way out the door, as though instructing me to go raise hell. I did my best to take his advice, but it never made me happy.

Bob and I left Jack's apartment mid-morning to walk on the beach. We held hands as we strolled over the wet sand. The waves were breaking about ten yards closer than normal. Our hands stayed locked together, as though the solidarity between us would keep us safe from the unforeseeable future.

❖❖❖❖

Bob, Anne, and I were milling around the apartment later that day when there was a knock on our door. I peeked out, and found Ed standing in the hall.

"I figured I'd stop by and make sure you chicks survived our surprise this morning," he said. "How's it going? The question of the day is, what were you doing when the earthquake struck?"

I stepped out into the hall and closed the door behind me as Ed gave me a quick kiss.

"We're fine. I was awake, then we got stoned."

He smiled. "Listen, the reason I came by is I finally got some acid. I promised you next time I scored, I'd turn you on to it since you've never tried it. Want to come over tonight and trip with me?"

I hesitated, wondering if Bob had heard. I had been wanting to try LSD, but since Bob was around, I wanted to stay with him.

"I can tell you have company, I didn't mean to interrupt," Ed acknowledged, backing away.

I heard the rattle of Bob's car keys before I heard his voice, and I knew what it meant.

Bob opened the door and brushed by us on his way out. "I'm meeting Jack," he said without looking at me. "See you around."

I felt the familiar ache I was growing used to as I watched him leave. I knew he would be gone for more than the afternoon. Was he leaving anyway, or leaving because of Ed? I wished I could turn off my feelings as easily as Bob seemed to and simply have a good time, like he kept saying I should.

During Bob's absences, I'd started visiting Ed, figuring this constituted not being good but happy. I pretended I was wild and free, but I didn't feel wild and free. I felt confused. I wanted Ed as a friend, but sex was part of the package for him. At thirty-three years old, he was gifted in the art of manipulation far beyond my insight. His interest flattered me, although I wasn't sure if I was glad for it or upset by it. I felt I needed to prove myself to him because of my age, and he seemed to enjoy this advantage. I listened when he told me what to do since he was older and wiser, and the person who knew everything about life in Venice.

Ed's friendship wasn't only about sex, however. We had thought-provoking conversations that I didn't have with anyone else, including Bob. All the hip books were on his bookshelf, and he encouraged me to read them. Herman Hesse's *Siddartha*, Alan Watts's *The Way of Zen*, Robert Heinlein's *I Will Fear No Evil*. He took great pleasure in introducing me to concepts and ideas I'd never heard of, as though he were molding me into who he thought I should be. Having no idea who I was, I followed his lead.

"Sure, I'll trip with you," I told Ed. "Why not?"

I went over to Ed's house in the early evening, feeling I was about to be initiated into a hippie fraternity. He handed me a tiny yellow-orange pill called Orange Sunshine.

"I've been told this is really good stuff," Ed warned me. "Get ready."

I swallowed, and we went into the kitchen to make popcorn while we waited for it to take effect. About ten minutes later, I jumped as I noticed movement in the darkened pantry to my left. Nothing was there. I felt mildly apprehensive.

"See something?" Ed asked.

I nodded.

"We're starting to get off already. We better go sit down. We're in for one hell of a ride."

The mescaline I'd taken in the past needed an hour or two to take effect, then increased gradually, then peaked for a few hours before wearing off. By the time I sat in the living room, I was losing my ability to stand.

The next several hours were an onslaught of uncontrollable thoughts, dreams, hallucinations, fears, and visions. I never moved from the floor. All sense of time and space vanished. Colors pulsated with sound, music danced before my eyes, dizzying patterns collided randomly. During moments of coherency, I attempted to analyze what was happening so I could describe it in detail to Anne. The thought of what must be going on in my brain frightened me. It was as though all my neurological circuits had crossed, causing one sense to have the experiences of another.

At one point, I noticed an annoying buzzing that wouldn't go away, try as I did to ignore it. Then I realized it was Ed's voice, speaking into my ear.

"Listen to me, listen to my voice. That's better, now pay attention to my words. You're getting too far away, you need to come back."

I was desperate to have it end. "I want to come down," I pleaded. "Please help me come down."

"That's what I'm doing now. I'm talking you down. I'm helping you control it."

"Is that all you can do is talk? Isn't there anything you can give me to make it stop? I can't take it anymore!"

"You think I can give you some magic pill and turn it off? Sorry. You'll have to ride it out."

The hallucinations were astounding. I focused on Ed's face for a while, watching as it changed. Once he had heavy wrinkles and graying hair. Then the wrinkles disappeared, and he had no eyes, just a forehead. Then his head was free-floating, without a body. I saw him as an Indian medicine man, and as a head with arms sticking out of his ears, like something I used to draw as a little kid. Once during this time, I watched torment writhe on his face until he broke into tears. I could tell my brain hadn't manufactured this vision; he was truly crying.

Hours later, as normalcy returned, Ed suggested we step outside—a total lunar eclipse was in progress. Standing by the canal, watching the dark red moon with colors swirling around it, I wondered, *Is this real, or am I still hallucinating?* I felt like I'd experienced baptism by fire and survived.

Later, Ed discovered we had each taken four-way sunshine, a pill intended for four people to share, not one. We had taken enough LSD to get eight people high.

One afternoon, Anne and I received a certified letter from our parents. Stunned, we tore it open and we read how they had been searching for us, and someone had finally shared our address. We had mailed it to a few select friends we trusted.

We called home collect on the pay phone in the hall, huddling together to hear their voices through the earpiece, although that was unnecessary when the shouting began. They demanded that I return home at once; Anne, they said, was free to do what she wanted. I threatened to leave Venice and go elsewhere, although I didn't want to. By the end of the call, I was worried that they may have the police come get me.

It took a couple of more calls to finally reach an agreement. Their local police advised them not to force me to return because if I left again, they might never find me. My parents decided to take that advice and settle for contact. We had to write letters every few days, and they would call us once a week on the pay phone in the hall. But they hoped we'd choose to come back before long.

❦❦❦❦

Bob returned a couple of days after my LSD trip with no more explanation than he had given when he left. I knew the drill. I wouldn't ask; he wouldn't ask. But it pained me not to discuss it. "I got some pot seeds I've been saving," he said that day. "Thought I'd plant them in Topanga Canyon. Wanna take a ride?"

We spent the next few days together sharing greeting card experiences. We rode through the canyon and stopped at another beach, watched sunsets from the rock jetty near our house, and stayed up together until dawn. We sat on our rooftop eating spaghetti for breakfast and watching the sun rise. One afternoon as we laid together with our bodies intertwined, listening to the Crosby, Stills and Nash album, he looked into my green eyes and sang along with the haunting song "Guinnevere." The intimacy between us was growing.

A revelation had emerged during my acid trip with Ed about how deeply I loved Bob. Like psychedelic truth serum, there was no lying to myself, no feigning nonchalance. I wanted to tell him, but I was afraid. So I wrote him a letter.

When evening came, I handed it to him, announced that I was taking a walk, and fled the apartment. I circled the block, wondering if I had done the right thing, but our noncommittal relationship was becoming painful enough that I didn't care as long as something changed.

As I approached my building, I had a clear view into our dimly lit apartment. Bob had his jacket on and was leaning over my dresser, writing something. Immediately, I regretted my decision and was sure I'd driven him away.

Not wanting to face him, I raced to the third-floor roof of our building. I burst into tears as I watched his small red car weave its way up Pacific Avenue.

❮❮❯❯

I need some time to think, his note said. That didn't sound menacing. But the waiting left me fidgety the next day. I finally went for a brisk walk toward the grocery store, so lost in thought that I didn't notice when a car pulled up beside me.

"Hey, Foxy, want a ride?" Bob's familiar voice caught me by surprise. When the Triumph stopped, my trembling hand struggled to open the door. As I climbed into the seat next to him, my heart raced.

He leaned over and kissed me tenderly, lingering for a moment to gaze into my eyes.

"Where're you going?" he asked, turning his attention back to driving.

As we drove to the grocery store, I tried to contain my excitement. I had expected him to be gone for several days, but not even twenty-four hours had passed. And that kiss! When we reached the parking lot, we sat in his car.

"Guess what?" he asked. "I got a job. I'm going to be working replacing glass for this company in Malibu, right in the Malibu movie colony. Far out, huh? It's a good thing, too, cause my unemployment just ended."

I gulped, realizing he would be here all the time now. "That's really far out. I've been looking, too. There was an ad in the paper at the phone company for operators. It said no experience required. I'm going to apply."

A rolled-up poster behind the seat caught my eye. It was new, and my curiosity got the better of me.

"What's this?" I asked. "Can I see it?"

"No."

"Why not?"

"Because. . . Never mind. I'll show it to you later."

This worried me. What was he hiding?

"If you're going to show it to me later, why can't I see it now?" I pressed.

I could see he was becoming irritated, but I couldn't stop myself. Too many unanswered questions left me impatient.

"Okay. If you want to see it that bad, I'll show it to you. It was supposed to be a surprise for later." He smirked as he reached for the poster in the backseat and handed it to me.

I unrolled it to find a picture of a long-haired girl sitting on a rock jetty, gazing out at the sunset over the ocean. Three simple phrases were printed in one corner:

> *I believe in the sun, even when it does not shine.*
> *I believe in God, even when he is silent.*
> *I believe in love, even when I am alone.*

He studied my face as I read the words, their meaning filling me like a rush of heat.

"I was going to give it to you tonight," he explained. "I was going to wait until we were making love to tell you I love you. Then I was going to surprise you with the poster."

I rolled it up carefully, speechless from his romantic gesture. Looking into his eyes, I saw affection and uncertainty as he awaited my reaction. I fell into his arms, ecstatic.

 **Chapter 8**

February 1971
Venice, California

Sunlight filled the room as I awoke the morning after Bob discovered he had lost his job. He had only been there a couple of weeks, but work had been slow. Through my half-closed eyes, I saw Bob's face leaning over me. As I forced myself awake, I realized he had his coat on. There was sadness in his eyes that frightened me.

"I have to leave for a while," he said.

I felt my stomach muscles tighten, waiting for the sledgehammer to fall.

"I'm not sure when I'll be back. Jack's going with me for a few days. But I will be back, I promise. I'm going to leave the quilt my mother made here. You keep it. That way, you know I'm really coming back."

He kissed me long and slow, like it would have to last, and I held on to him, afraid to let him out of my arms, afraid to face a day without him in it. Our plan to get a two-bedroom apartment together in Santa Monica with Anne once she and I found jobs was shattered.

"I love you," he assured me in a whisper.

I choked out my reply. "I love you, too. I'm going to miss you so much."

He looked away toward the window, and I saw the dampness in his eyes. His lips gripped together in what looked like a silent plea for self-control even as my own tears exploded.

He rose from the bed and grabbed his fully packed bag.

He hesitated by the door. "I will be back," he emphasized, then turned and left.

❖ ❖ ❖ ❖

Anne understood my hurt. She licked my wounds like only a sister can and tried her best to take my mind off him. She'd become involved with Bill, Jack's roommate, and the two of them decided I should not be left alone.

Toward evening, Bill was getting fidgety, which was normal for Bill, since speed was his favorite drug. He popped the little white pills on a regular basis; they made him animated and talkative to extremes. Jack found Bill's behavior highly irritating, and the two of them were barely speaking by this point. So Jack's absence left Bill in a celebratory mood.

"Either of you been to the Sunset Strip?" he asked, his mustache wiggling as he licked his dry lips side to side.

"No, we haven't, except on the bus when we first got here," Anne said. "But I've heard a lot about it."

"Yeah, it's a real trip. When they say freaks there, they mean it." Bill giggled in short, quick laughs as he shuffled through his stuff, then jumped up and looked through Jack's ashtray for a cigarette butt. "But there's a whole bunch of clubs and you don't have to be twenty-one to go in all of them. There's always music. You want to go?"

"How will we get there?" Anne asked. "It's going to be dark soon."
"We'll hitch. I do it all the time." He gave a *why not* kind of shrug.
Anything that'd help me stop brooding about Bob was worth
a try.

◈ ◈ ◈ ◈

We arrived at the Strip in the middle of chaos. Flashing neon lights
and blasting music surrounded us as we wove our way through the
human congestion on the sidewalk. Men in cars honked and yelled
out to women nearby.

A guy leaned forward from the crowd as I passed and spoke
into my ear. "Purple barrel acid. Two bucks. Reds, yellows, mescaline, anything you want."

Bill seized both our hands and pulled us into the nearest
shop. It was lit by black lights. Posters of Jimi Hendrix and Janis
Joplin adorned the walls next to pictures of huge marijuana leaves
and motorcycle emblems. Santana's music poured from the speakers at decibel levels designed to block out conversation. I toyed with
the small glass vials of liquid in rows on the counter. They were
labeled "Essential Oils" and had names like Jasmine, Sandalwood,
and Patchouli.

I touched Anne's arm and yelled in her ear, "This is that
patchouli oil Ed was talking about! The stuff he said all hippie
chicks wear and he can't stand!"

"I wish I could afford it." She picked up a bottle and sniffed
before handing it to Bill to smell, but he was already familiar
with it.

We giggled over the idea of a repellent that could keep Ed
at a distance, then Bill pulled out his money for the cashier and
handed the bottle to Anne. We walked back into the street and
began dousing ourselves with it.

"Do you think it keeps away all the assholes?" Anne yelled to me as I rubbed the deep brown oil onto my arms and neck.

"I don't know, but this smells weird. I think I like it!" I yelled back.

"Let's find a place to get a drink," Bill said.

We passed by the checkerboard walls of the Whiskey A-Go-Go; its cover charge exceeded our budget, but a bar nearby had free admission and allowed minors. We went in.

The bar was dark, with black walls and ceilings. Over the stage was a sign that read OPEN JAM NIGHT, and a terrible band whose members looked like high school students blasted their guitars.

We sat around a table as far from the band as possible. An attractive, stoned-looking man wearing a tie-dyed tank top started dancing near our table, then asked me to join him. I stood and bounced around to the monotonous beat. For the moment my sadness faded, replaced by a hollow feeling of indifference.

"Ever do psilocybin?" he shouted in my ear over the noise of the band.

"Yeah, a few times." An image of sitting on a curb tripping with Bob, laughing and out of breath from our sprint along Pacific Avenue, came to mind. I tried to shut it off.

"I'm doing some right now. It's pretty good." He reached into his pocket and pulled out a small, oatmeal colored pill, handing it to me. "Here. It's on me."

Feeling careless, I slipped it into my mouth, thinking this would make the night fun. Soon after I swallowed, I regretted it. What if this was anything like the acid I did with Ed? I didn't know this guy; he could have given me anything. *Don't get paranoid*, I told myself. *Anne won't let anything bad happen to me.*

He talked and danced with the three of us as I slowly lost coherency and stumbled around. After some time, Anne and Bill decided it was time to head home. On the return trip, I got despondent, crying on and off. It felt like hours getting back to Venice, moving from car to car as we caught rides through dark, confusing neighborhoods.

During one ride, the opening notes of Marvin Gaye's new song "What's Going On" came over the radio followed by his haunting voice—and a chill shot through me; it was as though I was feeling his song in my body. I leaned my head back against the seat and closed my eyes, dreaming awake, wondering how life would ever feel right again.

When we reached Venice, it was after midnight. Bill and Anne wanted to go to sleep, but I was still tripping and wide awake.

"I'm going over to Ed's house to get downers," I told Anne. "I need to sleep."

"Be careful on the bridge," Anne said.

Ed's house was near the canal, and occasionally there was a homeless guy under the bridge, but he never bothered me.

I wasn't too high to walk, but it was difficult to see, as I kept crying. When I arrived, it took Ed a few minutes to answer.

"Come in, it's good to see you. You haven't been by in a while." He looked me over for a minute as I stood in his living room. "You don't look good. What's the matter?"

"I'm tripping, and I don't want to be. Someone gave me psilocybin and I can't sleep. I need downers."

"Okay, I can do that. Have a seat. Is that all that's bothering you?"

My tear-streaked face must have given me away.

"That guy from Texas I was living with left this morning."

"You weren't in love with him, were you?" he asked.

I burst into tears.

"What did you do that for? Didn't I tell you to stay away from these transient guys? They're here, they're gone. I warned you. You don't want to go falling in love, you're too young. You haven't even lived for yourself yet."

"Yeah, but he's coming back. He said he was."

He looked at me and slowly shook his head. "Don't count on it, sweetheart," he said softly.

It's not like that, I wanted to say. *He's not one of those transient guys, this is different.* But Ed knew more about everything than I did. I wished I could have stopped myself from falling in love.

"Don't you worry about a thing. Doctor Ed will fix you right up." He pulled out a small wooden pipe with a bowl no bigger than a thumbtack, then unrolled a piece of foil, revealing a nugget of dark brown hashish. He snapped off a chunk, placed it in the pipe, and held his lighter over it while first I inhaled, then he did.

"Is that patchouli oil you're wearing?" he asked with a frown. "I thought you said you never heard of it."

"I hadn't. We bought it tonight on the Sunset Strip."

"God, I hate that stuff. Don't wear it anymore."

"I wasn't planning on coming here, but I didn't know where else to go."

"Well, you came to the right place." He stroked my hair and whispered, "You're so sweet, you don't ever need to worry, someone will always take care of you."

I tried to smile at his compliment, but underneath a nagging anger stirred that I didn't understand. Why did this make me uncomfortable? I should be pleased. I liked the idea of being taken care of. After all, I wasn't having any luck finding a job. Would someone always take care of me? Was I truly that sweet, that helpless, that useless?

I smoked more hash and put the thought deep in the back of my mind. For this moment, at least, Ed would take care of me.

He reached around me and started to remove my shirt.

"Ed, don't. I really don't want to do this, that's not why I came here. Can't we just talk?"

"Yeah, we can talk," he replied gently, continuing to pull at my clothes. "Aren't we talking?"

"You know what I mean. Stop it, please. I can't do this."

I struggled to push him away, but Ed wasn't hearing no. I knew he didn't believe me, why should I expect him to? It was a game to him, and he enjoyed playing it. I yelled for him to stop and pummeled his chest and arms with my fists. He covered my mouth with one hand and pinned my hands behind my back with the other. I bit him on the hand, the shoulder, anywhere I could reach, but he only grew more excited. I knew I was losing the battle.

"You're mine, you're mine," he repeated over and over in my ear when I finally gave up the fight.

A few days later, Anne and I were making lunch when a pounding on our apartment window startled us. She stuck her head around the corner from the kitchen to see who it was.

"It's Ed. I wonder what he wants."

Neither one of us wanted to see him, but she let him in at his urging.

"You both have to get to the clinic right away," he said. "I've got the clap, so you have it, too. Listen, I have to run, I've got a lot of other stops to make. See you both later."

He was gone as quickly as he arrived. Anne was avoiding looking me in the eye.

"You slept with him too?" I was stunned that I didn't know.
I thought we talked about everything.

"Yeah. I don't know why, he's such a sleaze. He asked me not to say
anything to you. I probably should have, but I was too embarrassed."

"It's not your fault," I told her. "I wish I'd stayed away from
him, too. I feel gross. I wonder how long he's had it."

A wave of anxiety swept over me as I recalled the conversation
Bob and I had the night before he left.

"I have to know something," he had asked me. "Have you
slept with anyone else since you've been out here?"

I couldn't imagine why he was asking. Had he already been
experiencing symptoms? Was that why he'd left?

I had told him the truth, because I never lied to someone I
loved. Maybe it was a flaw of mine, this total honesty. I hadn't yet
learned that many men couldn't handle honesty. I also hadn't learned
that I could ask the same question of him. Instead I accepted the
blame, carrying it with me like a scarlet letter, never questioning if
only I was at fault. I had slept with two men, so I deserved whatever
I got. Tramp. Slut. The words all fit, and I had the disease to prove it.

❦❦❧❧

The humiliation continued at the clinic. People jammed the tiny
waiting room. I put my name on the list under "Venereal Disease
checkup." After half an hour, the woman at the desk called on me.

"I need to know the names and addresses of all your sexual
partners in the last month," she ordered.

That was easy. I gave her the two, pointing out that one of
them had left Los Angeles.

"Is that all of them?" She looked doubtful. "Because if there
are any more, we need to know. That's the only way we can stop
this from spreading."

"Really. That's all." Wasn't two enough? Was I that unusual?

Three and a half hours later, I finally had my turn to see the doctor.

"The tests won't be back for a few days, but since you know you've been exposed, we'll give you the medication anyhow."

He handed me a small brown envelope containing mint green capsules. Vibramycin. Two a day. No sex or alcohol for two weeks.

❮❮ ❯❯

Right after Bob left, Anne had cut her hand on a piece of glass while taking out the garbage. Several days later, her arm grew swollen and red. Ed was the only person we knew with a car, and he reluctantly agreed to help.

"You're going to have to go to an LA County hospital since you don't have insurance," he explained, grabbing his car keys and leading us out the back door. "There's only two. One downtown and one in Torrance, twenty miles south of here. I think it will go quicker at Harbor General in Torrance. The gunshot wounds and OD's will all be downtown."

Several hours later, they admitted her and gave her IV antibiotics for the next week, leaving me in Venice on my own for the first time. Over the next few days, I dodged the landlady, who kept pounding on our door for the rent and threatening to put us out on the street. I explained that Anne had the money, but I couldn't get it out of her bank account because she was in the hospital. I don't think she believed me.

I was also penniless without Anne. Bill showed me how to cook brown rice so I would have food to eat until she returned. Between that and pancake mix, I wouldn't starve. He also hitchhiked with me to Torrance to visit her.

Still pining for Bob, I sometimes ran to the window thinking

I'd seen his car return, then broke into tears when I realized it wasn't him. I had never known pain like this before, pain that crept into my dreams and got under my skin. There was a new hit Janis Joplin song called "Me and Bobby Magee" that was on the radio constantly. I cried along with her every time she wailed about how much she missed holding Bobby, and I felt like I too had nothing left to lose.

❄❄❄❄

Later that week, Jack returned from the desert. When he knocked on my door, I was ecstatic.

"Where's Bob? Did you ride back together?" I asked.

He grinned. "Last time I saw Bob, he was wasted out of his mind, tearing across the desert on his way to Houston."

I choked back the anguish rising in my throat. I didn't want Jack to see me cry and look vulnerable.

"I see you're all alone. Must be pretty lonely with Bob being gone. Want to take a walk?"

"Sure, I'd love to get out of here for a while," I said. I went on to explain about Anne being in the hospital.

We walked for ages, talking, following the beachfront path all the way to the Santa Monica pier and beyond. We stopped and watched the men work out at Muscle Beach, watched the sun dip into the ocean and the night sky appear. We walked along the water's edge and smoked a joint, and when we felt we couldn't walk any farther, we crossed the beach out to Highway 1 and hitchhiked back to the apartment house. I had never cared for Jack, but this evening I was grateful for his company. He was being nice, and I needed a friend.

When we reached my door, I told Jack how much I enjoyed the evening and wished him goodnight.

"Aren't you going to invite me in?" he asked.

"No, I'm going to sleep." I turned and unlocked the door.

"Not yet you're not." In one motion, he scooped me over his shoulder, pushed his way through the door, and slammed it behind him with his foot.

"Cut it out, Jack!" I yelled at him as he threw me on the bed.

"What are you doing? I thought you and Bob were good buddies."

"Well Bob's not here, is he?" He threw himself on top of me and held me motionless.

I lay there thinking to myself, *Go ahead, you bastard, rape me. You're going to get the clap, and you deserve it.*

Instead, he did nothing but look at me. Finally, he said, "You know, I could do anything I wanted to you right now and there'd be nothing you could do to stop me." He had that smug expression on his face he always had when he thought he was right and wanted you to know there was no point in arguing. "But I'm not gonna." He let go of me and I pulled away from him and moved toward the door.

"There's something I gotta tell you," he said, still lying on the bed. "I got a message to you from Bob. Seems that before he left, you gave him some kind of disease." He waited for my reaction, a cross between a smile and a sneer on his lips. Blood rushed to my cheeks, as though betrayal had slapped me in the face. How could Bob have humiliated me by telling Jack? Couldn't he have written a letter? Called me on the pay phone? Anything? At least Ed had the guts to tell me to my face.

"He was pretty pissed off," Jack continued. He gloated with superiority, grinning at me like he had the times he'd reminisced about torching hootches and killing gooks.

If this was a contest, Jack had won. I had been reduced to dirt.

He stood, walked out the door, and slammed it behind him.

 **Chapter 9**

April 1971
Venice, California

Life had settled into a routine over the two months since Bob left. Anne and I spent most days making trips to the library for books, hitchhiking to interesting parks, neighborhoods, or free museums, and low-key socializing. We had a few new friends, and hardly ever saw Ed or Jack anymore. Bill had moved across the hall away from Jack and was descending into severe drug abuse, so Anne had distanced herself from him. Our nights were filled with reading and not much else.

Walking along Pacific Avenue on one early evening in mid-April, we ran into Arnie, a friend of ours who lived nearby. He was moving to Hawaii and invited us to join him at his good-bye party where he was heading. We were thrilled.

We walked a few blocks to Marina del Rey, where he led us down an alley to the back entrance of a townhouse.

As we followed him to the door, he turned to us. "Don't drink anything in the refrigerator if it's open unless you want to be tripping. This, by the way, is the entrance for friends."

He walked in without knocking, and we squeezed our way past people standing in the hall and into the overcrowded living room. The sweet aroma of pot and incense flooded the air, and Mick Jagger's voice wailed about wild horses from the stereo speakers, mixing with the loud drone of conversation.

A cheer rose from the crowd as they spotted Arnie, and I realized we had made the grandest entrance possible by arriving with him. Along with Arnie, we waved hello to the crowd, and then Anne and I settled into an open spot on the floor while he greeted old friends.

In the four months we had lived in Venice, we had never been to a party of this magnitude—probably forty people were there when we arrived. We smiled approval at each other. The evening showed promise.

The center of activity was a huge, boat-shaped candle. Incense cones had burned into the wax, forming molten pools and acting as flaming wicks, and streams of jasmine and frangipani drifted into the marijuana haze. A man sat cross-legged beside the candle, rolling a joint from a garbage bag half-full of pot. He twisted the ends tightly between his lips and lined it up with a dozen more that already sat along the edges of the boat like torpedoes.

"Hey Joe, fire up another one!" someone yelled.

He raised a new joint in acknowledgment, flicked on his lighter, inhaled, and snorted the smoke before passing it on. He intrigued me. He looked Italian with his olive skin, curly black hair cut like a short afro, a trimmed beard, and a wide, contagious smile. I took a swig of Boones Farm Apple Wine when the bottle came my way, welcoming the relief for my dry mouth, without taking my eyes off him. Looking up, he caught me staring and smiled. I blushed and turned away.

I pretended to ignore him, but each time I glanced back he was watching me, beaming across the candle centerpiece with a wide, obvious grin. I felt honored to be acknowledged by this attractive man whose position at the party was one of respect and importance. He turned from one side to the next, replying to comments and witticisms, joining in the laughter of a nearby conversation and shouting to a friend as he entered the room. A blond woman in a star-covered halter top walked over, knelt behind him, and massaged his shoulders, her hair falling onto his face. When she leaned over to whisper in his ear, he smiled at her remark and turned to kiss her on the lips. *Oh, he's taken*, I thought, feeling a touch disappointed, but then she put on her fringed jacket to leave. Moments later he was grinning at me again as he continued his mass production of joints.

"What are all of you?" I turned to see a wild-eyed Englishman with blond curls dangling in his face holding a red magic marker. Several people laughed as he began drawing across the wall, creating a full size, floor-to-ceiling mural depicting a genderless person with rays shooting from their head, heart, and genital area. He raged on about something the rest of us missed while the party went on around him.

Hours later, the crowd had dwindled, and Arnie had left. Seven of us remained encircling the candle, including Anne and me.

"This has been a really far-out night." Joe lit another joint before passing it on to the smaller group. "There's been lots of great vibes in the room. Let's not stop yet. I'm feeling like a trip to the desert and I know my bus can fit all of us. Shall we go?"

"Sure," replied a woman I recognized as the person who'd drank too much Dr. Pepper from the fridge earlier in the evening and was obviously still tripping.

The Englishman, who I now knew as English Mike, propped himself on his elbows from a spot where he was lying on floor. "Onward!"

I turned to Anne, who nodded in agreement and told Joe we were in. Joe filled a couple of small plastic bags with pot from the garbage bag and stuffed the rest under the couch.

❦❦❦❦

Joe's '59 Volkswagen bus was covered in colorful, hand-painted designs. The inside was equipped with a bed, Indian print curtains across the windows, bells that tinkled as you moved around, clothes, books, and blankets. "This bus is my home most of the time, but I've been staying here at the house the last few weeks." He opened the passenger door and held it for me. "Sit up front with me."

I welcomed the invitation, flattered by his continued attention. Anne climbed in back with English Mike, a couple of others, and a fourteen-year-old girl who English Mike had named Cosmic Kitten.

Joe and I didn't speak as he drove. Occasionally, we smiled at one another while the noisy contingency in back tried to get organized and find the rolling papers.

"Whoa, wait a minute." Joe looked startled. "This isn't the way to the desert. The bus must be on automatic pilot. It's taking us up Highway 1 to Big Sur instead."

He relaxed again and shrugged. "Hey, guys," he yelled toward the back, "looks like we're going to Big Sur. Anybody find the dope yet? Aw, *shit*, the Highway Patrol!"

Flashing red lights glanced off the rearview mirrors as Joe grimaced. He took his time slowing the bus to pull over while the backseat crew scrambled around. I heard one of them panicking. "Eat this, quick. I can't take anymore. I've already swallowed three."

My pulse began to race.

"Everybody get out," Joe ordered when we came to a stop. "Maintain."

We spilled onto the gravel shoulder of the road, doing our best to look cooperative. Joe sauntered over to a grassy area and sat cross-legged, his knit Mexican poncho covering his body. Two cops approached us, their high black boots clumping over the pavement as they sneered at the psychedelic bus.

"Who's the owner of this vehicle?" one of them demanded. Joe rose to speak with him as the other began taking names and birth dates, calling them into the dispatcher on the radio for wants and warrants. I knew I had to appear calm, but my palms were sweating. Had anyone found all the dope before we got pulled over? Would the cops find it? They pulled apart duffel bags, checked the pockets of the clothes hanging against the windows, and ripped pillows from the homemade seats and reached inside them.

"What do we have here?" One of them rummaged through a pile of blankets and found Cosmic Kitten lying on the floor. They exchanged satisfied smiles. "Why are you hiding?"

She inched from beneath the covers, rubbing her eyes, cowering from the smirking, uniformed man. "I wasn't hiding, I fell asleep."

"Sure you did. How old are you?"

"Nineteen."

"Let's have some ID."

"I left it at home."

He escorted her away from the rest of us while he questioned her and ran checks on the radio. Then he slipped her into the squad car and placed handcuffs on her tiny wrists. When he stepped away from the backseat, English Mike forced himself between the car and the cop. "What is she charged with?"

"She's not charged with anything. We suspect she's a runaway. We're taking her in for questioning."

"You can't take her, she's my wife." Mike puffed up his chest, still standing between the car and the cop.

The cop snickered. "Can you prove that?"

"She's my common-law wife."

The two policemen exchanged knowing glances, then gave Mike a look of disgust. "If this girl is your common law wife, then I think I'm going to have to take you in as well for statutory rape. She's not over eighteen. She can't legally consent to anything. You're out of line here."

Joe walked over to them, a look of concern on his face. "Can I talk to you a minute, Officer?" he asked, using a quiet, respectful tone.

The two of them walked away from the car but I was standing close enough to overhear.

"Listen, Mike hasn't done anything wrong here. He doesn't even know this girl. He's from England and he doesn't understand the laws in America. He's a crazy artist who's trying to be gallant, save the damsel in distress. He intends no harm."

The cop looked hesitant but let Joe lead Mike away from the cruiser.

"Drop it Mike," he muttered. "Let her go. You can't help her."

As Mike let out a sob, the cop shook his head and left him alone.

They turned their attention to me and Anne. I pulled out my Venice, California library card for identification and Anne showed them her passport that she carried as ID proving she was twenty-one. They took her aside from me and asked us both for my date of birth. I lied confidently and hoped Anne would too. We had practiced our routine, subtracting two years from my actual date of birth to make me eighteen. They believed us when nothing appeared on the dispatch. Relief felt sweet, but I concealed my happiness.

Two others were each placed in the cruiser due to warrants.

"It's some stupid parking tickets," the man told Joe through the window, his eyes wide and glassy. "This is a bummer. Get me a lawyer, will you, Joe?"

Joe nodded.

As the highway patrol left with a carload, Joe, Mike, Anne, and I crawled back into the bus and turned around. The sun was rising over the eastern rim of the mountains as we headed back home.

"I wonder why they never found those two lids we were missing?" I asked Joe.

"Oh, those. I found them before they reached us. I stashed them under my poncho and stuck them in the tall grass when I sat. I'll get them later."

As we drove up the hill into Santa Monica, the bus stalled. The four of us got out and pushed it to the side of the road. Mike ran ahead, crying about the cruelty of life, and Anne, Joe, and I hitchhiked back to our apartment.

≪ ≪ ≫ ≫

"You live here?" Joe looked surprised when we arrived at our building. "My good friend Dale lives down the hall. Let's go see him."

Anne told us she was going to sleep.

Joe took my hand, leading me to Dale's apartment, who was also a friend of ours. It was barely daybreak and I wondered if Dale would welcome us, but Joe didn't seem concerned. After several knocks, Dale's bleary eyes peered through the door opening. Seeming surprised and pleased to see Joe and me together, he invited us in.

Dale had a one-room apartment like Anne and me but had turned his closet into a bed chamber. He'd built a high platform for his mattress and painted the closet walls deep blue, with stars in DayGlo paint.

He invited us to make ourselves at home, then crawled back onto his platform mattress and pulled his curtain across the closet entrance.

Joe and I sat on the floor against large pillows. He pulled out an aluminum film canister and a joint from his pocket that he had stuffed in his pants during the search. We smoked a little, then he offered me LSD from the film canister.

"I just got this stuff, but it's really pure, not cut with anything. Seven hundred fifty micrograms on each side of a Vitamin C tablet. See, it's good for you, you need your Vitamin C."

I was nervous about LSD after my trip with Ed, which had been terrifying. I explained my reluctance to Joe.

"This won't do that to you. I know the chemist. He's good people, not some Mafia slimeball. You probably got acid cut with speed or strychnine. You can't have a bad trip on the pure stuff. Take a quarter if you're scared."

I didn't want to disappoint him after hoping all night that I could get to know him. I was blown away by how he had chosen me rather than one of the worldly, beautiful women who'd been at the party.

"Okay. I'll take a small piece."

While we waited for the journey to begin, we smoked what pot was left, and then he lit a candle and a stick of incense. He began to kiss me—long, lingering kisses—and I enjoyed the drug-induced sensations we were experiencing, a culmination of all those hours of flirting.

I knew where this was leading, but I still wasn't comfortable with casual sex. My Catholic upbringing insisted on no sex before marriage. Any indiscretion was a mortal sin, punishable by going straight to hell unless one confessed and asked for forgiveness. I had done neither, nor would I accept hell as my fate. But having thrown off the Catholic teachings and that of my parents, I'd been left with a blank slate. I was convinced that total abstinence was not the answer—but was total indulgence any better? I envied those who freely abandoned convention. If I had sex with Joe, was I being a tramp or being liberated? It seemed like someone else was always making these decisions for me, telling me what rules to follow, whether it was the church, my parents, or the man I was with. I had no idea what it was *I* wanted.

When I finally had sex with Joe, it was he who made the decision.

As the morning continued, the acid created gentle hallucinations. We dressed and he led me outside to pick wildflowers. Back inside, we placed them in a glass of water next to the candle and the incense. He was right about the acid. I wasn't having any paranoid thoughts like during my previous trip. Instead, I was overwhelmed with joy. When Joe spoke, I felt like I was in a dream, almost like we were communicating telepathically.

See, I told you, Sharon. LSD will show you the way. Don't be sad, life is beautiful. Love all the people. It's a new world.

The meandering smoke glided from the incense like a slow-motion drawing, its scent pungent, almost holy.

Don't believe in God, be God. Feel yourself filling the universe.

The smoke drifted, twirled, settled, and stretched as a single strand of white. I began to feel it, the wondrous glory around me.

Oh Joe, the walls, they're rich as velvet. The petals of flowers are soft as silk, and the tiny fuzzy centers, each like the bristles on a brush. How have I walked through the world and never seen all this? It's amazing. Thank you for showing me. I want to cry. I am seeing it with god eyes!

Every vein of each leaf demanded my attention, enraptured me with its beauty. My face hurt from smiling and was wet with tears from the fierce splendor engulfing me. Each nerve in my body seemed to tingle with joy.

In that moment, I experienced a new kind of love—a love that Joe was teaching me, and I wanted to learn. A love that could be shared with everyone and would never hurt you. I was becoming part of this new world. From now on, I would believe in this universal love and never need to feel any pain again.

❋ Chapter 10

April 1971
Marina del Rey, California

I was enjoying the way the waterbed conformed, womb-like, to my body. I didn't want to wake up. I hoped Guy never returned from Hawaii, where he'd gone with Arnie following his party, so Joe and I could keep sleeping in his room like we'd been doing all week. Joe was crashing there now that his VW bus had been towed away.

A wave sent me bouncing and swaying as Joe leaned onto the bed, and I smelled the smoke before my eyes were fully open.

"Want a hit? It's almost gone."

I reached for the joint and forced myself into a sitting position.

All three roommates at the Marina del Rey townhouse who had bedrooms were from Chicago. Two of them, including Guy, ran a successful leather shop. The third, Rob, was a bum like the rest of us, living off unemployment after quitting his computer programming job to come west. He had become a good friend of mine.

When the joint was finished, Joe lit another Marlborough and went to take a shower. I could hear music from the next room, so I figured Rob was awake and walked next door to visit.

Rob was sitting on the floor, leaning against his bed, listening to music through his headphones. Tall and thin, with sharp, bony features, he had fine, ragged hair that was already receding at the age of twenty-six; its light brown color made it nearly invisible as it faded against his tanned skin. He wore wintry Chicago clothes: a corduroy shirt with a tiny flowered print and wide-wale corduroy pants rubbed thin at the knees from wear and age.

"Hey, Sharon, what's happening? Is that old man of yours talking this morning, or is he in one of his moods?" He slid the headphones around his neck as I settled on the floor beside him.

"Joe's fine. He's very intense, that's all."

"Intense is right. He needs to lighten up."

I had become used to confiding in Rob about Joe because I could talk to Rob about anything. I shared with him what was bothering me. "I feel like I'm doing something wrong, like I ought to be able to make him happy."

"Lady, there is nothing wrong with you." He smiled and shook his head in my direction. "He's the one with the problem. You could make anybody happy. Listen, I love Joe like my own brother, but I can't relate to his trip. He's all fucked up over his divorce."

"What should I do?"

"That's easy. Leave him alone. Let him brood if he wants to."

He removed the headphones from his neck and placed the pillow-like plastic cups over my ears. The music vibrated through my bones as though I were directly plugged into an amplifier. I closed my eyes and listened to Cat Stevens singing "Wild World" and I felt like the refrain could be about me. It made me sad.

After a couple of tunes, Rob took back his headphones.

"Earth to Sharon. Hey! Want to go for a ride on my bike?"

"I guess so," I said. "I'm stoned, I can handle it. As long as you promise not to drive too fast and scare the shit out of me."

Rob stood and pulled me to my feet. "You've never seen me ride *fast*. I only get really cranking when I'm alone, never with anyone on the back. Don't worry. You're safe."

I poked my head next door to grab my jacket and say goodbye to Joe, who was sitting on the bed deep in thought, smoking another joint. He gave me a nod in acknowledgement.

I followed Rob downstairs to the garage. He unlocked his modified 650 Triumph Chopper and rolled it into the driveway. The front wheel extended a few feet ahead of the bike and its handlebars stretched toward the sky.

Rob ran his wire-rimmed sunglasses around his ears, mounted the bike, and backed it out of the driveway before kick starting it.

"Hop on!" he yelled above the roar. I pulled down the stirrups and climbed onto the higher level of the two-tiered seat, leaning back against the support bar as I had done several times before, and we took off. Since I was riding higher than Rob, I could feel the wind hitting me in the face and rattling my long hair, yanking it into tangles.

We turned up a canyon road, leaning through the turns first one way and then the other, the pavement within arm's reach as we spun around hairpin corners on the edge of cliffs. Was there enough aerodynamic force at work to keep us from skidding sideways across the blacktop? I gripped Rob tighter and closed my eyes, terrified that an oncoming car waited for us around the next curve as the bike moved faster and faster.

Finally, I couldn't stand it any longer. "Stop! Stop! I'm getting off!"

I had threatened before to walk away into an unrecognizable part of LA County—day or night, it didn't matter. When he pushed me to the point that I thought the end of my life was moments away, I was prepared to get home by thumb.

He pulled over and let me dismount.

"That's it! I'm hitching home! I don't know why I always ride with you. You get a charge out of this, don't you?"

His laughter showed I was right. "Aw, c'mon. I wasn't even going that fast. Why you always spoiling my fun?"

"You're a maniac."

"C'mon. Get on. I'll be good."

"I'm not going with you next time."

"Yeah, I know. That's what you said last time. Admit it, you love it."

Reluctantly, I mounted the bike again. He pulled back onto the road.

It was April 24th, the day of the San Francisco March for Peace, which was being held in coordination with a march that was happening in Washington DC the same day. Joe, Rob, Anne, and I had made the spontaneous decision to drive north so we could join in with thousands of others and experience the energy of that many caring people in one place, protesting the Vietnam War. This would be a historic event, the largest of its kind to be held in San Francisco.

Joe had an additional agenda. His ex-wife, Nancy, and four-year-old daughter lived nearby, and this was an opportunity for him to visit them.

I stood next to Rob's black and yellow '54 Chevy truck, which he affectionately called The Bubble Bee, and stared out between two mountains to the Pacific Ocean. I hadn't seen a sky that blue in months due to the smog in Venice, and the bright sun felt blinding.

We'd slept on the side of the road in Mt. Tamalpais State Park, Rob in a sleeping bag on the roof, Joe across the front seat, Anne and I sharing a mattress in the back. Now Joe was preparing breakfast on the two-burner Coleman stove—steamy black coffee in one pan and hard-boiled eggs in the other. I wrapped myself in his poncho against the crisp morning air. A Volkswagen beetle drove by and the driver waved, as did a young woman riding up the side of the mountain on a ten-speed bicycle.

"See what I mean about this place?" Joe threw his arms open. "It's great isn't it? People around here are like a bunch of little elves. They just appear out of the woods. This is the way it's supposed to be, not like that rat race back in LA." He poured me a cup of black coffee and I wrapped my hands around it to warm them. "Can you imagine my daughter growing up here? She'll be a little elf, just like them."

When Anne emerged from the truck, she looked pasty and stared at the ground, looking up only to make a face that I recognized as meaning she felt terrible. On the drive there the day before, she had taken LSD for the first time, and she had tossed and turned all night. I could tell she regretted her impulsive decision, and I felt sorry that I'd encouraged her.

Anne had always been more cautious than me. Since leaving home, I knew she'd been feeling the weight of responsibility, while I allowed myself to blunder into each new experience without concern for the consequences. I never worried about buying groceries or paying rent. Anne took care of supporting me with her unemployment and savings.

I also knew that when she didn't feel well, she was stubborn and inconsolable.

"I didn't sleep at all. I think I'm going to throw up." She leaned against the truck.

"Maybe you need to eat something."

"Eggs. Ugh. That will make me even sicker. Is there a piece of bread around here?"

Joe found part of a loaf tucked under a jacket and handed the bag to Anne.

"I have to go home. There is no way I'm going to walk around San Francisco in a crowd of people feeling like this." She tore a piece of bread from a slice and stuffed it into her mouth.

"Aw, c'mon. Be a sport." Rob walked over and put his arm around Anne to hug her.

"Fuck you." She threw off his arm and walked to the other side of the truck.

"What did I do?" Rob shook his head at Joe and me.

I shrugged. "It's not your fault. She gets this way when she doesn't feel good."

Joe stared at the ground, rubbing his beard for a moment, before looking up. "There's a bus station in Mill Valley. I bet she could get a bus back to LA from there."

Two hours later, I was waving good-bye to Anne at the bus station. It felt strange not having her with me while exploring a new place. It was the beginning of a split that would deepen with time.

By the time the bus arrived, it was too late to get to the demonstration before they closed the roads. We'd been warned the city would be shut down once they did. So Joe, Rob, and I spent the rest of the morning meandering around Marin County, exploring Stinson Beach, Bolinas, and Mt. Tamalpais. When we reached Nancy's house in San Anselmo late in the afternoon, we watched the news and learned that 150,000 or more people had marched down Geary Avenue. I was disappointed we hadn't been part of it.

Nancy was pretty, as I had expected—slender and feminine, with straight, dark, nicely trimmed hair. She oozed confidence and sarcasm; she seemed not a woman beaten by divorce but one freed by it. I couldn't help comparing myself to her, an exercise that left me miserable. For one thing, she was at least ten years older than me. I was still sixteen. I had nothing interesting to say, or even a single enlightened statement to make. During my months in Venice, I'd gained weight from gorging on junk food after getting stoned. Now my clothes fit too snugly, and next to svelte, delicate Nancy, I looked blubber-like. Joe insisted we were cosmic sisters, but I felt like a cosmic klutz as I tried to be useful in the kitchen. As Nancy chopped salad, I did my best to cut through the carrots, but my knife kept slipping and I almost cut myself. She graciously asked if I could set the table as she took over the carrots.

Meanwhile, their daughter hovered around Joe, climbing on and off his lap and making a fuss when he wasn't paying attention to her.

Nancy rented the room she inhabited with their daughter from a man who worked for a music magazine. We spent hours listening to music I hadn't heard before from the demo copies he'd brought home from work. When the time came to go to bed, Joe suggested that he and I could sleep in the truck, but Nancy teased him, asking, "What's the matter, Joe, can't handle two old ladies in the same house?"

As a result, Joe insisted we sleep on the floor in the living room, right outside of where Nancy slept with their daughter in a double bed behind a curtain. Rob slept on the other end of the living room on the couch. No one asked what I thought, and I felt unworthy of offering an opinion. I was extremely uncomfortable and barely spoke throughout our stay. I wished I could disappear.

❖❖❖❖

In the morning, still lying on the floor in the living room, I heard Joe arguing with Nancy in the kitchen. I wished I didn't have to listen to this. Joe had told me previously that one of the reasons he wanted to visit her was to talk her out of pressing him for child support payments he owed, claiming it was unsisterly of her. As they spoke, he accused her of being too hung up on security and suggested she trust all her brothers and sisters to take care of her.

"How come you never want to see your daughter?" she demanded.

"I don't want her to get hung up on the idea of me as her father. Everyone's her father. Richard's her father, Tom's her father, Rob's her father—"

"I don't want to be a father!" Rob called out from the living room, looking over at me with a smirk and shaking his head.

Nancy wasn't giving in. "You don't care about her at all. You even gave all her clothes to somebody else."

I believed Joe wasn't saying these things out of selfishness but from of a belief that by relinquishing material belongings, you became a better person. This apparently connected you with the vast universal consciousness where we all became one. At twelve, I had read books about saints, aching inside for the strength to be as good as them and capable of devoting myself to faith. In Joe I sensed that same devotion, a belief strong enough that ordinary human relationships paled in comparison. In my mind, he couldn't do or say anything wrong. If I didn't agree with him, then I must be at fault.

Yet as I lay there, something nagged at me, and I couldn't help but sympathize with Nancy. A child had to eat, after all.

And why had he given away all her clothes? Couldn't he have given them to her?

"I'm the one who's taking care of her. I'm the one who goes to work every day so she can have a home and food on her table. What do you do?"

"You've sold out to the system," he argued back. "I won't do that. I will not support this warmongering society where all that matters is how much money you have. We're making a new world—no, a new universe. Our consciousness is going to move beyond all of this, to a place where there are no mothers and fathers, only equals, only brothers and sisters, can't you see that? Can't you be part of that?"

"My job does not support warmongers. Come on! I work for a leather shop! We're making a new society, but it's a society that can feed you while you step outside of the bounds of tradition. And what about you? I mean, you were a hairstylist, for Christ's sake. How is that supporting the war?"

"It was Beverly Hills! That's as warmongering as you can get. I styled hair for all those people shopping at Georgio and driving Lincolns. It was starting to make me sick. Where do you think their money came from? Someone was burning babies to get rich."

"Joe, you've even abandoned your music. What's happening to you?"

I rolled over and peered into the kitchen. Joe was silent, but fidgety. He dug into his cigarette pack, only to find it empty, then crumpled it into a ball. Nancy handed him one of hers.

"I'm moving on. I'm casting off everything. That stuff was my ego. When it's all gone, I'll be a free man, one with the universe. I'll have reached a state of perfect consciousness."

I studied Joe from the living room floor, saddened by that too-familiar look of anguish on his tense face. I wanted to believe in him—he was my man, after all—but I feared he was wrong.

❖ ❖ ❖ ❖

Back in LA a few days later, Joe was indeed casting off everything.
"That was a good thing for me when my bus was towed with most of my belongings," he said. We were getting stoned in Rob's room with the music playing. "Now I don't have to be hung up on needing it. You're lucky, Sharon. You never got involved in owning stuff. You're pure, uncorrupted, a true child of the universe. That's beautiful. Me, I have to reach bottom before I can be truly pure, before I can find my way back up. I'm not there yet. I'm still on the way down."

He opened his film canister of crushed LSD, licked his finger, jabbed it into the white powder, and sucked it off like a child eating icing from a cake before handing it to me. I was careful to take a small amount. Rob reached for the canister as well.

It had become a ritual since we'd returned from San Francisco, eating small amounts of acid each day for the purpose of maintaining an ongoing higher consciousness. I was spending nearly all my time at their house, and Anne seldom joined us anymore, since she preferred to forgo the tripping.

Joe turned his head from side to side and rolled his shoulders—what he always did to ease tension. "I met this guy Jeff today. He's hitching around on the coast with only a Frisbee for luggage. Far out, huh? Anyhow, he lives on this commune in Eureka, and he's here looking for new members. It's way out in a redwood forest: no locks on the doors, no cops, no bullshit. That's the place for me. For all of us! We should all go. How trippy would that be?"

Rob nodded. "Sounds great. I could get into it. I've had it with this bullshit going on around here. This dude was telling me there's a major drug bust coming, like three hundred John Doe warrants coming out just for Venice. LA sucks. We're going to have to deep-clean the house."

I'd never heard of a John Doe warrant. Rob explained how all they needed was an address to come and search your house, not the names of people living there.

"I heard it's coming this weekend. We're going to have to lock all the doors for once. You got a key, Joe?"

"I don't need one. I won't be here. I'm leaving with Jeff on Thursday."

I was startled and hurt by this news, feeling a cross between *Why didn't you tell me* and *Why can't I go*? It was obvious from Joe's remark that he meant to go alone, and I felt like I'd failed. My hero was leaving me behind. He was casting off attachments, and after a few weeks together, I had become one.

He looked into my eyes and raised his eyebrow, as though asking how I was taking the news. I made an effort to smile and he grinned back at me, nodding. *It's going to be all right*, his eyes said.

"Rob, you going to come to Eureka?"

"Yeah, I think I will. I'm ready to bust out of here. I'll need a trailer for my bike to tow it with the Bubble Bee." He looked at the floor as though mulling over the necessary activities for a few moments. "Yeah, I'd say in about two weeks I could be ready to go."

Joe turned to me. "Why don't you ride along with Rob when he comes?"

I was confused. Did this mean Joe wanted me to be with him, or was he trying to pair me up with Rob? Perhaps the pairing made sense to him, since I had always been closer to Rob than I was to him. Then it dawned on me: Joe believed we were all one consciousness—all friends, all lovers. He wanted me there because I was part of his universe, pure and uncorrupted, like Eureka.

I nodded back. "Okay."

He was grinning as wide as the Santa Monica Freeway now.

❖❖❖❖

Hot rumors blew in with the Santa Ana winds, making everyone jumpy. We heard the bust was delayed, but it was still on. I helped the roommates vacuum the shag carpeting for roaches and pills, clean out the sofas, empty the ashtrays, and throw out the vacuum cleaner bags. What few drugs Rob had left he stashed inside the gas tank of his motorcycle, sealed in a plastic bag. I was still staying there most nights, even though Joe had left a few days earlier. I wanted that emotional connection.

In preparation for the bust, the house was clean of drugs and the doors were all locked. It was quiet until morning, when we heard a sudden pounding on the front door that sounded frantic.

Rob sprang to the window to check for cops. "Aw fuck, it's only Jeff. What a jerk. I thought he had a key." He bounced down the stairs to the front door. He had never liked Jeff. He only tolerated him because he was Joe's friend.

"Jesus, what's your problem?" I heard Rob yell as he unlocked the door.

"You fucking asshole!" Jeff shouted as he entered. "I've been banging on this door all night. I was having a bad trip and I couldn't even get in my own house. You left me out there! How come you never answered the door, asshole?"

"Hey, man, I thought you had a key," I heard Rob reply. "I never heard any knocking until now. You must have been knocking on another door."

I could see Jeff now, and his eyes were wild. He raised his fist and swung at Rob, landing a smack to his jaw and then another quick blow to his stomach. Rob doubled over for a moment, caught

off guard. Between the grunts and punches I heard myself screaming, "Stop it, Jeff. Stop it! He didn't lock you out. *STOP IT!*"

Jeff ignored me and backed Rob against a wall next to a
dresser. Rob's years in Chicago seemed to instinctively return.
His eyes were frantic, scanning the dresser top, and I barely saw
his hand snatch an open jackknife and raise it toward Jeff's throat.

I flew from the room and raced downstairs, not bothering to
shut the front door, not looking back to see what had happened. My
heart pounded as my feet ran. I needed to get out of there. What
was happening? Was all this talk of loving each other and building
a new world bullshit? I was sick of Venice, sick of the paranoia, sick
of feeling manipulated, sick of the idealism that disappeared when
anything went wrong. How would Eureka be any better?

I was nearly home when I heard the roar of Rob's motorcycle
behind me. I couldn't stand to look at him, or talk to him, or begin
to think about what happened.

"Sharon, wait! I need to talk to you!"

I ducked into an alley that led to the back of my apartment
house and stood by the back door, shaking and crying. If I waited
awhile, if he didn't find me, maybe he'd go away, I thought.

A few minutes later, he burst into the alley. I started to run,
but he grabbed me before I could get away.

"Where are you going? What did I do? I was just trying to
defend myself! Soon as I held up that knife, Jeff backed down. But
there I was, numb with pain, trying not to get beaten up, and I turn
around and you've run out. What's going on?"

I didn't know how to explain. I couldn't put into words the
flood of emotions and horrible doubt.

"Rob, I don't want to go to Eureka. It's going to be more of
this same shit. Jeff's going, too. How's it going to be any different
from Venice?"

"There won't be any locked doors in Eureka. Everyone's uptight because of what's going on around here. Once we get out of LA, things will be better. Really. I know they will."

He put his arms around me and stroked my hair as I buried my head in his chest and let the tears run onto his shirt. I couldn't find it in myself to believe anything would be better in Eureka. I felt burnt out and depressed and yearned for a stable relationship with someone who truly loved *me*, not just all humanity.

We walked inside to my apartment and Anne was there. She gave me an odd look and I wondered why.

"A letter came for you from Boston." Her voice was monotone.

Boston? Who did I know in Boston?

I was shocked when I discovered it was from Eddie. It seemed like another lifetime when I knew him.

Rob told me he would talk to me later and left.

I miss you, the letter said. *I've been looking all over for you. Carolyn gave me your address. Here is my number and the code to make up phone credit card numbers so you can call me for free. I still love you. Eddie.*

Wow. Eddie missed me and had gone through trouble to look for me? I was stunned. There was a time when there was nothing I'd wanted to hear more than words like this from him, but now I wasn't sure how I felt.

I walked to a pay phone on the street so they couldn't trace the call to our building, and moments later, Eddie was on the phone.

"Hey babe, I found you, this is great! You should see this place I'm living in right now. I got a great apartment on Beacon Hill. I'm getting into a work training program. The only thing missing is you. I want you back."

I was speechless.

"Hello?"

"I'm still here. I don't know what to say."

"Say you'll come back to me. I know I screwed up. I know I wasn't always good to you the way I should have been, but this will be different."

"Why don't you come visit me in California? We can see how things go."

"I hate fucking California. But if that's what you want, okay. I'll come to California. I have to get some new tires first. I don't know if the Dodge is gonna make it on these tires. I drove her all the way back to Boston, and to Florida and back. Pretty good car, huh?"

"The best," I agreed, feeling nostalgic.

"I'll call you in a few days and tell you when I'm coming."

Everything felt confusing. I thought back to a time less than six months earlier when I'd believed all my problems would be solved if I left home, that everything wrong with my life was because of my parents. And in a sense, I was right. The problems I had then had all been solved. Only now I had new problems, ones that were far more complex than I'd ever imagined. I'd had no idea life would be so difficult once I had the freedom to make my own decisions.

Eddie called a few days later.

"The Dodge isn't gonna make it. Besides, if I come to California, I'll miss getting into that training program at Mass General. Why don't you come to Boston? I'll send you the money to fly."

Eddie cared enough that he would send me plane fare? He really had changed!

"Let me think about it."

I thought about everything that had happened since I'd arrived in California. How Bob had broken my heart, how Joe needed to cast me off, how the cops hounded all of us whatever we were doing, how any happiness I found was soon destroyed. I felt drained and unable to put faith in the unknown that waited in Eureka, and staying in California with Anne felt like more of the same.

I couldn't think of a reason to stay in Venice any longer. Eddie said he wanted to make a life with me and make me happy, and in this moment of vulnerability, I trusted him one more time.

Chapter 11

May 1971
Boston, Massachusetts

I stared out the airplane window at blackness, glad my stomach felt better, wishing I could sleep. I was nervous on my first flight, and turbulence set in quickly as we took off. Before we reached flying altitude, I reached for the barf bag.

Now I had long, dark hours to worry about seeing Eddie again, and to reflect upon how different I felt leaving California from when I arrived. Anne and I had exchanged a tearful good-bye at the airport. She'd wished me luck, but I knew she thought I was making a mistake.

I tried to remember how it felt to love Eddie, but the memory was cloudy. Eddie begging me to come back to him proved there was justice, didn't it? He had come to his senses and realized he loved me. He would be different now, I was sure of that. And now that I was on my own, with no more interfering parents, what could go wrong?

I had some pure acid left. I'd hidden it under my floor-length, purple dress, tucked away with a few downers in case of a difficult LSD crash. This was a special gift. Eddie and I would trip together, and this would help us renew our love and feel close again. I tried to remember feeling close to Eddie, but all my memories were vague.

From thirty thousand feet, I watched morning unfold as a pale, faint light seeping across the sky. The golden glow on the horizon reminded me of religious book covers showing the awakening of faith. The vision filled me with hope for this new day in a new life.

≪≪≫≫

When we landed, I retrieved my US Army backpack from the baggage claim and hobbled to the pay phone. Two weeks earlier, I had dislocated my knee while prancing downstairs. The swelling wasn't as bad now, but I still had it wrapped it in an ace bandage and winced from pain if I tried walking normal.

"Call me when you arrive," Eddie had told me. "I don't want to park. I'll pick you up in front of the terminal."

After the call, I limped out front and waited for the Dodge to make its appearance, waited to rush into Eddie's arms and have him tell me how much he missed me.

Ten minutes . . . twenty minutes . . . a half-hour. Was I standing in the wrong spot? Had he gotten lost? Caught in traffic?

Another half-hour later, I spotted the Dodge as it pulled alongside the curb. There was the dark, shaggy hair I remembered, the mustache, the narrow eyes, the Eddie scowl. I rushed forward and opened the passenger's side door.

"Get in!" he yelled from the driver's seat, barely glancing at me, his focus glued to the rearview mirror.

I managed a smile as I shoved my pack into the front and shimmied in after it.

"You got fat," he growled. His scowl continued and I felt ashamed. Shifting into drive, he pulled away from the curb and began the drive to my new home with neither a kiss nor a hello.

"This is the worst fucking time to be driving to the airport, right in the middle of fucking rush hour."

I stared at the angry profile fidgeting with the mirrors and hanging onto the steering wheel like he was attacking it. A wave of heat began to creep along my arms. Oh my lord, what had I done? I recognized the Eddie I had managed to forget. No wonder my memory was cloudy. Why would I want to remember this?

Eddie cursed and ranted while we inched through traffic. A jumble of red brick buildings rose up a hill on my right. He turned up one of the streets and climbed the one-way road, rounded the block, and then pulled between two cars in an area marked NO PARKING that was full of cars.

As we got out, he explained. "They only tow the cars on each end. As long as I park in the middle, they don't fuck with me."

I took a deep breath to calm myself and scanned the neighborhood.

Four-story brick buildings poised themselves like prison walls, locking in the humid, still air; the stench of garbage and dog feces rose from the sidewalk. I longed for that breeze off the ocean.

We walked downhill. Eddie stopped at a building and unlocked the black, wooden door at the entrance. The musty smell of age hit me as I entered.

"We're on the third floor." He climbed the stairs, leaving me to carry my bag. "Hurry up, you need the exercise, you gotta lose a few pounds." His voice began fading as he ascended. "Sure didn't take care of yourself out there, did you? What's taking you so long?"

It was useless trying to tell him about my knee. I finally caught up as he stopped to unlock the door. I might have been angry if I wasn't in such a state of shock, half numb from the long flight and no sleep. Disbelief overwhelmed my emotions, as did the realization that I was stuck here: I'd come on a one-way ticket.

A clean-cut man with strawberry-blond hair, freckles, and glasses, wearing a button-down shirt and a tie, arrived at the door to great us.

"You must be Sharon." He extended his hand with a smile as I entered. "I'm Bill, the roommate. Ignore the rags, I'm on my way to work. This is *not* the real me. How was your flight?"

"Long and bumpy. I got sick at the beginning, but I was all right after that. Where do you work?" I stood near the entrance, not sure what to do next.

"At a bank. It sucks, but it pays the rent. I don't plan to be there any longer than I have to. Once I have enough money, I'm going hit the road like everyone else. Except I want my own wheels and money in my pocket. I'm not cut out for poverty."

Ed took over speaking for both of us. "She'll be getting a job soon, too. And when this program starts at the hospital, I'll be making money."

"Hey, don't sweat it. I know you'll come through. See you both later." He gave another smile as he left.

"Put your stuff over there." Eddie motioned toward a mattress on the floor in the corner of the living room next to some boxes. "That's my bed. Bill has the bedroom. You got to start working right away 'cause we owe Bill money for rent and the plane ticket. I had to borrow that from him. I heard they're hiring at Stop and Shop down the street. We'll take a walk over there later."

I wanted to work. My inability to get hired for anything haunted me. Maybe Eddie would be nicer if we both had jobs. At least I could give him a chance.

He sat on the mattress next to me as I unpacked my small bag and dug through my things. When nothing of interest appeared, he grabbed my pocketbook and started rummaging through it without asking. Before I could object, he held up my birth control pills.

"What are these for?" he demanded.

"What do you think they're for? So I don't get pregnant, of course."

"You been doing it with another guy? Couldn't you wait for me?" His face twisted into an accusing look.

"Eddie, I didn't even know where you were. I didn't expect to ever hear from you again."

"Well, you don't need these now. I won't get you pregnant." He paused giving me a sideways glance. "And even if you did get pregnant, wouldn't that be far out? Wouldn't you love to have a little baby girl with long black hair who'd wear pretty dresses?"

"No, I really don't think I'm ready for that."

Especially with you, I wanted to blurt out, but I kept silent, just like I had for all the other wrongs I'd felt that morning. How could he even think about having a child while living on a mattress in someone's living room? Maybe I did stupid things, but I knew having a baby was serious. A baby needed a home, and parents who loved her. No matter how much I'd fought with or disagreed with my parents, I'd never once doubted their love.

As I thought about my parents, I missed them for the first time, deeply missed them. It was too bad I couldn't stand to live with them. I had no plans of telling them I was in Boston; it was only two hours away, and if they knew I was that close, they would try to make me come back. I would keep calling them, but I would pretend I was in still in California. How could I possibly go live there and relinquish control to them again after everything

I had experienced? If I'd felt suffocated before, it would be even worse now.

I finished unpacking, then slipped the leather pouch out from under my dress that I'd brought the drugs in.

"What you got there?" Eddie looked interested.

"I have pure LSD. It's the best, made by a chemist a friend of mine knew. I thought we could trip together. There're downers to crash with too." I hoped he would understand what a wonderful gift I had brought for us.

"Let me see those." He reached out to me, took the pouch, and shook the contents into his hand. After picking out the downers, I followed him into the bathroom, where he threw the LSD into the toilet, and flushed it. My mouth dropped open.

"That stuff's garbage. It'll fuck with your head. I can't believe people are still doing that shit." He grinned as he waved the downers in front of me. "Now these I can use."

Reaching into the medicine cabinet, he pulled out a syringe and a bent spoon. He opened the red gelatin capsules and emptied them into the spoon, added a few drops of water, and flicked on his lighter, heating the liquid to dissolve it. After drawing it into the syringe, he pulled his belt off, sat on the toilet, and wrapped the belt around his arm. As he pulled it through the loop and tugged it in the opposite direction, my last hope for our relationship vanished and I felt like I might vomit.

"This isn't working. You're going to have to help me out here." He motioned for me to take the end of the belt and I followed his instructions, fearful of his reaction if I refused. "Pull on this . . . tight . . . *tighter* . . . come *on*, you can do better than that, what are you, weak?"

I tried not to shake, following his orders silently, looking away out the window. If he had beaten me, it couldn't have hurt any worse. What a terrible mistake I had made coming here. I had to get back to California. I could get a job, hide the money, I'd find a way back. I had to. I couldn't possibly live like this.

««»»

Later that night, on his mattress with the lights out, I went through the motions he expected of me.

"I love you," he told me.

I didn't care.

"I love you, too." My tongue felt clumsy, stumbling on the lie. How wrong it felt to be wasting those words on Eddie. Daggers of guilt dug into me for speaking them. I remembered the joy I'd felt when I'd said them to Bob, the way my whole being had responded when he'd whispered them to me. I wondered how long it would take to stop remembering, stop hurting over losing that love. I waited until Eddie fell asleep, then I buried my head in the pillow and wept.

««»»

Climbing the three floors to the apartment still hurt my knee, especially now that I'd spent all day on my feet at the grocery store. I'd gotten hired by Stop and Shop the day after I arrived, and now it was nearly three weeks later. The joy of finally getting a job had disappeared as soon as I had to run a cash register.

The Stop and Shop at the Charles River Plaza was one of the busiest of its stores in New England. As the only grocery store within walking distance of the heavily populated Beacon Hill, and next door to Massachusetts General Hospital, the lines stretched out from the moment I began work until I punched the clock at the end of the day. Customers glared at me for not moving fast enough. I tried to hurry as I manually entered the price of each item on the clunky cash register, then bagged it. Older people dragging shopping carts insisted I divide their groceries so the bags didn't weigh much and complained if one bag had too many cans and another too many vegetables, then wanted me to repack them. I made mistakes making change, which people pointed out when I shorted them. I figured I overpaid sometimes too, but of course no one ever mentioned that. Nearly every day my register was a little short, and I worried they would think I was stealing money.

Eddie's training program never did start, and I wasn't surprised. I had abandoned faking a relationship with him. I concentrated on trying to find a ride back to California and avoided being in the apartment as much as possible.

I retrieved the key from my pocket that Bill had given me when he moved and unlocked the door. Bill had figured Eddie out not long after I had and had decided to dump the freeloader by moving elsewhere. Out of sympathy, he'd given me his bedroom and his key, telling me I could stay for the last two weeks since the rent was paid. I hoped I would find a ride back west before the time ran out.

Using the fake phone credit card, I called Anne daily; she kept me updated on her life in Venice, and I rehashed how she'd been right about Eddie. She was kind enough not to say I told you so, offering sympathy and hope for a return ride.

As I pushed the door open, the safety chain blocked it.

"Eddie, open the door, it's me!" I heard his voice muttering, and then a girl giggled. No one approached the door. "Eddie, I know you're in there. Open the goddamn door! I don't care who you're in bed with. Let me in!"

There was heavy breathing, but no footsteps. I kicked the door and yelled, but to no avail. Finally, I sat on the steps and waited with my grocery bag.

A few minutes later, Eddie opened the chain and a young, dark-haired girl brushed past me. I stormed past Eddie to the kitchen.

"You're really rude, banging on the door like that. I just wanted a little privacy. Why didn't you go take a walk or something?"

"I don't want to walk. I've been working all day. I'm hungry and I want to eat!"

Roaches scurried into the drain as I shifted dishes from the counter into the sink. No one washed dishes except me, and each day when I returned from work, I found that more had appeared. Thankfully, with Bill gone, I no longer had to clean for him, so I'd quit. I washed what I needed and left the rest to rot.

I waited for Eddie to leave the apartment before emptying my bag. The refrigerator was empty of edible food. I hid the bread and eggs on a low shelf behind slimy lettuce. Eighteen cents for a loaf of junky white bread and twenty-seven cents for six small eggs was the cheapest solution I could find to feed myself. I had change back from my two quarters. Perhaps with only dirty pans for cooking, Eddie might not be tempted to steal my food. This had to last two more days, until my paycheck.

After eating, I walked over to the band shell by the Charles River. There were free concerts on Thursday nights, and on my two other visits I'd met local hippies and transients. We'd gotten stoned, exchanged stories, and listened to whatever music was being performed.

When I reached the park, only a few people were mulling around, and the stage was empty.

"The concert was canceled."

I turned around to see a man with dark hair and a mustache sitting on a concrete wall. He was wearing a long-sleeve shirt and jeans, smiling at me, and holding an unlit cigarette in his hand. "Got a light?"

"Sure." I dug through my bag for the matches I always carried in case a joint was offered. "That's a bummer. I wonder who was playing?"

"Got me. Me and my buddies figured we'd go over to the Music Hall." He lit his cigarette and handed the matches back to me. "The James Gang's playing."

"Really? I love the James Gang." They were one of the bands Rob, Joe, Anne, and I had often listened to in Rob's room in Venice. "I never hear them here but they're popular in California."

"You from California?"

"No, but I was living there until a few weeks ago. I'm trying to find a ride back. My sister lives there."

His expression showed interest. "Oh yeah? I might be driving out there in a couple of weeks. I just got discharged from the Army. Got back from 'Nam a few weeks ago. I live in Worcester, but I can't go hanging around there. I think I'm gonna look up an old Army buddy out west. You could come along for the ride if I go. Wanna get high?"

I nodded. *This could be my lucky night*, I thought, hoping this could turn into the ride I needed.

He reached into his pocket for a joint, lit it with the end of his cigarette, and inhaled before passing it to me. He introduced himself as Paul, and then we sat together on the wall and smoked, telling each other about our lives. I explained how I had run away and was sixteen but had found a job in Boston. I could contribute money for gas.

He had his own holdup. "I gotta kick this smack habit I picked up in 'Nam. Everybody was doing it; you wouldn't believe the vets with habits."

"I thought the Army had treatment centers for that."

"No way in hell I'm going to those Army hospitals." He cringed. "People die in there. I'll do it myself. I keep cutting back little by little. I'm down to about a bag a day, enough to keep from getting sick. Couple more weeks and I'm clean."

A younger guy who looked very much like Paul strolled over to us.

"This is my brother, Mark." Mark nodded toward me in acknowledgment and Paul asked him where the others were.

"Waiting for you, over by the walkway. You coming?"

"Sure. Sharon's coming to the concert too, aren't you?" Paul asked.

"Are you guys buying tickets? Because I don't have any money." Paul shook his head. "We don't have any money either. We're gonna try to sneak in."

With that, we left, joining three more guys and two girls for the long walk to the theater district, crossing the Boston Common through landscaped shrubbery, towering maple trees, and park benches. Squirrels scampered across the sidewalk and pigeons fluttered out of our path, interrupted from dining on the bread-crumbs tossed to them by an aging lady sitting in layers of clothing. On another bench, a man slept covered in newspapers, his arm dangling from under them toward a wrinkled paper bag that lay beneath the bench, a bottle neck protruding from it.

"Hey, Gramps," one of the guys in the group yelled at him as he kicked the bottle from under the bench. A wizened, startled face popped up and the newspapers slid to the ground. Three of the guys laughed, shoving and punching at each other over the joke. I felt sorry for the old drunk. Why did they have to harass him? He wasn't bothering anyone.

When we reached the other end of the Common, they all headed into a donut shop. The two other girls walked off by them-selves and turned their backs, having a private conversation. The three guys who'd been walking with them yelled over, "Hey, what's with you chicks? You coming with us?"

The girls shook their heads no and walked off. I felt apprehensive being the only girl left with the group as I didn't care for Paul's three friends, but I was looking forward to the concert and growing impatient.

After a long while of us doing nothing, the manager of the donut shop announced we had to go if we weren't going to order anything, or he'd call the cops. I was grateful.

We split up when we reached the concert hall for the purpose of sneaking in. After a few minutes, Mark walked over to where Paul and I were standing and told us to follow him.

"This guy will let us in at the side door," he explained as we followed. "He said they hardly sold any tickets."

No one paid any attention when we walked into the lobby.

Rita Coolidge and Kris Kristofferson were on stage with her band, playing the warm-up set. A large block of rows in the back was empty. I sat next to Mark, who was sitting at the end of the group. Mark shared a joint with me and we laughed together. By the time the James Gang was on stage, I had a good buzz and was ready for rock and roll.

As the band pumped electrical sound into the audience, the six of us wound our way to the area in front of the stage and stayed there for over an hour during the rest of the set. Joe Walsh's wailing guitar riffs got me moving to the music. I danced in rhythm to the pounding bass, hooting and stomping; the guys jumped like madmen and played air guitar. It felt good to finally enjoy myself, to have fun and get a bit wild.

After the concert, I announced I needed to get home because I had to work in the morning. I hadn't expected to be out this late.

"Let's hang out for a while," Mark said. "There's no hurry. We'll walk you back."

I didn't feel like hanging out—I was exhausted—but I also

didn't relish the idea of making the long, lonely walk to the other side of the park by myself. It was after midnight, and Boston never felt safe to me even in the daytime. I decided to wait until they were ready to move on.

They lurked around, two or three of them at a time off alone, talking, laughing, like there was a joke I wouldn't get. The tone in their voices was making me uncomfortable. There was a side glance, a snicker. I was growing anxious and finally announced I was heading home, hoping this would get them moving.

It did.

"Let's cut through this way," Mark ordered. "It's shorter."

There was a giggle. Paul hung back from the others. I didn't like walking straight through the park, as there were no lights off the main sidewalk. I couldn't see very well, and I was still limping. Suddenly, Mark reached over and took my hand, and one of the others took my other hand, and they started running, pulling me along faster and faster. I didn't understand why. The grass flew under my feet as I looked at the ground and tried not to trip. I couldn't run that fast, my knee would collapse. *"Don't run!"* I shouted. *"Slow down!"* But they were laughing like they didn't hear me, and then I either tripped or they pulled me to the ground.

I slammed my hip when I landed because I couldn't put out my hands to stop myself. Why were they doing this? Where was Paul? I thought he liked me. Why was he ignoring what was happening?

Mark and one of the others pinned my arms down. A third one was unbuttoning my pants, pulling them off. They were laughing, excited, like craziness was in the still summer air, and they didn't care who I was, only what I was. "She's been asking for it all night," one of them said. He didn't speak to me directly, only to the others, as if I wasn't there. "She's been asking for it all night, now she's gonna get it."

How could this be happening? I thought we were all friends—getting high, dancing, singing, having fun. I was one of them, wasn't I? I was like one of the guys.

But of course, I wasn't. I could never be one of them. That would make us equals and give me a choice, and I had no choice. They were making that clear. It was their choice. It had nothing to do with me.

Someone was unbuckling his belt, kneeling over me. Adrenaline shot through me, causing my heart to pound, and I pulled at both my arms to break free, but one of them dug their fingers into my skin like claws, strong enough to keep me still, and I couldn't budge. I began to cry, but I didn't try to stop them, because I was broken and could do nothing. They had won.

I turned away and looked at the ground as I cried, wishing I could cover my face, staring at the patchy grass worn thin by too many feet crisscrossing that park, too many squirrels, pigeons, too many old ladies whose lives were in shopping bags, too many young punks with pumped up blood who kicked old drunks and raped women. This thin grass had seen it all, had told this story too many times, could barely sustain itself against the beating it took each day as it was systematically ground into dirt.

"Stop!" Paul's voice interrupted like a loudspeaker in the execution room, coming from a place where he had separated himself and could avoid participating in the group slaughter. "Hey guys, I don't think we should be doing this."

There was a moment of hesitation while all of them froze, like in a child's game when someone spins around and yells, "RED LIGHT!"

"She's only sixteen. We're gonna fuck up her head. This is not cool. I really think we should not be doing this."

The guy kneeling over me who was about to violate me first backed away. One of them let go of an arm, and a moment later, the other let go, too. I sprang to my feet, pulled on my pants, and ran for the direction of Beacon Hill, stumbling over unseen bumps and holes in the darkness, my knee sending sharp jolts of pain with each step.

When I was out of breath, I walked. No one was following, I was probably safe. *Close one*, I thought, but it was okay, everything would be okay. I was breathing fast, my heart racing, my palms cold. What had I done wrong? Why did they think they could do this to me?

"Sharon!" I heard Paul's voice calling. "Sharon, wait a minute. I need to talk to you. I'm not going to hurt you."

I couldn't run if I wanted to. I was panting, and my knee throbbed. He caught up to me as I walked, heart pounding, wondering what might happen next.

"Listen, I'm sorry. It wasn't supposed to happen like this. We all got carried away. They all have something they want to say to you, too."

The others sauntered behind him, looking at the ground, and each muttered a forced "sorry." Evidently Paul was in charge here, and they looked to him for their approval.

"See guys, I told you she has a good head. The fact that she's even listening to us after what happened proves that. Come on. We'll walk you home. No hassles, I promise."

The rest of the walk home was uneventful. They goofed around as though nothing had happened and I tried to act like that was true as I watched for any hint of danger, hurrying along and occasionally getting ahead of them. When we reached my building, Eddie was walking out the door and held it open for me. "Who's your friends?"

"No one."

I told the others good-bye and went inside, even more depressed that my only hope for a ride had evaporated.

❖❖❖❖

The next day, work went badly. I made more mistakes than usual. I hated the way people looked at me. Did they know? Did it show, whatever it was those guys had seen that had made them act that way—did it show to everyone? I had to forget about it, put it out of my mind. I called Anne, but I didn't tell her about it. No one must know. Ever. My secret. My shame.

My boss called me into his office and told me my register was short again, this time by twelve dollars.

"I can't do this job, it's too hard. I quit." I choked back tears. I had to get out of there, had to get away from his accusing eyes that told me I was no good. I already knew I wasn't.

 **Chapter 12**

July 1971
Province de Quebec, Canada

"*Merci beaucoup*," I told the driver as Pat and I unloaded our packs from the back seat. Perhaps those grammar school French classes would finally come in useful. I now wished I had continued the language beyond the eighth grade instead of switching to Spanish in high school.

The Chateau Frontenac, a European-style grand hotel that resembled a castle with its tarnished copper peaks and turrets perched upon stone walls, caused a shiver of delight to run through me. I felt I had stepped off the continent into a magical land.

I'd met Pat in Boston the week before, right after I quit my job at Stop and Shop. Like me, he was looking to move on from Boston. A ride to California felt hopeless to me now, and Pat was passing through from Toledo.

"If you could go anywhere, where would you go?" he'd asked me over coffee.

"I wish I could go back to California. My sister's still there. But I can't find a ride. So I would choose Canada. I went to Montreal with my parents twice, but I've always wanted to go to Quebec City. They speak nothing but French there, it sounds far out."

Anne and I had often fantasized about living in Montreal after we visited there on vacation. Recently I had heard Quebec City was even better, a gem of a place for those on the road. With Canada's reputation as a haven for draft dodgers escaping the Vietnam War, it felt like a beacon of peace and freedom.

"Let's go." Despite our only knowing each other for an hour, Pat was ready to join me. "You want to travel together to Quebec?"

I'd felt immediately energized. There was no reason not to go. I had nothing to keep me in Boston. With Pat by my side, I could hitchhike and feel safe.

A few days later, I used a fake ID that said I was eighteen at a quiet border crossing in Maine and arrived in Quebec City not long after.

Once in the city, we saw several hippies like us with backpacks and sleeping bags. Pat approached one and asked if he knew where the youth hostel was. The young man replied in an American accent. "You see that road over there?" He pointed uphill in the direction of the Chateau Frontenac. "You follow it to this huge park called the Plains of Abraham. Walk along it until you see this old stone prison. That's the youth hostel. Pretty cool, huh? A prison converted to a youth hostel? Canada's far out."

We agreed and thanked him.

I loaded my pack onto my back, but Pat hesitated.

"Now that we're here, I'm going to go my own way. You know where the youth hostel is, so you'll be fine."

Panic hit me. Although I wasn't emotionally attached to Pat and had known him for less than a week, I already depended on him to feel safe. Without him, I was completely alone in a strange country with thirty-five dollars in my pocket. How would

I survive on my own? I didn't even speak the language. I nearly broke into tears.

"What's wrong? Are you mad at me about something?"

"No, not at all. I just need my space. Listen, I'll probably see you at the youth hostel later. There will be lots of other people there. I know you'll be fine. Don't worry, okay?"

"Okay. I'll see you later." I realized there was nothing I could do to change his mind.

Pat threw his duffel bag over his shoulder. I watched him walk off, then took a deep breath and left to find the youth hostel, reminding myself that this had been my idea. Although I was glad to be out of Boston, I felt swamped by loneliness, and being in a new city only accentuated that feeling.

As I expected, signs in Quebec City were written only in French, and people other than tourists seemed to speak no English. I couldn't wait to reach the youth hostel, where I was certain to find other English-speaking travelers. Unfortunately, it was closed when I arrived.

"You can leave your pack 'ere. We check it for you," a young woman instructed me at the door. "We open at eight o'clock." I handed over my pack and checked my watch. I had nearly four hours to kill. I decided to take a walk around the gated city.

It was after seven when I discovered *Terrasse Dufferin,* a promenade built upon a stone wall that overlooked the St. Lawrence River and lower Quebec City. Lined with park benches, this appeared to be the center of social activity in the city. Crowds of tourists, hippies, and locals swarmed along the boardwalk. I joined in, hoping for a familiar face, or at least a friendly one.

"*Pardonez-moi.*" A handsome young man with shoulder-length brown hair and wide, doe-like eyes was speaking to me, rambling something too fast for me to understand.

I replied with two French sentences I hoped would get me through anything. *"Je ne parle Francais. Parlez vous Anglais?"* ("I don't speak French. Do you speak English?")

"A little bit. I try." He hesitated for a moment then spoke slowly. "Do you 'ave ten cent?"

Ah! He was panhandling. The poor begging from the destitute. I smiled at the irony. But he was so cute, I wanted to keep talking to him. He looked harmless enough. A taller friend was with him, and they both looked close to my age.

"What do you need the money for?" I inquired.

"For to, 'ow you say, pot?" He held his hand to his lips and made a motion like he was smoking a joint. This was great. Not only was he cute, but also, he intended to score some pot. This could be an opportunity to meet some local heads.

"If I help you get some money, can I smoke it with you?" I had panhandled before, so I knew how this worked.

He and his friend exchanged some words in French.

"Yes. Okay. I tell you 'ow to ask. We ask for ten cent, always. People will give you dis. Say, *'Voulez-vous donnez moi dix cents, s'il vous plait?'"*

I tried it two or three times as he corrected me, until I finally had it right. I recognized the phrase as using the formal version of you, with please at the end. *How polite*, I thought.

"What is your name?" I asked.

"Eve," he answered.

That can't be right, I thought, *that's a woman's name.* "What did you say?"

"Y, V, E, S—Yves."

"Oh. Yves. I get it. I'm Sharon."

"I am Jean," his friend introduced himself. I knew that was the French version of John.

We agreed to meet back in an hour by pointing at our watches. The evening became fun as I nabbed tourists, asking for money in French. It didn't seem degrading like when I asked in English. It felt like a game. Several times, people began speaking rapidly and I had to explain that I only spoke French *"un peu"* ("a little"), but I frequently received a dime, occasionally more. When Yves, Jean, and I met up, I added my change to theirs and Yves counted it.

"Five dollarz. Okay. We 'ave it. Come."

"Where do we have to go for the pot?" I followed them away from the promenade.

I didn't understand what he answered, only that we needed to walk somewhere. I followed them downstairs and around a few corners until they turned into a dead-end alley. I hesitated at the entrance; my mouth went dry, and my stomach clenched tight. I wondered if I should turn and run. Nothing about their behavior suggested anything was odd, but I couldn't imagine why they'd walked in there. Were they meeting their connection? Was this a trap?

Yves and Jean reached behind a dumpster and pulled out two bicycles, and I almost laughed with relief.

"We ride dere," Yves said. "Sit on de seat. I pedal."

This is different, I thought. I hadn't been on a bicycle since I was eleven, and it was tricky leaning back on the seat while Yves stood on the pedals, my feet dangling beside the back wheel. I held on to the luggage rack and did my best not to upset his balance. I had seen kids riding twos on bikes when I was a child, but I'd never been allowed to participate. I felt a childish pleasure from the experience as we biked past buildings and headed over a bridge out of the city.

"Where are we going?"

Yves turned his head to answer me without stopping. "Loretteville."

"How far is that?"

"Ten miles."

I was flabbergasted. No wonder they had hesitated when I first asked about joining them.

We rode through the Quebec countryside as I listened to the peep frogs chirping a rhythm that sounded like the whirling bicycle tires. The steady swoosh, swoosh, swoosh of Yves and Jean pedaling as they took turns riding me on the back of their bikes was the only human sound in the night, as few cars passed by. I leaned my head back and gazed at the star-filled sky; a band of white that I knew was the Milky Way stretched from horizon to horizon.

The trip seemed to take hours. At times we all walked while the three of us talked. When I told them I had lived in California, they seemed impressed.

"California? Oh, *oui*, dat is where I go . . . Someday, maybe." Yves's voice sounded dreamlike. "Do you see 'ollywood? Go to beach? Maybe I 'itch 'ike when I finish school."

I was charmed by Yves's innocence, not unlike the innocence I'd had only months earlier. I knew I could never feel that way again, that my dreams of California had been permanently tainted. I smiled with a kind of sadness, the way older children do when little ones talk about Santa Claus.

"California's nice, but it's nice here too. In fact, it's beautiful here."

"*Ah, oui*, it is beautiful. I live 'ere always. Maybe I visit California, but 'ere I live."

I thought how great it must be to feel that way about your home and hoped I would find a place that meant as much to me.

When we finally reached Stephan's house, it was near midnight. Stephan was their connection and friend. Since his parents were away for the weekend, the music was blasting, and the pot began flowing.

"Stephan, he learn Spanish in school. He not want to learn English," Jean explained as we sat cross-legged on the floor. "Dey English, dey treat us like dogs. In Montreal, dey'ave all de jobs, all de money, all de power. Dey call us stupid for 'ow we talk. Someday we 'ave our own country, you will see. *Libre Quebec!*"

"*Libre Quebec!*" I mimicked before turning to Stephan. "*Hola Stephan. Se habla Español?*"

Stephan broke into a wide smile as Yves and Jean giggled.

The four of us sat around the living room smoking pot, speaking words or phrases in English, French, and Spanish, pointing at pictures and gesturing, making hand and body motions as though we were playing charades, then breaking into uncontrollable laughter when we finally reached an understanding.

I was surprised when I saw the faint light of dawn squeaking through the window. I wanted this night to last forever. It had been months since I had laughed so hard or enjoyed the simple pleasure of new friends.

"Do you want to walk?" Yves asked. "I 'ave somet'ing to show you. Please, come."

Yves and I walked out into the morning, crossed the street, and strolled into a field of tall grass. My sandals and jeans became wet with dew as we stepped through the thigh-high pasture, the scent of wildflowers and meadow grasses tickling my nose in a pleasant way. I loved being outdoors as daylight arrived. A low fog hung among the trees beyond the meadow. Here and there, dew-covered spider webs appeared. Violets were blooming in bunches and Yves picked one and handed it to me with a tender smile.

"*Le fleur de violette.*" He spoke in almost a whisper, as though he didn't want to wake the morning, continuing the French/ English lesson we'd been carrying on all night.

I was touched by his gentle act of kindness, and I realized it had been too long since anyone had been nice to me.

We were quiet as I followed him into the woods. Only the sound of leaves crunching and twigs crackling under our footsteps, along with the warning calls of birds signaling our approach, broke the silence, until I heard water ahead. Mist still hung over the rushing stream, and I could feel the coolness of it as we approached. We followed the river upstream in silence, until Yves stopped and faced me.

"Shhh." He held his finger to his lips and stood nearly motionless. Then he pointed to his ear and nodded in the direction we were walking. I heard water still, but also a louder, crashing sound. I gave him a questioning look. He smiled and began walking again, beckoning me with his finger. The sound grew louder, and I realized there must be a waterfall ahead, but I was still unprepared for what finally emerged. A spectacular fall that looked a hundred feet high poured from the side of a cliff into the river we'd been following. Yves beamed with pride, his face radiant, as he watched the amazement on mine.

"I keep telling Blanche she must learn to speak better English or she will be a prisoner in Quebec." Blanche's mother wiped her hands on the dishtowel. "She wants to hitchhike around the country like you, but how can she when no one else on the continent speaks French? Maybe *you* can get her to understand!"

Blanche smiled at me from beneath her mane of dark curls in the way teenagers do when their parents repeat what they've heard before, as if we were both in on a secret. I helped Blanche clear the dinner table as her mother talked, realizing this could be why her parents had invited me into their home. How lucky she was to have such understanding parents who would invite a stranger to stay with them and accept that their daughter also wanted to hit the road, I thought.

For two nights I had stayed with Blanche, a friend of Yves, in her family's guest room, and tomorrow I was moving on to Lise's house at her parents' invite. It was lovely sleeping in clean, white sheets, snuggling under the covers at night safe and alone, waking to the smell of sizzling bacon drifting from a kitchen filled with family chatter.

Blanche's mother was an English teacher, so Blanche spoke better English than most of the kids. She asked me questions about places I'd been and told me how she too wanted to travel the next summer, after high school and before starting college. She had seen so many young people passing through, like me, and wanted to join in.

"It can be hard sometimes," I told her. "It is better if you have someone with you."

"Ah," she said, looking puzzled. "But you travel alone."

"It didn't start out that way. It wasn't what I wanted but my friend left me. I was lucky to meet Yves and Jean and come here."

She smiled and nodded. "They are nice."

A few days later, I joined Blanche, Yves, Jean, and Lise for a canoe trip into the woods. To repay their generosity, I bought a gallon of loganberry wine, Yves's favorite, with my fake ID at the provincial liquor store. I had barely spent any money while staying in Loretteville so I felt I could afford that small token of thanks.

We had to squeeze together to fit all five of us, and the water level wasn't far below the edge of the canoe. I didn't understand their words, but I knew from the laughing and facial expressions that the slightest tip would send us into the river. I had never been in a canoe before, and didn't know how to swim, so every movement sent me into a panic. I tried to calm myself by concentrating on the beauty of the stream we paddled along, lined in towering evergreens. Blanche explained that we were riding to where Jean's brother was camped for the summer in a tent in the woods.

When we arrived, the camp was empty, but a ring of stones for a campfire and a large log beside it were all we needed for our party. We huddled together on the log, passing the gallon jug and a few joints back and forth, swatting mosquitoes and stamping out sparks as they flew onto the needle-covered ground. The others were joking back and forth to one another, but I had lost the gist of the conversation, as it moved too fast. They weren't speaking English to me as much as before and it was tiring for me to try to understand their French. I felt suddenly alone, as I hadn't felt since I'd arrived in Loretteville. I loved their countryside and this group of happy friends. But it wasn't my home. As much as I wanted to, I didn't belong there. I didn't know where I belonged.

❦ ❦ ❧ ❧

I had retrieved my backpack from the youth hostel midway through staying in Loretteville and had not run into Pat again. Three days after the canoe trip, my pack beside me, I stood on the highway onramp heading for Montreal, hoping the familiar city would be welcoming.

Chapter 13

July 1971
Montreal, Canada

The Montreal youth hostel was on the top two floors of a high-rise that also housed a McGill University dorm on Sherbrooke Street. One floor was for men and one for women, but no one policed the premises to enforce this rule until after curfew. At midnight the doors to the building were locked, and you were either in or out, with everyone on their appropriate floor until morning. For fifty cents a night, I found it to be an ideal place to stay—plus I knew the downtown area from my visits with my family.

I'd spoken to Anne in Venice when I first arrived, but when I called again a few days later, the person answering said she had moved out. I was shocked.

"Where did she go?" My pulse raced from panic.

"I think somewhere back east."

We had discussed how she might come to Canada, but nothing had sounded imminent. I guessed she'd gone home, but

I couldn't imagine why she would suddenly do that. What if she hadn't gone home? How would I find her? I decided to call home to see if she was there.

When I called collect, my mother answered, accepting the charges. "We're coming to Montreal," she announced soon after she answered. "Anne is home and she wants to go there with you, so I told her we would drive her. I don't want her hitchhiking. We want to see you. Where are you staying?"

For a moment, I felt worried. Would they try to force me to return home? Our agreement was they would not as long as I kept in touch, and I'd been doing that.

"I'm staying at the youth hostel. It's on Sherbrooke Avenue, so it's fine." My mother knew that was a nice area, so I hoped this would reassure her. "They have cots, with separate rooms for guys and girls. It's only fifty cents a night."

"Why don't you come home for a few days too?" I could hear the pleading in her voice.

I gulped, my throat stiffening from guilt and sadness. "I can't do that. I'll meet you at the border, but I'm staying here."

Despite how difficult my life had become, the thought of returning to my old life was even more depressing. What would I do then? Resume where I'd left off? Pretend nothing had changed and face the same bleak future? They would never stop trying to control my life, my actions, my friends, my future. They'd made it clear that Anne wasn't allowed to move from home or drive until she was twenty-one, and she'd even had to ask permission to go out on a date at nineteen. Here at least, anything could improve at any time, couldn't it?

"We just want to see you, even if it's only for a few hours. We'll meet you at the border, if that's what you want. We won't try to make you come back, even though we want you to."

We agreed on a time and place. I felt strangely excited at the prospect of seeing my parents again for the first time since I'd left home six months earlier, even though the meeting made me apprehensive.

"Can I talk to Anne?"

"Sure, she's right here."

There was shuffling on the other end, and then Anne's voice greeted me.

"What happened?" I asked. "How come you left so quickly?"

There was a half snicker, half chuckle on the other end. "That guy Jim I was living with, we had a big fight," she said softly into the phone. "He's always trying to tell me what to do, then he wanted to get married and move to Hawaii, so I knew it was time to leave. What's Montreal like?"

"It's great. I can't wait until you get here. Hippies are everywhere, the cops don't bother anyone, it's far out. What's it like being home?"

"Strange. I don't know if I could stand it for very long, but in a way, it's a nice break from all the hassles. I need some time to mellow out and get my head back together."

After we hung up, I was pumped about seeing Anne in a few days. I was sure I'd feel better having her with me again.

❖ ❖ ❖ ❖

That night, I decided to sleep early at the youth hostel. By ten o'clock, I'd curled up on my narrow mattress and laid my head on my backpack, like I always did to prevent being robbed. I was almost asleep when a noisy group of guys wandered in with a girl and sat against the wall. I kept my eyes shut, hoping they would realize someone was sleeping and leave, but to no avail.

I finally got fed up. I leaned onto one elbow and squinted against the lights they had turned on. "Can you guys be quiet?"

"Hell, no, it's too early to be quiet. What are you doing sleeping so early, anyhow?"

"Yeah, get up and party with us, don't be such a drag." They all began to giggle.

Realizing they weren't going away, I decided I might as well socialize. I propped myself into a cross-legged position. "Are you all stoned?"

A nice-looking guy with a mop of thick, dark hair streaked in gray leaned forward. "Shit, no. We've been at the bar around the corner, chugging some brews. This Canadian beer is some good shit. Ever try it?"

"No, I don't drink, except to have a swig of wine when I'm smoking sometimes."

"Why not? It's legal, it's cheap, and it gets you high. You have to come try some of this stuff."

Despite the gray hair, I could tell he was only about twenty. He didn't even look like he shaved yet, but he was older than me.

"I'm not old enough. I'm only sixteen."

"That doesn't matter. They don't even check. C'mon, I'm buying, okay?"

I'd never had a drink in a bar before. Curiosity was getting the better of me, and the words *I'm buying* didn't hurt either.

"Okay, okay, I'll go." I stood, flung my pack over my shoulder, and strode to the elevator with him.

He had a mischievous smile that might have been from drunkenness, but in a non-threatening sort of way. "My name's Steve, from Chicago. Just hitched here this morning. Where are you from?"

"Boston, most recently, but California before that, and originally Connecticut. I'm Sharon."

We walked the two blocks to Le Chat Noir, a bar on the ground floor of a round-sided high rise, and just as Steve had promised, no one said a word as I entered. Inside the door I hesitated, intimidated by the dark, noisy bar crammed with people of all ages. Steve took my hand and pulled me through the throng of standing patrons jammed between the bar and the tiny tables lining the wall. I could hear a band playing pop music in the adjoining lounge, but I couldn't see past the crowd. Clouds of smoke, along with a strong smell of beer, nearly overwhelmed me. Wedged between the wall and the far end of the bar was a small, unoccupied, round table, and Steve led me there to sit. I slipped into the wooden chair and stuffed my pack on the floor between my legs.

"What should I drink?" I yelled to him as he leaned forward to hear.

"Labatt 50. That's what I've been drinking, it's the best."

The waiter brought two chilled bottles with glasses, and Steve showed me how to pour the beer down the side of the glass to keep it from foaming. I had tasted beer once before in my life as a child, on a rare occasion when my father brought home a can of beer and insisted I take a sip of it to satiate my curiosity. I remembered gagging from the bitter taste as he laughed, telling me he hoped I would never want to drink again. But bitter flavors had become tolerant to me as my taste matured, so this time the malty ale slid through my mouth like cold, buttered silk, and within moments rushed straight to my head. He was right. I liked this stuff. By the time my second bottle arrived, I was flying.

"I don't get it!" I said. "Why should pot be illegal and this stuff isn't? I'm more buzzed now than when I get stoned!"

"Now you know what a sham the whole thing is!" He leaned across the table as he shouted to me. "Booze is the socially acceptable drug. It lets the straight world get tanked up and pretend they're morally superior to us. You know, R.J. Reynolds and all those corporations can't wait for the day marijuana gets legalized.

When that day comes, you'll wish it never did. They get their hands on it and they'll pump it full of chemicals and sell you crap."

"You sound cynical."

"I have my reasons." Steve began staring at his bottle and peeling the label away. After a while he looked at me. "This is a fucked-up world. Before I came to Montreal, I was traveling with this chick from Nova Scotia. She was a gypsy and I was so in love with her." He stopped and lit a cigarette; he offered one to me, but I shook my head no.

He grabbed the ashtray and pulled it toward him, fingering it as he talked. "One night, we were tripping our brains out outside of Toronto, and we were hitching. These two drunk guys stopped. I didn't like the way they looked, but she thought it was cool, so we took the ride. It was a major bummer." He looked away from me to his beer and kept his eyes riveted there. "They drove us out to the woods and punched me in the head, then they beat her up and raped her. I just lay there and couldn't even move. What a useless piece of crap I was, huh?"

He shuffled around in his seat, taking a long puff on his cigarette, and I felt like my own stomach had been punched hearing this, immediately flashing back on those moments on the Boston Common.

"The world sucks. She and I made a vow to go to Death Valley and kill ourselves, but then we had a fight and she took off. I've been trying to find her. I think she was on her way back to Nova Scotia. That's where I'm going."

I could barely move, unsure of how to reply.

Steve looked into my eyes as though he were pleading. "So, you tell me. What's so great about living, anyway?"

Goose bumps covered my body as my own pain came rushing at me, and after two beers, I felt defenseless to bury it. The near rape in Boston, the way Eddie had treated me like dirt, how no one I loved ever seemed to love me back. Steve had a point. The world had a way of dishing out misery, and my life was growing emptier day by day. It seemed like the more places I traveled to, the more hopeless I felt. The Yveses of the world were too few and far between, and I never felt I belonged with such people anyhow.

I thought I could stay a step ahead of those fears as long as I dwelled on the future. Anne would be here soon, my old sidekick, the person who kept me from sinking too low. With Anne nearby, I believed I'd be fine.

I turned toward the bar, where the face of a clock was illuminated by yellowish light shining through nicotine-stained glass.

"It's almost midnight. We need to get back to the youth hostel before they lock the doors."

He stood. "Let's get out of here."

A few days later, it was time to meet my parents and Anne at the border. I stuffed my backpack into a locker at the train station as insurance to keep me in Canada. During the sixty-mile, uneventful hitchhiking trip to the border, I was filled with nervousness, excitement, and guilt. Certainly, my parents had become more understanding, but surely they hadn't changed. I doubted they were ready to accept me running my own life.

It was hard to imagine that I'd ever had a life like my old one, where my biggest worry was getting out of the house. It seemed silly to think of having to follow someone else's rules. There's a power that comes from knowing that nobody controls your life. I had that power now, and I was not willing to relinquish it. Yet my toughness and strength were fragile. It could shatter with the next nasty comment toward me, or a casual rejection from someone I liked. I was glad I would have Anne back with me again. I needed her. I was running on empty and short on ideas about how to keep going, but I didn't dare let on to my parents that anything was less than perfect.

The green metallic Ford Falcon was parked on the Canadian side of the border when I arrived. My mother walked toward me, older than I remembered her. She had more gray in her streaked hair and heavy wrinkles below her eyes that made it look like she cried all the time. She seemed so small. I hadn't realized she was shorter than me before, and I didn't recognize her cotton home-made blouse with its tiny calico flowers.

We wrapped our arms around each other, and I remembered how soft she felt, like a comforting pillow that always made me feel better.

"I promised myself I wasn't going to cry," she blurted out as her tears came rushing down. "I'm sorry."

I burst into tears too. Of course, she could cry. Why shouldn't she?

"It's okay," I reassured her through my gulps. Anne had joined in and my father wiped his own eyes as I turned to hug him, too. The shell I had built around myself to keep from missing my family was cracking, but it had yet to break.

"My goodness, what's happened to you?" My mother stood back and looked me over. "You look terrible. You've gained a lot of weight."

Was it that bad? I hardly noticed anymore, I was so used to it, but the extra fifteen or twenty pounds was a shock to my mother. I was sure she was trying to make me feel bad, to convince me I wasn't doing well on my own and needed her to fix me. It was true that I wasn't doing well, but I also knew she couldn't fix me.

"Well, we better get going. Your father has to work tomorrow, and it's a seven-hour drive back." I could tell she was controlling how critical she was, because normally she wouldn't have stopped with my weight. My mother's critique on everything wrong about me grew lengthy at times when it wasn't aimed at Anne or my father.

"We'll take you to the youth hostel, but we won't have time to stop. Unless you want to come back with us, that is."

"No. I don't think so."

"I figured as much. We won't try to make you. Maybe someday you'll be ready to come back because you want to." I heard her voice crack as her lip trembled. I knew this had to be hard for her, and it pained me to watch her suffer.

For a moment, remorse nearly overtook me, and I felt a shiver of wanting to say I would return. I was relieved when the moment passed.

I climbed into the backseat with Anne, exhaling as I felt the tension fade. She and I smiled at each other. She lifted the hem of her bellbottom jeans and slid her hand inside her boot, pulling the end of a rolled-up baggy out just enough to reveal the pot inside. She winked, then shoved the bag back down into her boot.

✳ Chapter 14

July 1971
Province de Quebec, Canada

A couple of days after Anne arrived, we heard there was a concert in Quebec City with two bands: Deep Purple and the Faces, including Rod Stewart. Anne, Steve, and I agreed to hitchhike the 160 miles together and stay overnight at the Quebec City youth hostel. Steve pointed out that he was heading that direction anyhow, and I knew he meant toward Nova Scotia. I suspected he would not be returning with us to Montreal, but I was still hoping he might change his mind and hang around, as I was getting to like him.

Inside the arena, we found seats near the floor in a boxed-in area next to what would be the ice rink when they played hockey. While we waited for the concert to begin, Steve wandered off. A while later, he returned with a little white pill.

"Someone gave me this acid." He held the pill between his thumb and forefinger and raised his eyebrows into a question. "Want to trip with me? We can split it."

I hadn't tripped since California, and I was nervous about it. There was always the question of what you were getting in strange offered pills. Anne gave me a warning look, letting me know she didn't approve. But Steve stood there staring down at me, hovering close.

"Take a little. A little isn't going to hurt you."

I didn't want to disappoint him. "Okay. A tiny piece."

He held the pill out in his hand while I broke off a section with my thumb nail, then he turned and offered some to Anne.

"No thanks." She frowned. "I'm not into mystery drugs."

The concert was delayed for over an hour. When Rod Stewart and the Faces finally took the stage, I was feeling high, but not the nice mellow kind like I had with the pure acid back in California. I could tell this was cut with speed, because my heartbeat was accelerating, and my stomach felt like there was a storm going on in there. Looking around at the audience, I saw a lot of angry people wandering around, yelling and pushing each other, and it seemed like a fight might break out at any moment. Or was I being paranoid? Were they really fighting? Or fooling around? I ground my teeth until my jaw hurt. Fortunately, I was coherent, but I spent more time feeling anxious and distracted than watching the concert.

"Yeah, England," Rod screamed into the microphone, staggering across the stage, as the predominantly French audience booed. "Maggie Mae" was a hit song, but Rod Stewart was making no fans with his obnoxious remarks. He appeared to be drunk and the crowd began chanting, "Deep Purple, Deep Purple, Deep Purple."

Steve's eyes had widened into saucers from the acid. He used his height to scan the crowd, ignoring the performance. After a while he wandered off again, leaving me with Anne.

Rod Stewart finished performing, then we waited another hour. Finally, an announcement came over the loudspeaker in French and the audience booed as the lights came on.

"What did they say?" Anne asked a girl next to us.

"They say Deep Purple is not to play. We leave, they give us the pass. We see them here another time."

"What a bummer," Anne said. "We won't get to see them."

This whole concert had turned into a bummer, as far as I was concerned. I wished we hadn't come.

As we watched the crowd emptying out of the coliseum, I grew nervous: Steve hadn't returned yet, and I didn't see him anywhere. He knew where we were, and I hadn't moved, so why hadn't he come back? I had a bad feeling about his absence. Once again, I wished I wasn't tripping. Why had I let Steve talk me into this?

"We should get going, it's eleven o'clock." Anne shuffled from one foot to the other, looking at me as though she were annoyed. "If he doesn't show up soon, we should leave without him or we won't get to the youth hostel before curfew."

I didn't want to abandon him while he was tripping. "We can't. He doesn't know where the youth hostel is."

We continued to wait while Anne and I scanned the crowd. I could see she was getting increasingly annoyed. I avoided making eye contact.

Finally, I spotted his familiar mop of streaked gray hair bobbing toward us. Relief swept over me, and I ran to greet him.

"Where have you been? I've been looking all over for you. We have to get going to the youth hostel."

"I'm not going," he announced, then looked away into the remaining crowd. "I came back to tell you."

I felt like the floor was collapsing below me. What had I done wrong?

"Steve, that's not fair. You asked me to trip with you, and I did. I wouldn't have done this on my own. Where are you going?"

He turned back to look at me, but his voice sounded sullen and depressed. "I don't know. Who cares? I'm just going."

"Then why did you ask me to trip with you? *You have no right to do this!*" I couldn't distinguish the anger from the hurt; they felt like one emotion.

"You're right." He nodded his head, a vacant look on his face. "Life sucks." He paused. "That's why I'd rather be dead."

His response hit me like a physical blow. It was happening again. People were always failing me. Life was one big hurt after the next, and no matter where I went it never got any better. I seemed to be chasing a string of falling dominoes, one tumbling over after the next as I raced toward the inevitable end. Perhaps Steve had the only solution.

I watched him walk back into the crowd, and I turned and dove out the nearest exit with Anne racing behind me. I didn't care if she followed or not. The night had turned stormy. Torrents of rain pelted me, soaking my hair and my clothes, as I stumbled along the side of the road, my sandaled feet sloshing through unseen puddles. Warm tears ran down my face, the only warm part of me.

"Sharon! Sharon!" Anne chased after me. "Which way's the youth hostel? We have to hitch to the youth hostel." She caught up and grabbed my jacket to get me to stop.

"I don't know. What difference does it make? I don't care what happens to me."

"Come on. We're hitching." Anne grabbed hold of my upper arm and pulled me to the other side of the road, where the traffic was driving out of the coliseum parking lot. I let her lead me blindly, the glare of the oncoming headlights jabbing at my dilated eyes. I shut my eyes against the pain.

When a car stopped, Anne pushed me inside and begged the driver to take us to the youth hostel, saying we were lost. He must have agreed, as the next thing I was aware of, we were there.

Inside the old prison walls, the air was damp and musty. Anne crawled into a bunk with my pack tucked beside her, but I knew sleeping would be out of the question for me after doing the acid. Most of the high had worn off, but the residual effects of too much speed and my anxious state kept me wired and awake.

I found my way downstairs to the cafeteria, a mostly underground room with a concrete floor and tiny, high windows. For ten cents, I bought a hot chocolate and sat at an empty picnic table. They'd been painted in bright red gloss. Pens and markers left the stories of the travelers. GEORGE M NYC 6/71; Ronnie, Derek, Jack, Mike on their way to Toronto—July 3, 1971. Peace, Peggy & Jim 7-9-71; *Nicole et Jean sur le chemin du Montréal.*

I wondered what I would write if I had a pen. Where was I from? Boston? California? Connecticut? Where was I going? I had no destination to write beside my name, no lover to include as my accomplice in getting there, no words of wisdom to add to this wooden slab of history and poetry. It didn't seem to matter that I had been here at all, and I couldn't imagine who would care if I wasn't. Well, Anne and my parents would, of course, but that didn't mean anyone else ever would.

The hot chocolate didn't warm me, since my sandaled feet and hair were soaked. A few other ghoulish-looking souls loitered at tables, but no one seemed friendly. I probably looked deathly myself.

It was many hours before a pale light came in the windows. I wondered if it was too early to wake Anne. Surely, she had slept enough, I decided, and headed upstairs.

❮❮❯❯

Anne and I spent the day wandering around Quebec. I was glad to have her for company. During my sleepless night, I had adjusted to the fact that Steve had taken off—that he had his mission and had to follow it. Still, I hated feeling like I had been abandoned again.

By evening, I was exhausted. With the youth hostel closed all day, there was no napping to compensate for lost sleep. I thought about crashing early, but a new crowd had arrived, and I didn't want to miss anything. In the main hall, a group of people sat on the floor facing two guitarists who had settled onto metal folding chairs to perform, a guitar case open between them for donations. They had worked the crowd into a sing-along with a Pete Seeger song about garbage. The performers sang the story about garbage thrown into the oceans and pollution in the air, while the gathered audience sang along to the chorus. I joined in.

Fifteen people sat before them, then twenty, thirty or more. Most of the youth hostel occupants were being drawn into the music. When the song was over, the troubadours jumped to their feet and, like Pied Pipers, began leading us through hallways and tunnels and past locked unused prison cells, a cold dampness hovering in the air. I followed with the group, hypnotized by the music that had joined us together, singing now and then when I knew the lyrics. We were all journeying on the road to somewhere, or nowhere, with the music to unite us.

At last the musicians stooped to crawl into an arch-shaped stone dungeon lit by one red light bulb hanging from the ceiling. Those still with us followed, crouching into the space and sitting cross-legged on the icy stone floor. They began singing a Bob Dylan song, "Like a Rolling Stone." It had been a hit when I was younger, but now I felt like it was my song, a story of homelessness and life on the road, of being lost and searching.

A kind of sadness seemed to prevail in the room as we sang, because it was everyone's story; we were all drifters, searchers, looking for answers and some kind of meaning, as though it might exist in the next city, with the next ride, or the next lover, or the next drug. Where was that dream we had grown up believing? That television happiness that *Ozzie and Harriet* and *Leave It to Beaver* had promised us in our childhood? We were disillusioned, awakened, fallen angels. We knew the dream was a fraud because every day young people were dying in Vietnam for no reason, sent there by leaders who were desperate to convince us they hadn't screwed up. If middle-class America didn't have the answers, perhaps we could find them here.

While the raw, moldy air penetrated our nostrils, ghostly spirits seemed to drift from within the prison walls, as though they were haunting us, envying our freedom and filling our souls with the weight of theirs. Tonight, on the Plains of Abraham, in the dimly lit corridors of Le Petite Bastille, the restless spirits of old and new danced together—the dance of the hopeless souls, the dance of reckless abandon, a flirtation with the devil himself.

❖ ❖ ❖ ❖

Once Anne and I were back in Montreal, I made the decision to kill myself. No half-assed, swallow a dozen pills and get your stomach pumped kind of attempt but a serious, fool-proof death. If I was to kill myself, it would have to be done quickly and thoroughly, with no turning back.

It seemed the obvious solution to my problems, and ever since Steve had first suggested it, I'd felt the idea seeping into my veins in a slow, steady drip.

The truth was, I had lost my nerve to go on. I had grown suspicious of everyone I met, afraid of every car that drove too slow next to me when I was walking. My stomach muscles would tighten with anxiety if a man whistled or made a comment in my direction. What was he thinking? Was I safe? I realized I was avoiding meeting new people and keeping to myself much of the time. I wasn't enjoying living like this, but I couldn't face going back to my old life in South Windsor, either. Afraid to go on, afraid to go back, I was frozen into a state of depression and fear. Death clawed at me with tempting fingers, whispering promises of relief as it blew in my ear. With death, I could stop being afraid. With death, I wouldn't have to hurt anymore. With death, I could be joyously empty of all these feelings I wanted so desperately to go away.

Once I made the decision, it was as though a weight had been lifted from me. I thought it strange how my depression vanished as soon as I reached this conclusion, knowing it would all be over soon.

But how would I do it?

I could jump in front of a speeding vehicle. That would be effective, and it would be worth a few minutes of agony to put an end to this misery I called my life. I stood on the sidewalk of Sherbrooke Street, studying four lanes of aggressive traffic. Intent on beating the lights before they turned red, the vehicles rushed forward, oblivious to me, as I stood on the side of the road in a semi-hypnotic state, wondering if a little voice would urge me forward, making this the final moment. When a line of traffic stopped in front of me waiting for red to become green, I noticed the face of a woman turning to smile at her young daughter, as the girl held her doll at the window.

I took a step back. Was it fair for me to put this trip on some unsuspecting driver? Would their life be ruined by killing me?

The pedestrian light turned white and I joined a group of people crossing the road, knowing I would have to find some other way.

A leap from a high building was a possibility. There were plenty to choose from. In fact, the youth hostel itself had a rooftop exit, I had heard. The youth hostel was a bad option, though. I knew something like a suicide would mean immediate closure. That was no way to treat the place that was home for so many other travelers like me.

But surely some other monstrous building was available. When I reached St. Catherine Street, I found myself staring up at Place Ville-Marie, a cross-shaped building named for the Virgin Mary, the highest structure in the city. That would be a fitting place to die, wouldn't it? And the top floor was open for tours, making it an easy access.

I had reservations about the actual fall, however. Was it true you died of fright before you hit the ground? Would it seem like an eternity during the drop? What if I changed my mind somewhere around the tenth floor? That would be terrible, knowing there was no turning back, just waiting for the impact. Better to go immediately.

I didn't want to think about my parents finding out. I tried to keep those thoughts far away, almost wanted to physically push my hand out in front of me to make them distant. I hated to do this to them, but they didn't have to live inside me, did they?

I turned away and walked past the Christ Church Cathedral, where I'd often sat on the wall and socialized with other transients that gathered downtown. I had no interest in joining them today, despite recognizing a couple of people from the Quebec City youth hostel that I'd spoken to before.

I walked back to the apartment where we were staying, a couple of blocks from the youth hostel, near McGill University.

Steve had found this place for the three of us before we left for Quebec. Now only Anne and I remained, along with a couple of other transients and the two renters.

Anne was stretched out on the sofa; she'd slept late. "Where have you been?"

"Out walking around, trying to decide what I want to do next."

I hadn't told Anne about how desperate I was feeling, or my plans. I knew she would be hurt, and probably try to talk me out of it. And why upset her any more than necessary? When it happened, that would be soon enough for her to know.

"I've been thinking, too." She sat up, pushing her hair behind her ears. "I think I'm going home for a few days. Maybe get some stuff and come back. I'm not sure. I don't feel like staying here anymore. This moving all over the place is getting old."

"I know. It's been getting to me, too."

"Why don't you come with me?"

I felt a spark, the strangest feeling of wanting to do that. I could go back and see my parents one last time. Unexpectedly, thoughts of death gave me new choices.

"You know, I think I will."

"Well, let's go." Anne stood and began gathering her belongings. "It's not that late. We could get there before dark."

Suddenly, I was eager to join her. "Okay. I'll grab my things."

Seven hours later, a ride was dropping us at the top of our street.

Chapter 15

August 1971
South Windsor, Connecticut

Anne and I hadn't called our parents to say we were coming home, so when my mother opened the door, a gasp of air jumped from her throat. She said nothing as she took me into her arms, and I felt a strange exhilaration as she held me. I was glad to be there. She didn't ask how we'd gotten there, or how long we were staying. Not at all like my mother.

Our shaggy miniature poodle, Herman, barked and yapped at my feet. He rolled onto his back and stretched out, exposing his belly, then jumped up again, nearly falling over himself in excitement. I crouched down and rubbed his belly; his dog tags shook as his legs kicked at the sky. I'd missed him more than I'd realized. I'd missed home more than I'd dared believe.

When my father arrived home from work soon after, there was more hugging and less arguing than I could ever remember. I had always believed that my parents would never change, that they moved like some giant ocean liner on its path toward a pre-defined destination. It felt weird how polite everyone was, now that we were all strangers.

❀❀❀❀

Over the next few days, as I settled into being at home, the arguments finally began. My parents knocked on my door one evening after dinner while I was sitting on the floor going through some old sketches I'd made. When I told them to come in, my mother said we needed to talk. I stiffened in anticipation of a confrontation.

My father sat on the edge of my bed while I remained cross-legged on the floor.

"Are you a drug addict?" he asked.

I shook my head. "No. I smoke pot, but I'm not a drug addict." I had decided to stop taking LSD and any other pills after the bummer trip in Quebec, so in my mind, that didn't warrant mentioning.

"Well, if you're not an addict, why don't you stop?" His face was locked in a stern frown that told me he was not open to any understanding on this matter. My mother sat beside him, frozen in proper posture, her feet flat on the floor and her hands folded in her lap, unusually silent.

"Because I don't want to. I like to smoke pot. It's fun."

"It's not fun, it's dangerous!" His voice boomed in the tiny room.

I continued to speak in my normal tone. "What do you know about it? Have you ever smoked pot? I know lots of people who smoke pot, and nothing bad has ever happened to them. You can't believe all that crap on TV, you know."

"And I suppose you know everything!"

"I've learned a lot of things you'll never know."

"Things I don't want to know!"

There was silence as my parents looked at one another, as though unsure of what to say next. Finally, my mother asked in a calm voice, "So what are you going to do now?"

"I haven't decided."

"Why don't you stay home?" I knew she'd wanted to ask this since I'd walked in the door a few days earlier.

I stared at the floor, speaking in a monotone voice. "I haven't decided if I want to keep living or not." It was difficult saying this to them, but I knew I had to.

My mother broke into tears.

"How can you say that?" my father shouted. "We're worried about you! You can't keep living like this!"

"That's what I mean. I can't keep living like this. I haven't decided what I'm going to do about that."

"What does that mean?" he roared. "We're not going to let you leave again if you're like this!"

"You know you can't make me stay. I have to figure it out for myself. What's so great to live for, anyway?" I looked at them, knowing they didn't have an answer. Their lives had been difficult for years, and I was making it even harder for them. I wondered how they could live with that pain when I was barely able to live with mine.

"See? Drugs are making you think these things. You never used to be like this." My father sounded exasperated.

"Drugs have absolutely nothing to do with anything. You couldn't possibly understand." I felt the fight go out of me. Drugs were just a diversion from my problems, not the cause. It was life's pain I couldn't face, and there wasn't enough joy to help me get beyond that. I'd tried to make a different life for myself from the one they were living, from the one they expected me to live, and it had turned into a failure. I believed the world had showed me what it was made of.

Variations of this argument continued for a few days, alternating with times of great politeness when I wondered if these were actually my parents. Meanwhile, Anne avoided getting dragged into any of these discussions by saying that she simply wanted to chill out and get her head together and was enjoying some peace and quiet.

I was still carrying a book Ed had given me in Venice from his collection of hippie literature. It was Robert Heinlein's *Stranger in a Strange Land*. I dove into its pages, immersing myself in the magic of the story. The main character, a man raised on Mars who had returned to earth and brought his Martian ways with him, had created a loving, idealistic commune of people around him whose ideologies closely matched hippie ideals of universal love, support for those you love, and no jealousy between lovers. He founded an inclusive religion for the world, and they called each other *water brothers*. I knew this had become a term of endearment among hippies in some places. The spirit of the book was infectious, and I found myself feeling uplifted by its message. My depression waned as I daydreamed that some kind of utopia was out there, that someone might have created a loving, spiritual community like that, and if they had, perhaps I could find it. This was something new for me to consider. Maybe I had not yet exhausted all the world's possibilities.

❖ ❖ ❖ ❖

One afternoon, I hitchhiked to the shopping plaza I'd hung around when I was still in school to see if anyone I knew was there. No one was. To kill time, I decided to walk home the two and a half miles.

On quiet Troy Road, not a car disturbed the tranquil summer afternoon. A long stretch of road was flanked by meadows of tall grass and flowering weeds. Crickets and grasshoppers screeched from deep within the field, and a fly buzzed and darted down each side of my head. I took a deep breath, taking in the scent, then put my foot up on an aging, split rail fence lining the road and stared across the pasture. A butterfly lighted on a nearby flower, hovered for a moment, then moved on to another. A bird called out as though warning the others that a stranger was in their midst. I stood, watching this familiar and splendid world that I had ridden by hundreds of times.

Why had I never noticed this brilliance, this energy, this magical thing called life that was right in front of my eyes? For the first time in months, I felt exuberant. I felt my own blood pulsing through my body, warmed from the sun. I noticed the clean, fresh air moving through my nose into my lungs. I felt alive and I loved it—I wanted nothing more than to be alive. What was left to be afraid of? Wasn't death the greatest fear that anyone could imagine? Yet I feared death no more. What worldly terror could possibly top death?

I stepped off the fence and started to skip, something I hadn't done in years. It didn't matter if someone drove by and saw me—who cared? I skipped, jumped, and even stopped and twirled around right there on the side of the road, drinking in the glorious sunshine, the soothing sounds of chirping and humming, the sense of peace I felt filling my being. I laughed, then giggled, as if I was high, as if I was Ebenezer Scrooge on Christmas morning, discovering I was still in the present and had time left to change my life. My three visiting spirits had come from Robert Heinlein's book, and combined themselves with this moment of awakening by nature.

It didn't matter what came next, as long as something came next. I could handle it. In fact, I could handle just about anything. I could even handle being at home.

❮❮➔➔

When September came, Anne got her job back at the Travelers Insurance Company and I started school. I took the plunge and abandoned junk food, smoking pot, and guys, at least for a while. I convinced my parents to get me a three-speed bicycle that I could ride around town instead of hitchhiking. I figured I could get into shape at the same time.

I felt like an alien from another planet when I returned to school. I had nothing in common with the high school students who used to be my friends, whose pettiness annoyed me as they whined about their parents, avoided doing homework, and sneaked around smoking pot. I missed having people I could relate to.

I spent my days and weeks working hard in school. In order to graduate with my class, I took both my sophomore and junior English classes over the year, along with additional credits. I realized I needed to graduate if I didn't want to end up working somewhere like Stop and Shop forever. I spent my free time riding my bike, reading books, writing poetry, embroidering, and doing macramé. On weekends I made granola and read *Mother Earth News*, a magazine that Anne gave me a subscription to for my seventeenth birthday in November. I got a job for the holidays at a department store and saved nearly all my money for the summer.

I felt healthy and whole, but my life grew boring. The weeks turned into months, and the boredom turned into discontent. By late spring, I felt the walls closing in on me, but I made sure I finished my junior year and received all my credits before leaving for the summer.

Chapter 16

June 1972
Patterson, New Jersey

The day after I finished my last final for my junior year of high school, Lynn and I stood on the westbound onramp for Interstate 80 in Patterson, New Jersey, with our thumbs out. After getting a late start from Connecticut, we'd reached there by late afternoon.

After only a couple of minutes, a dented metallic brown Chevy with two hippie guys and a girl in the front seat stopped for us.

"Where're you heading?" the driver asked as we slung our bags into the backseat, sliding in after them.

"Chicago," I replied.

"I'm on my way to the Pennsylvania border, so I can get you that far. I picked these two up and I'm taking them to a state park out there." He pulled back into the traffic and onto the highway as the rest of us began introductions.

"I'm Mike," the other guy said. "This is my girlfriend, Gina." He tipped his black bowler hat wrapped in rhinestones in our direction. As he turned toward us, I saw his T-shirt had the Rolling

Stones logo—a giant tongue—on the front. Gina, who looked about fifteen, smiled silently back at us from beneath curtains of dyed red hair with black roots as Mike wrapped all his limbs around her.

"I love your shirt," I told Mike. "That's why we're going to Chicago—to see the Stones. A friend of mine there scored tickets."

"Right on! You're gonna boogie." Mike lit a joint and passed it back to us. "Us, too. I got six front-row seats for the final show at Madison Square Garden. You can't imagine what I had to do to get them. What a fuckin' night that's gonna be."

"So you're just out driving people where they want to go?" Lynn asked the driver as she slid her chin-length, wavy brown hair behind her ears.

"You bet."

"Christ, you're a hell of a nice guy." She leaned on the back of his seat and held out her pack of cigarettes, offering him one. "Too bad everyone isn't like you. What's your name?"

"They call me Butch." He took her cigarette pack and shook one out. "It's an old nickname that stuck. You should've seen me in junior high, man, I was bald."

Lynn reached out and pulled back his thick, dark hair, holding it in the air with both her hands to show me how long it was. He laughed.

"Maybe you should get a new nickname," she said. "Look at all this, it's longer than mine. Almost as long as Marty's."

"Who's Marty? He your boyfriend?"

She dropped Butch's hair and took back her cigarettes. "Good question." She looked at me with a smirk and raised one eyebrow. "What do you think, Sharon? Is Marty my boyfriend?"

Lynn had joined me on this trip to Chicago to impress Marty with her independence. We'd met each other through a guy I'd been seeing, Dave, who was Marty's friend. Lynn spent hours sitting around Dave's apartment hoping Marty would stop by, prodding me for details about his activities when she wasn't there. She was a slightly chubby, traditional Italian girl stuck in an era that didn't fit her. Marriage was her number one priority, and she made no effort to disguise it. Marty took her riding on his motorcycle, and into his bed, but made no commitments.

Over the winter I had been exchanging letters with Rob from Venice, who now lived in Chicago. Recently he'd surprised me with a phone call telling me he had two extra tickets for the Rolling Stones concert there and inviting me and a friend to join him. I'd accepted, but finding a suitable companion to hitchhike there with had been difficult. Anne had flatly refused, having decided to return to Montreal. Two other friends of mine had left for other places.

Lynn was nineteen and hadn't traveled before, so she'd agreed to join me.

"I guess you could say I'm in love with Marty, but I'm not sure if he's my boyfriend. I miss him already. It sucks." Lynn paused to light a cigarette. "Mike and Gina look happy, anyhow."

Mike and Gina smiled, then kissed to demonstrate that she was right.

"How about you, Butch? You have a girlfriend?"

"Ain't nobody in my life right now." He stared ahead at the highway. "I had a girlfriend, but she left me. Can't blame her. She got sick of watching me kill myself with crystal." He took another drag on his cigarette. "I love my speed, but speed kills. You know it, I know it, Christ, they even wrote a song about it, but I got to have it. Thank God I found Jesus. As long as Jesus loves me, I know I got a chance, but my body, it's all fucked up. I don't eat, I don't sleep, but I gain weight. My body's breaking down and giving out, but I can't stop the stuff. I love this shit, makes me feel like God when I'm doing it, and don't get me wrong, I don't mean no disrespect to Jesus or nothing, 'cause Jesus, he's the only one who can get me out of this."

Crystal methamphetamine, a drug I had never had the desire to try. I had never even met a hardcore "speed freak" before. Even some druggies I knew considered the stuff too dangerous, more deadly than heroin because of the way it destroyed your body and could cause a heart attack.

While Gina and Mike necked in the front seat, Butch chain-smoked and rattled on with Lynn and me as his audience.

A couple of hours later, a sign for the exit for the park at the Pennsylvania line appeared where Mike and Gina had planned to go, and Butch made a proposal to the group.

"I got enough speed to last me until tomorrow afternoon. If we can get some gas in this tank, I'll keep driving. Gina, Mike, you two in? We got enough money to get us to Ohio and back?"

Mike seemed unconcerned about where they were heading, as long as Gina was in his arms while they went there. "Yeah, sure. Let's take Lynn and Sharon to Ohio. I got five bucks for the tank." He pulled the money from the pocket of his pink brocade bell-bottoms and tossed it into Butch's lap; Butch nodded his head in thanks. Lynn and I dug into our pockets and pulled out a few dollars more, and Lynn handed them over the seat.

"This will do it," Butch said. "I just have to watch the time, so I get home before I run out of speed. If I don't score, it gets nasty. Man, I hate to crash. Some people can't handle the crash at all, they end up killing themselves. Some take downers—takes the edge off, helps you sleep through it. Sometimes I sleep a little, but mostly I try to score so I can keep on going. Sooner or later it will kill you if you don't come down; problem is, when I'm up here,

I don't care, it feels so goddamn good, right on top of the whole fucking planet—"

"Well I'm a cigarette junkie," Lynn interrupted. "When we get to the gas station, I need a pack. I'm about out." She dug through her pocketbook, found her last two cigarettes, and handed one to Butch.

Sometime later we arrived at a 76 Truck Stop, and everyone but Butch ate. He only drank coffee, which he claimed helped him relax. Mike offered to drive for a while and Butch sat in back with Lynn and me, talking quietly, as we cruised through the long, dark stretches of Pennsylvania. I felt bad for him. Only his belief in Jesus offered him hope, and it made me want to believe too, for his sake. I thought back to the religious books I'd read as a child, where suffering people had their lives rescued through God's miracles. I'd grown to think of those books as fairy tales, children's stories designed to inspire piety and make them behave. But Butch needed those stories to be real, needed their magic and their healing power.

We made a few other stops during the night and reached Ohio as the sun was rising. Butch pulled off the highway to turn around, and Lynn and I got out. Everyone gave us their phone numbers, and we promised to get in touch on the way back through Patterson.

I hugged Butch good-bye. He looked terrible, with black areas beneath his eyes and skin like a plucked chicken. Lynn handed him her cigarette pack, saving herself a few, and kissed him on the cheek. They all took their places up front and we watched them drive away. Then I did something I hadn't done in a long time. I said a prayer to Jesus for Butch.

❖❖❖❖

That Sunday June morning was bright and sunny. Traffic was sparse, offering little hope of catching a ride. I wasn't worried about reaching Chicago, however. With all the progress we had made, we would reach it easily by afternoon. We sat on our packs at the onramp in between waiting for vehicles.

"I wonder what Marty's doing right now." Lynn pouted as she smoked her cigarette. "Probably in bed with some chickie."

"Maybe." I shrugged. "You know how guys are. Why don't you forget about him until we get back? Going to Chicago is good for you. Now Marty knows you can live without him. He'll probably even miss you."

"Think he'll miss me enough to put a ring on my finger?" She held up her left hand and wiggled her ring finger.

I laughed. It was hard for me to take the idea of marriage seriously, but to Lynn, it was the only thing worth taking seriously.

"I know. You think I'm nuts thinking Marty will ever marry me. I think I'm nuts, but I can dream, can't I?" Lynn ground her cigarette stub onto the pavement. "How'd you get so smart for seventeen?"

"The hard way," I said. "I'm a whole lot stronger than I was a year ago. I'm not putting up with anyone's crap anymore. I can take care of myself. So can you. You'll see. By the time we get back from Chicago, you'll be ready to make that train trip across Canada with me."

All winter I had been gathering information on passenger rail travel across Canada. Lynn had tentatively agreed to join me. Now that I had money saved from working in a store at Christmas and babysitting, I could afford a ticket. After this short trip to Chicago, I intended to return to Connecticut and prepare. My parents had agreed to notarize their written permission for me to cross the border, provided I took the train and returned by September.

It was still early when a car pulled over and the clean-cut, middle-aged driver leaned over the seat to talk to us out the passenger side window, sounding cheerful. "Good morning, girls. Which way are you heading?"

"West to Chicago." I wondered why this conservative-looking man in a suit had stopped. He didn't look like a pervert. Besides, wasn't it too early in the morning for perverts?

"Well, get in, I'm going that way."

Lynn and I looked at each other and then agreed to take the ride. We eased into the front seat together, holding our packs on our laps.

"I'm not going that far," the man began. "Actually, I'm on my way to church, and I wondered if you'd like to join me. I'd be happy to buy you breakfast after. Have you eaten?"

"Not yet," Lynn answered as my stomach growled. Free breakfast sounded appealing. While I was usually put off by religious zealots, this man did not seem overbearing.

Lynn and I had both been raised Catholic. I had grown up attending Sunday morning Mass, but I hadn't stepped inside a church for some time.

Lynn asked my opinion by raising her eyebrows at me. We had begun to read each other's expressions to reach agreement on decisions. I gave a little shrug that said, "fine if you want to."

"It's okay by us," she told the driver. "We're not in a hurry. It seems like the right thing to do after that ride yesterday. We had terrific luck getting here."

"Praise the Lord." The driver's face looked radiant.

Part of me cringed, but I pushed that feeling aside. It was difficult to feel anything but optimism this morning. The weather was perfect, and Butch's efforts on our behalf had touched my heart. I realized I missed having God in my life. A void now existed where the faith that had been important to me as a child had once resided.

I thought back to my first communion, when I believed God stood near me, along with Jesus and the Holy Ghost, and all the angels were fluttering behind my shoulder like the pictures in my catechism. As I prayed, I felt Jesus would be with me forever and I would never sin again.

As I'd passed through my teen years, however, the hypocrisy I'd witnessed throughout the Catholic Church first made me angry, then disbelieving. Initially it was the church's unwillingness to condemn the Vietnam War, then their stand against birth control in an overpopulated world. It didn't matter to me that masses were now in English instead of Latin, or that teenagers played guitars and sang "Blowing in the Wind" during services. These superficial changes didn't compensate for the way the Church had failed to be a socially responsible leader.

Nonetheless, I'd made an attempt to restore that childlike piety in recent years. While Anne and I lived in Venice, we'd decided to attend mass in Santa Monica one day. I'd poured my sins out to the priest in the confessional booth, certain he'd prescribe a penance of saying rosaries for days. Instead he'd responded, "You are a seriously troubled young woman. I want you to come see me after mass."

I'd been taken aback. I'd believed confession was confidential, hence the shielded booth. I'd also been taught that once sins were confessed, God forgave them. Why should I need to talk to this priest? Instead of helping me feel absolved from sin and reunited with the church, it was as though he had branded me with a scarlet letter. I felt alienated throughout the mass, and I didn't go speak with the priest afterwards. Many years later, when abuse began surfacing about Catholic priests, I suspected the worst—that he might have identified me as an easy target and intended to take advantage of me.

After mass, Anne and I stood on the side of the road hitch-hiking, watching the churchgoers drive past us, gaping and shaking their heads. They had seen us sit among them and take communion, but that didn't change anything. I wanted nothing to do with their hypocrisy, and I'd sworn I would never set foot in a Catholic church again. Yet without the Church, God himself eluded me. Not knowing what to believe, I had decided to label myself an agnostic.

The church that Thomas, our driver, took us to was a congregation of people who met in a school cafeteria. I felt self-conscious as we followed him between the rows of folding metal chairs, passing between people that knew each other well. Along the way, he stopped to greet many of them and introduced us by name. They were Midwesterners, farm people and suburbanites, dressed in simple, conservative Sunday clothes. Yet each of them smiled, some shaking our hands, others telling us how glad they were we could join them. I kept waiting for the look of disdain, the sneer of disapproval, but I never saw it. What made these people react so differently to us? No one could have been fooled into thinking we were one of them.

We sat as the service began. An elderly woman took her place at a portable organ, and the congregation broke into "Rock of Ages." I had never attended any service that wasn't Catholic, so I had no idea what to expect. When the minister stood up to the pulpit and spoke, he didn't speak about how guilty we should feel for being terrible sinners and the long, suffering pain of Jesus, like I had heard in church. Instead, he spoke about the joy of life, how great it was to share all the bounty the Lord had given us. He cracked jokes and the congregation laughed openly, and when they sang, they sang as if Jesus himself had bought a ticket and was waiting to be entertained.

By the time the service was over, I had to catch myself to keep from "Praising the Lord" right back to the friendly people who continued to thank us for coming. Thomas introduced us to the minister, who did not act as though I was "a seriously troubled young woman" but simply another member of the church who had come to pray that Sunday morning.

I realized then that what made these people different was they weren't mouthing empty words from a book or going to church as a duty. God was real to them, as real as he had been to me during my first communion, and it occurred to me that perhaps it wasn't faith in God that was riddled with hypocrisy, it was religion that was at fault. Religion had forgotten what these people knew—that God was for everyone, whatever path you traveled and however you chose to express yourself. Even if you were a hitchhiker on your way to Chicago.

As promised, Thomas took us to breakfast at McDonald's afterward.

"My mother's cooking a big spaghetti dinner this afternoon," he said. "You're welcome to stay and join us, if you like. The minister will be there, as will be a number of members of the congregation."

"That's nice of you to offer," Lynn answered. "Everyone has been so friendly to us, I can't believe it. But we have to be in Chicago for this concert on Tuesday, and if we don't get going, we might not make it."

"Thanks for everything," I added. "This was nice of you to buy us breakfast. Church was great. I didn't expect that."

"Well, if you girls change your mind, you know where we are. Stop in and see us on the way back."

"We'll do that," Lynn said.

❦❦❧❧

Once again at the onramp, Lynn and I marveled over the people we'd been meeting on our trip.

"Isn't this great?" I asked her. "And we can see everyone again on the return trip."

I had no way of knowing that Lynn and I would never get the chance to hitchhike back east.

Chapter 17

June 1972
Chicago, Illinois

It was still daylight when Lynn and I reached Chicago. We arrived in the backseat of a Cadillac convertible driven by a couple who agreed to drop us in Old Town, where Rob had said he would meet us.

I called him from a phone booth, and he told me he'd be there in five minutes.

We stood prominently on the sidewalk, where Rob could see us. I had no idea what he'd be driving, so when two motorcycles came roaring through traffic and jumped onto the wide sidewalk in front of us, Lynn almost fell into me getting out of their way. I was ready to scream at the laughing driver, but as he pulled off his sunglasses, I recognized Rob.

"Hey, Sharon, welcome to Chicago!" he shouted.

My mouth dropped open because of how different he looked. He had grown a beard and cut his hair shorter. He was wearing a brown leather fringed jacket and looked tougher, not like the laid-back acid head of Venice days. Even his bike had changed. It had been remodeled from a California chopper into a racing street bike with short forks and cropped handlebars. There was a streetwise kind of sexiness about Rob now that I had never seen before.

He stepped off his bike and engulfed me in his arms, then leaned over and kissed me. "This is a great city. You're going to love it here!"

I had a sense he was right.

"I want you to meet Frank." He motioned toward his riding partner. Frank was an attractive man with long, wavy hair and a full beard, as well as a dimpled smile. He nodded toward us. Lynn raised her eyebrows at me with a smile.

"I wonder what Marty would think of this?" Her tone was provocative. "So, Sharon, is it safe to ride with these guys?"

"Did you come all the way out here to be safe, or to have fun?" Rob teased, jumping back on his bike. "Come on, we'll take you back to the house."

Frank shot Lynn a wink as he reached behind him to pull down the passenger stirrups. She stepped on his bike as I adjusted the stirrups on Rob's and maneuvered on behind him.

As I reached my arms around Rob's waist, I felt both comfort and anxiety, anticipating the excitement and terror of the ride ahead. We took off, weaving through traffic at speeds that made my pulse race. After a few minutes, I began to relax and let myself trust his instincts, smiling over at Lynn as she watched for my reaction from the back of Frank's bike.

Too quickly, we arrived at a brick building where Rob lived on Sedgwick Avenue, in a section he referred to as New Town.

Lynn stepped off Frank's bike. "God! You guys are maniacs. You drive like that all the time, or just for our benefit?"

"That was nothing," I said. "You should have seen him out in California on those mountain roads!"

Rob dismounted and pulled his bike into the curb alongside Frank's. "Trouble with Chicago is the roads are so damn boring. They're one long, straight line. That's one thing I really miss about California."

He led us up the steps of a three-story brick building. "This is the new hot spot to live. Everybody's moving out of Old Town 'cause it's pretty scary there after dark."

When we reached the second-floor apartment, I gasped. No one I knew lived anywhere as nice. There was a huge bay window topped in stained glass in the living room, a fireplace framed in tile, a chandelier hanging from the high ceiling. Thick red shag carpeting covered the floor and one wall held framed concert posters. Brass hookah pipes and statues of Buddha were interspersed with baskets of trinkets.

"This is beautiful!"

"Yeah, that's Kendra's touch. She and Jim are my roommates. I've known him since high school. He's a great guy. I don't know how the hell he got hooked up with that broad, though. What a bitch she is. But she's a great decorator."

Frank reached into his pocket and pulled out a joint as we all settled on the carpet around the coffee table. "How about we welcome these ladies to Chicago properly?"

"Good idea. I got brews in the fridge. Sharon, you like beer?" Rob asked as he headed for the kitchen.

"Love it," I yelled after him.

Frank lit the joint and moved closer to Lynn as he passed it to her, smiling. It looked to me like he was flirting, and she seemed pleased; she smiled back at him before catching my eye and winking.

"Tell me," Rob called out as he returned down the hall with the beers, "how is that sister of yours? You know, I always liked her, but I never could figure that chick out. I don't know where her head was at. I don't think she knew, either. How come she wouldn't come out with you?"

I shook my head. "She wanted to go back to Montreal. If Lynn hadn't come with me, I probably wouldn't be here at all." I was pleased I'd been able to pull off this trip without her support, and that it was going well.

"We're glad she came," Frank said as we popped open our beer cans. "How about you, Lynn? You glad you came?"

"So far, this has been one hell of a trip." She laughed. "Anybody got any cigarettes? I ran out around Toledo."

Rob pulled out his pack and offered one to Lynn and then Frank. "She's the smart one." He motioned toward me. "You still don't smoke, do you?"

I shook my head. Smoking cigarettes had never made sense to me, and I was glad I hadn't started.

Rob struck a match and lit Lynn's cigarette, and then Frank's, but before he could light his own, Lynn sprang to her knees, leaned over, and blew the match out. "Three on a match is bad luck. Light yours off my cigarette."

Rob glared at her. "Oh, come on! You believe that shit? Don't do that again. I'll take my chances." He snatched the cigarette from her hand to light his, then handed it back, staring at her with his mouth open.

"You do what you want," Lynn told him. "I was only trying to help. I never go third on a match. I don't do last match in a pack either. That's even worse luck. I always throw the match book away when there's one left."

"You're nuts," Rob told her.

"Maybe. But so far, nothing really bad has ever happened to me, so I'm sticking with it."

Two days later, Lynn and I were squeezed together in the passenger's seat of Rob's '66 Dodge van as we arrived at Frank's place to pick him up for the concert. Frank climbed in front and pulled Lynn onto his lap after setting down his cooler of beer and tequila on the floor between his legs. Rob had brought hashish, and he pressed some into a pipe to pass as Frank opened the booze. By the time we reached the Coliseum parking lot we'd emptied several beers, drank shots of tequila from the bottle, smoked the hash, and had the 8-track tape player in Rob's van cranking Stones tunes at maximum decibels. We let out a few practice howls around the van to get the mood going.

Once inside the Coliseum, I was surprised to see twenty or thirty cops dressed in riot attire, blocking the area around the stage. I had never seen that many police inside a concert before.

When Mick Jagger burst onto the stage, the roar of the audience almost drowned him out. He was dressed in a skin-tight shirt and moved rapidly from one end of the stage to the other, jerking his microphone to the beat, gesturing to the audience to move closer despite the cops. At his command, we all pushed forward, climbing over rows upon rows of chairs, stomping on the metal seats in time to the music as we stood on them, yelling out the words we knew along with Mick's raspy voice. The energy in the room was electrifying, and one man alone controlled it. I yelled and hollered and jumped on my chair like the others around me, because it felt so damn good to do it.

Before their final song, the house lights came on and the riot squad linked arms, standing shoulder to shoulder and boot to boot across the front of the stage in defiance of the crowd, as Mick screamed out the lyrics to "Street Fighting Man." The song had been banned from Chicago radio stations in 1968 following the violence during the Democratic National Convention, where thousands of police and National Guardsmen had clashed with half as many anti-war demonstrators and hundreds had been injured. It had been released a week after the event. Now the Stones sang it like an anthem for the Chicago protestors, and the crowd responded.

We pumped our clenched fists in the air along with Mick in time to the music, inches from the faces of the cops, who stood there unflinching. It was like a battle played out in music. They had the clubs and the tear gas, but we had the power. It wasn't the sixties anymore, and we weren't some minor subculture that could be dismissed as a fringe element. We had turned into a steamroller of young, carefree, and defiant people, ready to stomp over anyone who got in our way. One string of cops in the midst of all that anarchy didn't do anything but block our view.

On Friday, Lynn and Frank, along with Rob and I, stood in Rob's kitchen planning out our evening. It was meant to be our last night in town, as Lynn and I figured we would hitchhike back on Saturday. But Rob and Frank had other thoughts.

"How come you chicks have to leave tomorrow?" Rob implored. "Frank and I finally have the day off. We could take the bikes and ride up the lake."

Frank nodded. "I know where we could go. There's that commune in Wisconsin farm country. Friends of mine moved out there and they've been bugging me to visit. We could take a ride there."

"That sounds like fun," I said. "What do you think, Lynn? You want to stay? I mean, what the heck, it's only one more day."

Lynn looked torn. "I don't know. I said I'd be back by Monday."

"If we get good rides, we'll be back by Monday night. Come on. It'll be fun." I had no reason to rush back, and we'd all been having a great time together. Plus I had never been to a commune, and I was curious.

Rob put the pressure on Lynn. "Don't be a party pooper. It's supposed to be seventy-five and sunny, the best bike riding day of the year."

"I'd really like you to stay and ride up with me." Frank reached out to take her hand.

She looked into Frank's eyes. "Oh Christ, talk about peer pressure. Okay. One day, that's it." She looked back at me. "We leave Sunday no matter what, okay?"

"Promise," I agreed, mentally leaping for joy.

"Shit, I need a cigarette." Frank handed them out to her and Rob and pulled a matchbook from his pocket. There was one match left inside.

"Oh no you don't!" Lynn stepped backwards. "I'm not using the last match." She rummaged through her pocketbook and dug out her BIC lighter. She flicked it a few times before moaning, "Shit, it's dead. I must have matches in here."

After more searching, she found nothing.

"Looks like it's this one or don't smoke." Rob took the match book from Frank and waved it in front of Lynn's face before striking it, lighting first Frank's cigarette, then his own.

"Last chance, take it or leave it, and I'm not giving you mine to light yours." Rob held the burning match in front of her. She scowled at him as she leaned over to let him light it. Rob and Frank chuckled as they watched her succumb.

"Thanks a lot, guys. Not only did I get the last match, but third on a match, too. Anything happens to me, it's your entire fault."

"The only thing that's going to happen to you is you'll get over your stupid superstition," Rob assured her.

"I hope so." Lynn frowned.

❖❖❖❖

It was mid-morning by the time the four of us were ready to leave.

"Frank, you ever ride along Sheridan Road through The Ravines?" Rob asked.

"Nope, I haven't."

Rob grinned. "Well, you're all in for a treat today. It's the only curvy, hilly road in the Midwest. When I get to missing California too badly, that's where I drive. It's a poor substitute, but it still gets me off. It's the best we can do out here in the flat lands."

"Well, I hope you don't scare me the way you did out there," I told him.

"We'll be good. We're going to take a leisurely ride along the lake, right Frank?"

"You got it!"

They both laughed.

I tied a bandanna over my hair and knotted it underneath in the back, in hopes the wind might not tangle it as much, and wrapped my jacket around my waist; the warmth of the day was already sufficient to ride without it. Rob pulled out first and Frank followed, with Lynn on back.

We merged into the traffic of Lake Shore Drive, that stretch of highway between the city and Lake Michigan that's lined with skyscrapers on one side and narrow strips of beach sand, parks, and paved walkways on the other. The sky and water were a matching blue, and at the horizon it was difficult to discern their beginnings and endings. Pure white light glared from both. The roar of the motorcycles drowned out the other traffic sounds as Rob and

Frank rode, sometimes side by side, sometimes one pulling in front of the other, casually meandering north.

Our road turned inland as the neighborhood gradually became suburban. Manicured lawns and hedges poked out from under numerous shade trees, and houses grew larger and farther from the road. We were starting to get gentle curves as Frank led the way. Our pace accelerated; I clung on tighter to Rob and began experiencing the part of the ride I feared, when his speed seemed to grow out of control.

Still we rode faster.

Before when we'd reached this point and it was just the two of us, I would scream at Rob to let me off. I wasn't having fun anymore. He was pushing too hard.

Still we rode faster, with Frank increasing his lead.

I had to shift close to Rob's ear and shout above the engine to make myself heard.

"Slow down, you're scaring me!"

"I'm trying to catch Frank!" he yelled back. "He doesn't know this road! I have to warn him there's a bad curve ahead."

I closed my eyes and felt my stomach lurch, grinding my teeth and hoping it would be over soon. Rob gunned the engine harder in an attempt to catch Frank, but when I opened my eyes, I could see he and Lynn were too far ahead.

Suddenly I saw Frank's bike turning too wide, heading toward a patch of sand in the road on the curve. His tires started skidding and sand flew into the air as he hit it. I heard Rob shout, "No! No! No!" and time and motion seemed to enter a different dimension, where every second was like a single frame of a movie, advancing frame by frame as though the moment might stretch on indefinitely. I'm not sure if I heard myself scream, or was I thinking, *Oh my God! Please, no!*

Before the bike dropped onto its side, Lynn was flung into the air and her body sailed like a rag doll over the guard rail, toward a driveway, and out of sight. I watched Frank, still hanging on to his bike as it slid violently beneath the guard rail with his leg trapped underneath, and I realized this was the moment I had always dreaded when riding with Rob. This was the kind of moment that altered lives, that I had sworn I would never let happen, but it was indeed happening.

In the seemingly endless stretch of time before we reached them, I thought about when I'd pondered getting into a motorcycle accident. I'd said I hoped I'd be killed instantly so I didn't become a vegetable. But now I begged God mercilessly for Lynn to be alive, and I knew how foolish it had been of me to ever wish for such a thing. I was terrified of what I'd see when we found her mangled body.

When we finally got to Frank, he was still moving, trying to drag himself out from under the bike. I was stunned to find Lynn not on the driveway, but lying on the lawn next to it, her eyes open, looking dazed. There was no blood on either of them, but Lynn couldn't move her leg. A metal reflector pole had been bent sideways from the weight of her body having crashed against it, but it appeared to have broken her fall and diverted her away from the pavement. It seemed the most unlikely fluke, as though someone had maneuvered her mid-flight into just the right position.

The following moments were a blur. As other drivers stopped to help Rob pull the motorcycle off of Frank, someone yelled, "I'll call an ambulance," and Lynn started asking what she was doing on the ground.

Frank hobbled over to her to begin what would be endless and repeated apologizing and self-deprecation. An ambulance and police seemed to arrive within seconds, but time was confusing to me. Frank hesitated to get in the ambulance, claiming he didn't deserve any medical treatment, but we insisted he stay with Lynn.

Tears of both heartbreak and relief ran from my eyes as I watched the ambulance take them away, and I knew I should never have asked her to stay one more day.

Over the next week, I called Lynn every day in the hospital, where she lay in traction. Rob and I went to visit her after he got home from work. Frank was usually sitting beside her, holding the cane he needed to walk with while he recovered from his fractures. Doctors had inserted a rod in Lynn's leg during surgery to support her weight while her femur, which had cracked completely in half, healed.

"What if it had been my head?" she asked, saying out loud what we had all been thinking. No one had been wearing a helmet. "I think it was that trip to church in Ohio that saved me. Even the doctor said it's a miracle I'm not dead."

Chills ran through me. Rob had ceased snickering over her superstitions and now bordered on becoming a believer.

Lynn's mother flew out to stay with her; she would bring her home as soon as she could be moved. The pin would have to come out a year later, in a surgery in Connecticut. Any urge Lynn had for adventure had now been squashed, right along with my plans for a cross-Canada rail journey that summer.

I stayed another week, trying to decide what next. July was nearing when I chose to head to Provincetown on Cape Cod, where I'd gone over Memorial Day weekend for the first time. I'd heard it was easy to get summer jobs there, so I decided to try that, and my friend Joanne agreed to join me. For $49, I bought a student-standby ticket back to Connecticut. Rob drove me to O'Hare Airport, where we hugged good-bye and promised to keep in touch.

🌸 Chapter 18

July 1972
Provincetown, Massachusetts

The Provincetown Tennis Club was a wood-shingled building with clay courts out back, a few blocks from the action
in town. The top floor had couches and privacy from the street,
and downstairs there were bathrooms with showers. It would be
our crash pad, thanks to Joanne; she had befriended one of the
employees of the club while in Boston, and he'd agreed to leave
the upstairs door unlocked for us.

Joanne knew how to enjoy herself, so I was optimistic we'd
have a fun summer together. She was the youngest of five sisters
who all considered her the spoiled baby. Her interests and prior-
ities centered on boys, parties, and getting high. As a tall, blond,
and cute fifteen-year-old, she found these easily.

As she was younger than me, I felt responsible for looking out
for her, but Joanne reminded me of a cat—able to land on her feet
in any situation, ready to spring off in another direction once she
did. She talked to everyone, and laughed and flirted with abandon,

but was quick to tell a guy who was annoying her, "Beat it, buster," in a convincing tone of voice.

From our prior visit on Memorial Day, we'd learned that the place to be in P-Town, as Provincetown was called, was the "meat racks," an area of park benches on Commercial Street that surrounded a little green in front of the town hall, so named for the pick-up activity that went on there. Hippies, college students, gays, and tourists crowded around the benches, while both men and women in tight shorts and tank tops strutted by, displaying themselves.

But the meat racks were more than a pick-up place. They were also the center of information, like an underground Chamber of Commerce. Here a person could learn where to crash or not, where you could get arrested for sleeping, where to score dope, where to find a party, where to find a job. The irony of the meat racks location was that the police station was housed in the basement of the town hall directly behind them. But the police didn't bother the alternative lifestyle crowd, predominantly because one of the reasons tourists came to P-Town was to people watch. We were the entertainment.

≪≪≫≫

A few days after we arrived, Joanne heard about a party that was taking place that afternoon in an apartment one block off Commercial Street. Lots of young people worked nights in bars and restaurants, so afternoon parties were common. I was already beginning to notice how little time was left in a day after I'd spent most of it washing and hanging sheets in the cottage motel where Joanne and I had found jobs working as chambermaids.

As we climbed the wooden back stairs to the second floor of the weather-worn, multi-family house, loud music drew us to the correct entrance. Inside, about a dozen people, mostly guys, were lazing around on couches and kitchen chairs. A piece of plywood over a set of cinder blocks comprised a table in the middle of the room. It was covered in empty beer bottles, full ashtrays, roach clips, and a half-empty bottle of vodka.

"Chicks! All right! Come on in." A guy with light brown hair in a ponytail and wire-rimmed sunglasses motioned for us to enter as we stood in the doorway. He handed Joanne the bottle of vodka from the table.

"Here, have some juice. Not much else left, but you can get a good buzz with this shit."

The song "Leroy Brown" was playing on the stereo; our host proceeded to dance around the room to the tune while Joanne took a swig of vodka and then passed it to me.

"You spending the summer here?" The question came from a cute guy with medium-length blond hair and a mustache, who was sitting on the couch.

"Yep. I got a job as a chambermaid in Truro. Joanne and I are crashing at the Provincetown Tennis Club as long as we can get away with it. You can't beat the rent."

He shifted over on the couch and reached out his arm toward the open spot next to him as an offer for me to sit. I accepted it, sitting sideways to face him with my leg bent under me on the couch.

"You lucked out. Unfortunately, we'll be thrown to the mercy of the vultures soon. The rent tripled for July, so we can't afford to live here anymore."

"How long have you been here?"

"About a month." He took out a cigarette pack from the pocket of his T-shirt and offered me one, but I shook my head no. He lit it and rested his other arm on the back of the couch as he faced me. "My buddy and I spent three weeks in Jamaica before this. We were going to cross Canada, but I ran out of money. He went without me. I stayed here to get a job and hang out for the rest of the summer. By the way, I'm Ernie. What's your name?"

I introduced myself, pleased that we had an interest in Canada in common. I told him about Lynn and her accident, about my previous plans for the Canadian train, and he described his Jamaican adventure.

We talked nonstop for a couple of hours, and I noticed the way he grew intently serious at times, depending on what we were discussing. I liked his depth of thought, as well as his quick humor.

Finally, Ernie had to go to work, washing dishes at a restaurant.

"Can you come back tomorrow?" he asked as he was leaving. "We'll probably be here for a couple of more days, I hope."

"I will." I'd enjoyed talking to him more than anyone I'd met since we'd arrived. I was also impressed that he hadn't hit on me right away, which was a nice change from a lot of guys.

Work went painfully slow the next day, as I was excited about visiting Ernie later. I kept reminding myself it was no big deal, but I felt pangs of anticipation gnawing at me.

When I arrived at the apartment, he was there. I sat on the couch next to him as though I belonged there, resuming where we'd left off.

"You stay late last night?" he asked.

"Not that late. Still, it was tough getting up this morning."

"It pisses me off having to work nights. I miss everything. I have to go to work in a few hours today, too. It sucks." His tone had an edge of anger to it.

"I know what you mean. All I do is work. I came here to have fun, but you spend all your time working so you can be here."

"You want to go for a walk?" he asked. "There's this great Army Navy surplus store over on Commercial Street. Have you been in there? The place with the shells and all the junk hanging on it?"

"Not yet."

"It's a trip. Come on, I'll show you."

Ernie took my hand as we walked, and I was touched by this act of innocent intimacy. We explored the Marine Specialties store, where we tried on foreign Navy hats and Army helmets, and we each bought a dried sand dollar—which, we knew, could be made into a pipe if you put a screen in the hole in the middle. We wandered into the HandiCraft Emporium next door to look at handmade jewelry and trinkets, then over to Spiritus Pizza for a slice each, which we discovered was a favorite for both of us. We agreed we wanted to see the movie *A Clockwork Orange*, which was playing at the movie theater near the meat racks, but we would have to save it for another day.

When the time came for Ernie to work, he asked me to walk over to the restaurant with him. Then I promised to return the next day.

❖ ❖ ❖ ❖

"Everyone get the hell out right now before I call the police."

I sprang from my sleeping bag to the sound of footsteps pounding up the stairs of the Tennis Club, not even fully awake yet as I scrambled around to grab my things.

"I find any of you here again, you're all getting arrested," the angry male voice shouted in the doorway as several guys darted down the fire escape and Joanne and I followed.

"Shit, shit, shit!" I stomped my feet in anger once outside. "What are we going to do now? That place was perfect. Damn. It's almost time for work. We better walk that way."

"I'm not going today," Joanne replied. "I'm going to go look for a place to stay."

I frowned. "But you didn't go yesterday, either. He's going to fire you if you keep skipping work."

"Oh, what do I care! I hate washing all those stupid sheets. I hate ironing them. Who irons sheets, anyway? And the way he makes us fold those dumb corners. I hope he does fire me. Otherwise, I'm going to have to quit."

I didn't want to go either, but I knew I had to or I'd run out of money. P-Town was too expensive.

We said good-bye and I took off for work while she turned toward town, headed for the meat racks.

❖❖❖❖

When I reached Ernie's apartment that afternoon, it was nearly empty. The door was wide open, and a guy I didn't recognize was carting out boxes.

"Everybody's gone," he told me. "He threw us out this morning."

"Do you know where Ernie went?" I was panicked.

"I think him and Joel went to get a room in town."

Not only was I out on the street but Ernie had also disappeared.

❖❖❖❖

At the meat racks, I found Joanne laughing and talking with a group of people, some of whom I'd come to know, including Cindy. She was a freckle-faced fourteen-year-old runaway, and though she was full of exuberance and naïve optimism, she worried me. She had no money, no way to get a job, and no place to live. Going home wasn't an option, as she had come to P-Town to hide from her father who beat her. I didn't think she'd be able to survive on the streets for long, and I didn't know how to help her. I'd bought her a big breakfast a couple of times, knowing she might not eat again that day.

One time she'd taken me aside, teary-eyed, and asked if I had a tampon; her period had come and she didn't know what to do, outside of stuffing toilet paper inside herself. I'd taken her to the drugstore and bought her a box of tampons, which was a large chunk of money for me, but I couldn't leave her in such a terrible situation. I also knew, though, that I couldn't afford to keep helping her. She'd told me she had thought about stealing them, but—she said this while fingering the gold cross hanging on a chain around her neck—she wasn't a thief and didn't want to become one.

But she was laughing now, her long blonde hair swinging around her shoulders. She and Joanne were both giggling like the school-age girls they were.

I joined the group.

"Sharon, I've been waiting for you," Joanne told me. "I saw Ernie. He got a room with Joel, and he said we could stay there. It's at this place called the A-House. I hear it's all gay, so they probably think the guys are a couple." She laughed. "Anyhow, he said to bring you over and bring our stuff."

"That's fantastic!" I was relieved to have a place to stay and thrilled that Ernie would be there—and that he wanted me there too. It felt like fate.

"Cindy, how are things going with you?" I was hoping for good news.

"Cool so far. I'm camping out in the woods with Bobby and Jean. There's a bunch of us, and so far, no one's bothered us."

"I've heard you can get busted for sleeping in the woods," I warned her.

"I know. But where else are we all going to go? The only bad thing is I'm covered in mosquito bites." She held out her arms to display the red bumps she'd been scratching.

"That sucks. I hope you're okay out there." I gestured to the backpack on my back. "We have to go bring our stuff over to Ernie's. We'll see you later."

"You chicks take care of yourselves, okay? I'm so happy for you that you've got a place." Cindy hugged me, and then I followed Joanne.

She already knew her way there, and as we walked down the narrow, dead-end side street, I realized this was where Ernie worked.

The A-House was short for The Atlantic House, a large, white, two-story building with a front porch stretched across it. The owner usually sat there in his rocking chair and chatted with the patrons and locals who stopped by.

Attached to the building was an extension that housed a popular gay men's bar with blasting music that started in the late afternoon and continued until closing time.

Joanne led me to the last room at the end of the hall, across from the shared bathroom with showers and toilets labeled "Ladies." As it turned out, we would be the only females to use it during our stay, since everyone else in the building was a guy and they shared the ladies' room too.

Ernie opened the door when we knocked. "Welcome to our humble abode." The room was barely big enough to fit the double bed mattress and box spring they had separated and laid on the floor, with only a narrow space to walk between them and the dresser to the other end of the room. I was glad to see Ernie had the mattress, which I guessed we would share, while his roommate had the box spring, where Joanne would have to sleep.

"You will note our unique decorative style, which we call Early Burned Out Building." He pointed to the corner of the room, where whole sections of the ceiling were missing, with rafters and floor planks from above showing through and charred stains stretching across the wallpaper below. The only artificial light in the room came from one light bulb that dangled from the ceiling, wires exposed.

"And don't talk too loud, you could wake the neighbors." He lifted a poster that was thumbtacked to the wall, revealing another hole about two feet in diameter that led directly into the room next to us.

I shook my head as I bit my lip. "No wonder they rented this room to hippies. No one else would live here! But as long as there's no cockroaches, it's okay by me."

"Haven't seen any. Feel free to use a drawer in the dresser. We have peanut butter and jelly in the top drawer if you want a sandwich."

I couldn't deny I was happy, burned out walls or not. Something was developing between Ernie and me that felt different from the relationships I'd had in the past. Ernie was already my friend, a person I could talk to and share ideas with. I wasn't worried about other girls in his life or wondering what kind of head game he was playing. Ernie was, plain and simple, a nice guy! And I was happy he would now become my lover.

❈❈❈❈

Ernie and I never left the room before noon on the days I didn't work. Joel and Joanne, who were sharing the other bed strictly for sleeping, would individually rise and leave in their separate directions during the morning, granting Ernie and me endless hours of lustful privacy. There never seemed to be a good enough reason to get dressed and go anywhere else, since we were totally consumed with each other.

In between making love, we'd tell each other stories, bits and pieces of our lives that began to fill in the blank spaces that still kept us strangers. It was in one of those dream-sharing moments that I mentioned regretting not crossing Canada.

"I still want to go, too. Why don't we explore it together?" Ernie asked, and I felt a warm, gushy feeling spread through my body. "I've amassed enough money. I don't have to stay here and toil over a sink all summer."

"I'd love to, but I don't have enough money left for the train."

"Screw the train. We'll thumb. Why blow all your hard-earned cash when the call of the open road beckons?"

"At least they have cheap youth hostels everywhere in Canada, but they make the girls and guys sleep in separate rooms."

"That would be an atrocity." Ernie leaned over to give me a lingering kiss. "We'll get a tent. Home becomes the earth under your feet wherever the road takes you. When it gets dark, you stake out a place in the woods. It's pure freedom."

"Wow. I've never camped before, but it sounds cool. When can you leave?"

"I'll discuss it at the slave palace tonight and see when I can get my check. Once I do, I'm as good as gone."

❖❖❖❖

The following morning, Joanne strolled back into the room not long after she'd left.

"Okay you guys, quit the nooky," she cooed as she entered. "I have to tell Sharon something crazy that happened."

I sat up in bed and pulled on my drawstring peasant shirt. "Tell me what?"

"I met this guy who knows you. He asked me where I was from, so I told him South Windsor, Connecticut, and he says, 'I went to Canada last year with a girl from there. Do you know Sharon?' I said you're never going to believe this but that's who I'm here with. His name is Pat. He's at the meat racks around the corner."

"Oh my God! Pat is here in P-Town? That's wild! Joanne, you have to go get him."

Joanne left on her errand, and Ernie crawled from bed and put on his jeans. "I'm going to go take a shower." He left the room without waiting for a reply, leading me to believe he was not happy about Pat.

Soon after, the door opened and in strolled Pat, taller than I remembered him, smiling more than he had a year ago, and we wrapped our arms around each other the way friends do.

"What a trip seeing you here," he said, and the two of us sat on the edge of the bed. "I remember we talked about coming to Cape Cod, but we never made it. Well, here we are after all."

"And you know what? I just decided to go back to Canada yesterday. Ernie and I are going, the guy I'm living with here. He's in the shower, but you'll meet him. Did you come here alone?"

"No. I'm with this terrific chick, René. She's a poet. I want you to meet her. I know you'll dig her. I've learned a lot from her. Everyone learns a lot from her. Where did you go after we split in Quebec?"

We talked until Ernie returned from the shower, his hair dripping wet, a cigarette in hand. I introduced them, and Pat bummed a cigarette. Then we hugged and said good-bye.

Ernie said nothing and seemed distant. I wondered if he was one of those jealous guys who would get upset any time I talked to another guy. He sat on the bed playing with the little gray kitten Joanne had brought home the day before, an orphan we felt compelled to feed. We left the window open so she could crawl in and out. Ernie snapped his fingers and watched her pounce towards them, then spun his hand around in circles as her body spun after the flying fingers. We laughed at the kitten's antics, and pretty soon he was smiling directly at me, and I knew everything was cool.

⋘⋙

I found Pat on Commercial Street in front of the drugstore, standing with a small, brown-skinned woman with charcoal eyes who I knew at once was René. Pat introduced us. She and I hugged and then he took off, leaving us to get to know each other.

"Pat says you're a poet from New Orleans."

"That's my trade. I sell my poems on the street to strangers, if they will pay, and if not, I give them away. I never ask for hand-outs. I always give back something in return for whatever I'm given, and poems are what I have to offer."

"I write poetry occasionally. But only for myself or a friend."

"That's good. Once you see the world as a poet, the world will never look the same to you again. No one can ever take that from you."

She bit into an apple she was carrying, and it made me think about how much junk food I'd been eating. I was a little embarrassed by the thick, black hair that covered her legs and the long strands that dangled from her armpits, protruding from the wide-open armholes of her tank top. I knew girls who didn't shave anymore, but they usually had fair hair that barely showed. René was flaunting her body hair, and this made me admire her even while I cringed. I wished I could be as self-assured as her, so unconcerned about the reactions of others that I felt free to be however I wanted.

I paused, realizing that this was a new type of freedom I hadn't considered before. Although I enjoyed wearing bizarre clothing that might make people stare, I still lived within my realm of what

I considered acceptable. Even I was a slave to fashion, although it was hippie fashion. René seemed to exist outside these boundaries.

"Let's hang out here for a while." She crouched down and leaned against the white-painted brick wall of a gift shop. I joined her, letting my back keep me balanced against the wall.

"You can deeply feel the vibes down here—the energy of this place, and all the people passing through it," she observed. "Sometimes I find people want to judge me by how I look, and of course women are judged by how they look from the day they are born, so by the time you're all grown up, you don't even know you how much you are compromising yourself." She turned her head so we were looking at one another, eye to eye. "So I have decided to throw off those female clichés, and let my soul shine through." As she spoke, she touched her hand to her heart for a moment. "I think that way people start to see who I truly am, not who they want me to be. Pat understands. He's a good man. I had to teach him a few things, and he still has a way to go, but he respects me and gives me my space."

"Last year he gave me too much space," I said. "I wasn't ready to be by myself, but he left anyway."

"You're always by yourself, even when you're with someone. You have to love yourself first, love yourself as a free, strong woman. You don't need a man to get you through. You survived last year, didn't you? And now you're stronger. This is who you need to trust, and everything else will be fine." She touched her three middle fingers near my heart. "Trust yourself in here. And learn to trust your sisters. Women have to get beyond all that man stuff that keeps them feeling like strangers with each other. Pat's not the center of my life, and he knows it. But I let him keep me company."

I couldn't imagine being in a situation where it was up to me what a guy could or could not do. Did guys actually agree to that? How did you get them to do that?

We spent much of the day strolling Commercial Street, stopping here and there. I barely noticed the crowds because René had me cradled in conversation, cutting through my layers of preconceived ideas and touching tender new spots. I didn't realize it then, but she was planting seeds, planting little bulbs deep in my soul that would take another season to blossom.

When René and Pat left the next day for Boston, it was this hypnotic little woman that I hated to lose.

"No good-byes," Pat said as he and René hugged me. "Just *hasta luego*."

"*Hasta luego*," I replied.

A day later, Joanne and I adopted a friendly dog without a home while we were hitchhiking. We named her Venus and slipped her into the A-House as stealthily as possible. The arrival of Venus did not escape anyone's attention, however. Four heterosexuals, one cat, and one dog in one room was more than the A-House could handle. The next day, Venus was not the only one living out on the street.

Ernie and I had a few days left before he could leave his job and get his check, and we had nowhere to live again. The owner of the restaurant offered to let Ernie sleep on the restaurant floor, as long as he didn't quit any earlier. He was desperate to have a dishwasher in the height of season, and Ernie's replacement couldn't start any sooner.

Joanne ran into an old friend of hers from Boston who knew her sister and had an apartment there now. She decided to bag P-Town and return to Beantown, since she had a ride. We squeezed each other good-bye and she took off, Venus at her side.

It felt strange watching everyone leave when I wanted to get going myself. I had already quit my job in preparation for leaving, so now I'd be alone from the time Ernie went to work until the following morning.

Something always comes up, I reminded myself.

At the meat racks, I heard about a new youth hostel that had opened at a church on the edge of town and wandered that way. At the top of a hill, I found the simple concrete building with a cross on the front and a sign reading "United Methodist Church." There was a wing attached, and a few young people were walking through the door. I followed.

Inside was a typical sixties-style building—low ceilings with drop-in tiles, metal doors, linoleum floors. The first room was a cafeteria with metal folding tables and chairs.

"Sharon!" a voice called out, and I turned to see Cindy sliding off the table she'd been sitting on, looking carefree and relaxed.

"It's great to see you!" I said. We came together for a hug. "We got thrown out of the A-House and Joanne went back to Boston. You look happy."

"I am. I really am. I'll miss Joanne. She's something else. But this is a great place! I love it here! Wait until you meet Tim. He's the minister, and he's really cool. This whole thing was his idea. Come on, I'll show you where you sign up to stay."

She walked ahead, leading me to the next room, cheerfully pointing out the facilities. I figured this place had to be okay if it had made her this happy.

I wrote my name on the top of the three-by-five index card an older girl gave me and I handed her my $1.50. She wrote PAID 7/13/72 on the first blank line and filed it in her card box.

We returned to the cafeteria and hung out for a while. Cindy pointed out Tim, who was busy with another group of transients. He was younger than I expected, and he even had longish hair and wore wire-rimmed glasses. He talked and laughed like he was one of them. I'd never seen a clergyman behave in this manner, and it made me optimistic about this place.

❊❊❊❊

The sound of people chatting as they folded their blankets and headed for the showers woke me up in the morning. I stretched out on my cot, feeling relaxed and lazy. It was nice not worrying about feeling safe and knowing I could sleep there again that night.

I missed Ernie, though. I wondered how I would survive without him beside me, now that I'd become used to his presence. This yearning for him, knowing he yearned equally for me, caused me both joy and anguish. It didn't seem fair that life had forced this cruel separation upon us. A few more days felt like an endless stretch of time I would never cross.

I folded my blanket and placed it at the foot of my cot, as instructed, then headed for the kitchen.

"Bowls and spoons are over there." Tim pointed toward a stack near the sink. "You wash your own when you're done. There's coffee, too, if you indulge. I'm Tim, head honcho around here." He reached out his arm toward me and we shook hands. "I opened the hostel July 1st, and we've been busy ever since. What's your name?"

"Sharon. I'm on my way to Canada in a few days."

"Beautiful country, Canada is. I've never been, but people say you see the wonders of God by looking out the window."

"I've only been to Quebec, but it was spectacular." I scooped oatmeal out of the pot, scraping the bottom.

"You arrived yesterday?" He leaned against the counter with his arms folded.

"Yeah. We were thrown out of our place. I was worried about having nowhere to go." I sat at the table and began eating.

"That's why we're here. If you need anything, if you want to talk about anything at all, I'm around. We have musicians playing here tonight about seven. Stop back early, it's a good crowd."

"Okay, I'll see. How come you're doing this? I've never seen a church do this stuff before. I mean, for people like us."

"It's what I believe Jesus wants me to do." He sat at the table across from me. "You ever read the Bible? The New Testament, not the old fire and brimstone stuff."

"A little bit. I grew up Catholic. They read it in church all the time."

"Well, the thing is, I believe what Jesus said in the Bible. I don't think it's a bunch of empty words you read to the congregation on Sunday morning. I believe it's a philosophy to live by. If I can make the Bible come alive in the way I live, I can help make it happen for others."

He paused, looked directly at me, propping up his chin, and leaned toward me. "How about you? What do you believe? Honestly. You don't have to invent something because I'm a minister. Do you believe in any kind of God?"

"Well, for a while, I didn't." I paused, giving this more thought, as I put down my spoon. "But all these things have been happening this summer that have made me think about God and religion. I was an atheist for a while last year, when I first left home, but now I feel differently. I think maybe its religion and not God that I don't agree with. So, I guess I believe in something, but I'm not sure what."

"Do you think Jesus existed?" He shifted back into his chair.

"Yeah, I do. But I think he was a real person, a highly evolved spiritual teacher like Buddha. I read a bunch of books last winter about higher spiritual plains. I think Jesus was there, too. He traveled to those spiritual levels and tried to teach about it, but of course it was too esoteric for most people, so he spoke in parables."

"You have a more traditional concept of Jesus than most young people I talk to. A lot of them visualize God in strange, abstract ways, like he's some kind of gas floating around us." He twirled his arms around his head.

I laughed a little and went back to finishing my oatmeal.

"Well, I'm certainly glad to have had a chance to listen to you this morning. I hope we see you later."

After he left the room, I felt oddly distracted, but I wasn't sure why.

❮❮❯❯

"Two days and counting!" Ernie almost shouted as he joined me in front of the restaurant where he worked, and now slept. "Christ, I can't wait to be done with this shit and get out of here. Summer is passing by and I'm missing it. Anyhow, I got my money from the bank, and I'm ready to shop. Let's go get camping stuff."

At the surplus store, Ernie led me through the aisles, examining army rations and rain ponchos, canteens and snake-bite kits. Knowing nothing about camping, I tried to imagine the uses for things, and hoped we wouldn't need the snake-bite kit.

"Hey, look, an Optimus camp stove! These are awe-inspiring." He pulled the small metallic blue box off the shelf. "It's Swedish, and it runs on gasoline. Since we can buy that anywhere, we don't have to worry about finding fuel."

I carried the stove while he grabbed a set of nesting aluminum pans. "Have you ever seen these?" he asked, and I shook my head no. He released the clip that kept them together and displayed the multiple parts. "You have bowls, plates, a pot and a frying pan all in one. See?" He held out the plate and turned it into a frying pan by hooking the clip onto the side like a handle. "What a profusion of equipment this place has!"

He pointed toward the ceiling, to a small, orange-sided tent with a blue floor above us. "That's our tent. It's the cheapest one here, and it's lightweight, too, so I can carry it. Just big enough for two."

He leaned over the counter and asked the clerk to get one for him, and I was surprised when he handed back a bag smaller than my sleeping bag.

I was dubious. "That's what we're going to sleep in?"

"Think about total privacy," Ernie said. "Think about no one but you and me, deep in the woods."

"Mmmm." I smiled. "Any place we can put it up here?"

We reached the cashier with bungee cords, water purification tablets, and all the other gear we'd accumulated throughout the store. Ernie paid without a glance in my direction, and I didn't object.

Cindy was near the coat closet when I got back to the church, and the moment she saw me, she rushed in my direction.

"Sharon, I'm so excited, I have to tell you about this. I've been saved. I've accepted Jesus as my savior, and now I have nothing to be afraid of anymore. Isn't it wonderful? Are you happy for me?"

She was ecstatic, nearly jumping up and down. I couldn't help but feel happy for her, with all she had been through.

"What did you have to do to get saved?" I asked her out of curiosity. "Did you go to church?"

"No, not at all. All you have to do is accept Jesus, and you can be saved. It's easy. Jesus already died to save everyone from their sins, so there's nothing else that needs to be done. You just accept him into your life. I did. And now I can save other people, too."

"How do you do that?"

"Exactly the same as it was done for me. You tell someone who has already accepted Jesus that you accept him as your savior.

You put your hand on the Bible, and you say it. So if they want to be saved, they can tell me." Her face grew serious. "There's something else, too. Tim talked to my parents. He talked to my dad about why I ran away and my dad feels really bad. They're going to come here to talk to me with Tim, and we're going to figure out a way to work things out so I can go home. I'm really nervous, but I know it will be okay because I have Jesus to help me now."

She was starting to cry, and I was getting teary-eyed with her, so I reached out and held her in my arms. As I felt her body shake from the tears, I cried too, because I knew how difficult this was for her. I knew how much she needed this to work, how much we all needed that strength, that magic, whether it was Cindy, or Butch, or Lynn as she was thrown through the air. In fact, maybe even I needed it. Maybe even I wanted to have that nice soft pillow of Jesus on my side, to hover around me like my guardian angel and keep me safe when I felt afraid. I felt suddenly inspired. Perhaps this was the answer to my feelings of always needing and searching for something I couldn't quite touch.

"I want to accept Jesus, too," I said. "I want to be saved."

She wiped at her tears and broke into laughter. "That's wonderful! We can use my New Testament. Tim will give you one, too. I can't wait to tell him." She ran into the closet and came out with the tiny, pocket-size black book. She extended her arm toward me, the Bible flat in the palm of her hand. "Put your right hand on top of this and tell Jesus you want him to save you."

I felt uneasy saying the words, but I kept my eyes focused on her red-rimmed blue ones, nearly obscured by those long, straight, blonde bangs that fell over her forehead like the Little Dutch Boy. I placed my hand over the book, feeling her fingers touching mine as I did.

"I accept Jesus as my savior," I told her. "I want Jesus to save me."

She exhaled deeply when I was done. "Wow. You're the first person I ever saved. Now I know you'll always be beside me, wherever I am."

She reached around behind her neck and unfastened the gold cross she wore on a chain.

"I want you to have this. To thank you for everything and remember me by."

I moved my hair so she could put it on me. Tears streamed down my face as she fastened the little gold necklace at the back of my neck.

She hugged me. "Praise the Lord."

"Praise the Lord," I echoed back, stumbling on the awkward new words.

 **Chapter 19**

July 1972
Montreal, Canada

We arrived in downtown Montreal around dusk after spending all day hitchhiking from Connecticut. I'd stopped there for two days to visit my parents before leaving, and had assured them I would send postcards frequently and call once a week. In exchange, they notarized my permission slip to cross the border.

Ernie and I walked a few blocks to the Christ Church Cathedral, the spot on St. Catherine Street that had been my hangout the previous summer, where I hoped we could be directed to the youth hostel. A few people were hanging around out front, but as we rounded the corner to the back of the church, I was surprised to find a campfire burning. Probably a dozen or more people were sitting around it and had pitched tents on the grass.

"My God." Ernie froze and his mouth dropped open. "I can't believe they're letting people camp right in the middle of downtown Montreal. This is incredible!"

A guy waved for us to join them. I could smell a hint of pot smoke mixing with the scent of burning logs.

"Come relax and stay awhile," a sprawled figure on the lawn said to us. "This is where it's at."

I untied my sleeping bag from my pack and spread it on the ground near the others, and we sat.

I slipped my hand into the pocket of my jacket and fingered the textured plastic cover of the New Testament I was carrying, given to me by Tim. Throughout the day, while waiting for a ride, I'd read from it occasionally. It was part religion, part good luck charm, and I believed the reason our rides had gone well was because I'd brought Jesus along.

I barely talked to Ernie about being saved. He didn't seem interested in God, and I'd made a promise to myself not to become one of those preachy people that I'd always hated. I'd explained to him that nothing would change between us, as I didn't want this newfound spirituality of mine to cause any friction. It wasn't like being Catholic, where sex was a sin and I'd have to adopt celibacy. With that established, Ernie seemed convinced that my being saved had no effect on him.

Spending our first night in Canada camping at the church felt like an auspicious beginning to our trip. There were good vibes from the group, and no one was rowdy or obnoxious.

"I hear you two are heading for Vancouver, eh?" said the man next to me. "You can sleep right on the beach there, no one bothers you. That goes for almost anywhere in Canada. As long as you're not on private property and you're not bothering anyone, they leave you alone."

"It really sucks getting rides through Ontario," a skinny blond guy with an accent from the Deep South told us. "Y'all can get stuck there for days. I hear they use army buses to round up stranded hitchhikers and haul 'em to the youth hostels, can you dig it? Them Canadians know how to put the army to good use."

Everyone laughed as the man next to me passed me a joint that was circling. I took a hit and passed it to Ernie.

"Yeah, can you see that in the States?" asked another American across the fire from me. "Goddamn Army picking up stranded hippies instead of nuking babies in 'Nam? This is my kind of country."

"I hear ya, brother," a dark-skinned man with a tall afro sitting next to him added.

A couple of people had guitars and began strumming. Soon, the music grew deep and bluesy, rising in volume, and the crowd grew quiet. Ernie carried three harmonicas with him, each in a different key. He walked over to sit closer to the musicians. After studying their notes and nodding his head to the music for a while, he reached into his pocket, pulled out one of his harmonicas, and joined in the jam.

I loved to listen to Ernie play. He could make that blues harp wail, then slide into short raspy sounds by vibrating the side of his hand over the holes. His ability to participate in the spontaneous music gave me chills of excitement.

I tilted my head back and gazed at the stars, surprised by the clear night sky I could see even with the city lights around me. The cool air tickled my back, but the heat of the fire kept me toasty warm in front. I rocked back and forth to the music, hugging my knees and breathing in the wood smoke, thinking, *This is how happiness feels.*

❮❮ ❯ ❯

We crossed the continent from east to west and back again, and each ride had a story to tell, enough stories to fill a volume by themselves. On our way west, we said Vancouver was our destination, but that wasn't completely true. When we stood on the side of the road, when we hopped in the next car or tractor trailer truck, we were already where we were going. If you were on the road, you understood this in your heart, the way nomads do.

It took about two-dozen rides to make the round trip of nearly six thousand miles—certainly many less than I would have guessed. Seldom did a driver take us less than two hundred miles, and one drove us over a thousand.

There were periods in the Prairie Provinces where I could see to the edge of the horizon in both directions and the highway was as straight as a plumb line leading out to the sky, vacant of any vehicles. At times I entertained myself by sitting cross-legged on the yellow dividing lines that chopped the east- and west-bound lanes of the Trans-Canada Highway into equal halves. Ernie's manner of dealing with the boredom was to pull out his harmonica and turn his back on the direction of what we wished was oncoming traffic. When a vehicle did finally approach, we had plenty of time to stand and position ourselves with our thumbs out.

❮❮❯❯

Three days out from Montreal, we reached Winnipeg, where we planned on using the YMCA for showers. As we walked away from downtown, I started to notice poverty among the people on the deteriorating streets. But it was who these people were that shocked me, for they were Indians (as we called most indigenous North American people at that time), and I had never seen Indians in a city slum.

Driving across country the prior year with Eddie, I had seen Indians in the desert, mostly driving by in pickup trucks or at gas stations. The only Indian I knew personally was Ed in Venice, and he was part white, so most of my perception of Indians came from Western movies I'd watched as a child—films where they wore headdresses and brandished tomahawks. I was enlightened enough to realize that this was a ridiculous perception. The book *Bury My Heart at Wounded Knee* had been a recent bestseller, and there was a group that had taken over Alcatraz, trying to reclaim it as Indian land and demanding Red Power. I knew the myths I grew up with were wrong and that Indians had been horribly mistreated a hundred years earlier. But it wasn't until I arrived in Winnipeg that I understood how that translated into the lives of living Indians in 1972.

We walked through that area where the paint peeled from buildings and the sidewalks were broken, and I saw them—people sitting in doorways looking at nothing, men holding crumpled paper bags concealing bottles, women with babies in their laps, and children playing in vacant lots with broken glass. None of these people looked at us as we walked by, or at anyone else from what I could tell. It was as if they didn't exist, as if they were ghosts sleepwalking through the afternoon, their spirits stolen from them.

Ernie and I found the YMCA and paid fifty cents each to take a shower. When we were finished, we walked back to the highway and caught a ride that allowed us to continue heading west, with the goal of getting as far as we could before dark. I stared out into the green prairie, watching the way the blowing wind made patterns in the field, like it was running through the grass and stirring it up. I began to imagine that same wind blowing through the fur of buffalo while they grazed, eagles soaring overhead, coyotes howling in the distance. Mostly I imagined those proud, free, people riding horses across this land we were driving through. Now hundreds of people like Ernie and me were traveling these roads, trying to capture our freedom, while theirs was lost.

✦✦✦✦

Dusk was approaching when we reached Portage la Prairie after leaving Winnipeg. We'd come to realize that sunset in July in this northern climate came late. Days were long and stretched on forever.

Portage La Prairie was the crossroads of every railroad track heading through the prairies, either on the southerly route that we were following or north toward Edmonton and Dawson Creek. Unlike the smaller towns we passed through, the side roads were paved instead of dirt, and there was a downtown with rows of stores built sometime this century.

This would be our first night sleeping in the prairies, away from the thick forests of Ontario. Ernie and I walked along the main road looking for a concealed spot to camp. We saw a vacant lot with a few trees on one street, but not enough to conceal a tent. I was discouraged. "I think we ought to find a youth hostel."

"I don't want to quit yet. Let's try these side streets." Ernie turned the corner. "Maybe we can camp behind a building where we won't be noticed."

"Ernie, we're going to get stuck with no place, or else we're going to get busted. You can't crash in the middle of town."

"Why not? We did in Montreal!" He walked faster ahead of me.

"That was different. I'm not ending up in jail!" I yelled back, my anger growing. I wondered if there was anything we could agree on anymore. It was starting to feel like every decision we encountered resulted in an argument.

"We're not going to get busted!" he shouted. "Trust me. Have I been wrong yet?"

"Oh, so I'm the one who's wrong all the time, is that it?"

"Do you think I'm stupid? Didn't I get us this far?"

"What do you mean, *you* got us this far! I'm the one who's been to Canada before. I'm the one who's been showing *you* around." I was furious that he was taking credit for our trip.

He stopped and faced me. "Give me a break. You'd be dead on the side of the road if I wasn't with you. And you don't know the first thing about camping. I'd like to see you pitch the tent in the dark." He threw his arms in the air and started walking again, the frame of his pack hanging at an angle from unevenly packed weight.

"I don't need you," I shouted after him, standing still. "I got along fine before you came along, and I can get along fine without you now. Why don't you put your tent up in a vacant lot, and I'll go sleep in the youth hostel!" I pulled my pack from my burning shoulders and threw it on the ground.

We stopped yelling as a group of would-be hippie young teens approached Ernie, who paused. There were about five guys, between maybe fourteen and sixteen, with something like awe on their faces. I donned my backpack again and joined them. They were wearing bellbottoms, and three of them had chin-length hair, which might be considered radical in this prairie town of barber shops and crew cuts we had noticed on our walk.

"You got a match?" the tallest of them asked Ernie, holding a cigarette.

"Yeah, right here." He dug into the pocket of his army jacket.

The kids gathered in closer and the same person spoke again, but quieter. "You got any pot in your rucksack?"

"No. Sorry," Ernie told them. "You can't be carrying that stuff around when you're hitching. Not much dope in town, huh?"

"Not at all. Not much of anything in this town. Why are *you* here?"

"We're looking for a place to sleep tonight. You know where we could pitch a tent?"

They huddled together for a couple of minutes, muttering to each other, then they turned back and a different one spoke.

"You can put it in my backyard if you don't mind the trains, eh?" They broke out laughing, and I wondered what the joke was.

"He lives across the street from the station," the first one explained. "They come through here all night long."

Ernie turned to me. "Do trains bother you?"

"I'm fine with trains," I said to the boy, "but will your parents mind? They won't throw us out, will they?"

"Oh no, they won't care. Just wait until it's a-boat dark so the neighbors don't say anything, eh? Come on, we'll take you over there now, if you want. The back door is always open, so you can use the washroom."

I was relieved the issue was settled. Ernie and I followed them, walking side by side again now that our problem was solved.

"Where can you buy beer this time of night?" Ernie asked as we walked toward the tracks.

"The beer store's closed but there's a hotel back over there, about two streets over. You buy it at the window inside. Since you're getting beer, you could get some for us too, eh?"

"Be happy to return the favor."

By the time we came back with the beer and assembled the tent, our fight was long forgotten, but I felt our arguments were growing worse on a daily basis. The more horrible they were, however, the more passionate our lovemaking, so I found myself either raging mad or ecstatically happy. I had no idea where this relationship was going, but I was definitely hooked.

"I see what they meant about the trains," Ernie said around midnight. "I've got them clocked at every fifteen minutes."

We giggled together beneath one sleeping bag, using it like a blanket as we lay on the other bag. As I laughed, my foot wiggled and I knocked over a beer bottle.

"Shit!" I scrambled from under the covers to set it upright, knocking into the wall of the tent. "I hope there wasn't anything in it."

I felt around the tent floor and it was dry. "Phew. I'd hate to have to sleep in a beer-soaked sleeping bag. Thank God it was empty."

"The Hawk is saved again," Ernie teased.

"What do you mean, the hawk?"

"Didn't you ever look at your nose? It looks like a hawk's beak."

"It does not. My nose isn't hooked."

"Hawk."

"I'm not a hawk." Half laughing, but fully angry, I lifted my fists to pound his chest and he grabbed both my arms, wrestled me back to the ground, and tickled me.

"Hawk, Hawk, Hawk."

I giggled from the tickles and screamed out loud as another train roared into the station, squirming around and trying to avoid the onslaught of his playful attack.

By the time the train pulled to a stop, we were quiet again, as Ernie's wrestling had turned to kissing. Soon, all that energy and anger and teasing turned into another round of hot sex.

Three days later, our ride dropped us at an intersection where the Trans-Canada Highway splits; we were continuing west from Banff, and the driver was heading north into Jasper.

The day before, I'd read the pamphlet we'd been given at the gate when we entered Banff National Park. It emphasized staying within official park campgrounds and on marked trails, and never leaving on a hike without first registering with a ranger. The reason for this caution was grizzly bears, who were known to be vicious and attack visitors without provocation.

"Are you sure we should be doing this?" I asked as I followed Ernie through the brush, pushing aside branches and stepping over thorny vines. "Maybe we should stay in a park campground."

He paused briefly. "What do you think mountain men did? Did they stay in park campgrounds? That's propaganda for the Winnebago people. Why would you want to do that when we have the wilderness?" He marched on, forging a path between larger trees where the underbrush was leaner. The sound of rushing water grew louder as we continued.

Despite my concern about bears, a sense of calm spread through me with each step I took; the deeper we got into the woods, the farther I got from my fears. I understood the appeal of the wilderness, this untamed, seemingly limitless world that surrounded me. *Ernie is right*, I thought as I gazed toward the tops of giant trees, squinting against the sunlight. *Let the people in the motor homes have the campgrounds. We have Eden.*

Ernie reached the river before I did and stopped. He slid his backpack off his shoulders, rested it against a tree, and unhooked our canteen from it.

"I'll bet we've never tasted water this delicious." He grinned at me, then turned to kneel beside the river and filled the canteen underwater. "Wow, this is cold. Stick your hand in here and feel this."

I tested the water with my fingers and quickly extracted them. "That's freezing!"

"It comes from the snow melting in the mountains. Look at this water. It's so clean you can see all the way to the bottom on the other side of the river." He handed me the full canteen and

I took a drink. Indeed, I had never tasted water so refreshing or thirst quenching.

"I bet there's great fishing here," Ernie said. "Let's camp nearby but away from the river, since animals probably come here to drink."

"Like grizzly bears?" I reminded him as we hoisted our gear and headed back into the woods.

He ignored my question.

After we finished setting up camp, Ernie broke off a tall sapling above the root and stripped off the sprouting branches to improvise a fishing pole. We returned to the river, where he found a piece of used fishing line, attached it to his branch, and secured the hook he had found to the end. He positioned himself on a couple of rocks a few steps into the river and cast his homemade rod out into the water.

Meanwhile, I sat on a downed tree log at the edge of the clearing, breathing in the clean, woodsy aroma of fallen needles, leaves, and moist, dark soil. Across the river, snow-capped mountains rose from behind acres of tall, straight evergreen trees. The river was loud enough to obscure any other sound besides its powerful flow.

I stood and began walking through the mammoth trees, keeping the river in sight. There was a hush in the forest as I entered it. The trees seemed to absorb all sound. It reminded me of reverence, like when you enter a church and voices grow dim and respectful. Except church was the exact opposite of this, as tamed and repressive as this was wild and expressive.

This really is Eden, I thought. *This is the earth the way it was created, before Europeans came along and destroyed much of it.*

But it was in the name of God that they destroyed it, I recalled with anguish. Destroyed it, and the Indians, and created that mess back in America with pollution and war—America, where money, power, and greed ruled. Not here, however. This felt like the soul of the planet, the heart of Mother Earth—not the creation of God but God himself, alive and breathing.

I stopped walking in a cluster of towering evergreens. My eyes followed the long trunks to the top of these magnificent timbers where they framed a piece of sky. Streams of sunlight poured down on me. I closed my eyes and breathed deeply, as though I could inhale the spirit surrounding me and feel it through my whole body. There was no way I could experience this sitting in a church pew or reading the New Testament that I still carried in my jacket pocket. Maybe that's what this trip across Canada was teaching me, that I needed to move close to nature. I had been expecting people to have the answers, when this deep, primeval need in me was outside the realm of humans. God wasn't in a book that had been written two thousand years ago. He was right here all around me, in the pulse of the river and the layers of soil beneath my feet. He and Mother Earth were one and the same.

 **Chapter 20**

August 1972
Hope, British Columbia

The day we left Vancouver traveling east, the temperature blew past 90 degrees and kept right on going. I never expected British Columbia would be stifling, so when the road sign read "Hell's Gate, 34 miles," I imagined heat pouring through that gate in our direction.

Our ride dropped us in Hope where we were heading north along the Fraser River.

We'd spent only two nights in Vancouver. It had been disappointing after our wilderness days and nights. In Gastown, a section of the city we'd been told was fun, I'd been shocked to see a man whose throat had clearly been slit carried out of a bar and dragged into an ambulance. On our second day, we left and arrived in Hope three hours later.

Even the blue jean shorts and halter top I was wearing made me hot, and I wished I had a rubber band to tie my hair back. Ernie had wrapped a navy-blue bandanna around his head as a sweatband, but sweat was still dripping down his face.

We planted ourselves on the side of the road near a Texaco gas station, where we used their restroom and bought a cold bottle of Pepsi from the soda machine. There was no shade near the road, so we were stuck standing in the sun waiting for a ride. A hot wind rippled my hair but did nothing to cool me.

"Shit!" Ernie shouted, spinning his head away from the wind. "Something blew in my eye. Damn it, this hurts!"

With his back to the breeze, he poked at his eye, with no success.

"Let me see if I can see anything." I leaned toward his face.

He pulled away. "Why? I can feel it, I know it's there. I'm going to the men's room to see if I can get it out." With his hand still over his eye, he disappeared into the restroom.

I knew this would be another of Ernie's moods. This happened when things didn't go his way. Frustrated, I sat on my pack to bake in the sun and gazed around in boredom at Hope. We had passed a few warehouses with names of fruit companies along the railroad tracks, a couple of timber yards, stores, a motel, and several side streets lined with 1950s-style ranch houses. Why would anyone want to live in this dreary town, I wondered?

When Ernie returned from the men's room, he was scowling. "I couldn't get it out. My God, it's hot here. We have *got* to get a ride soon. I can't stand this place."

"No shit," I agreed, wiping the sweat from my face.

Another half hour wore by. I was considering springing for another Pepsi when a faded, red pickup pulled over to the side of the road.

"Thank God!" I hauled my gear to the cab and tugged at the door handle. The long-haired driver leaned over and shoved the squealing door open, smiling at us through his full beard. I saw he was wearing a Mickey Mouse T-shirt.

"I'm not going far," he said after we climbed into the cab, and I wanted to cry. "But I can get you out of town and into the shade." He shifted into gear and we lurched forward. "Actually, where I'm heading is this righteous swimming hole up the road, and when I saw you two standing in the hot sun, I thought you might like to go for a dip. It's on your way."

"Wow! Were you sent from heaven, or what?" I turned to Ernie, who was smiling for the first time in two hours.

"A cold lake sounds fabulous," he agreed.

The driver introduced himself as Mike, and we exchanged conversation about where we were going to and coming from, and how our rides had been. We crossed a metal bridge over the Fraser River, drove about a mile, then pulled off on a stretch of worn dirt alongside the woods. Another pickup and a Volkswagen bug were parked there already.

"How deep is it?" That was my first question about any body of water, since I'd never learned to swim.

"Real deep. As soon as you leave the rocks it's over your head, but if you stay around the rocks and hang on to them, you can stand. It's cold enough to freeze your balls off, too, but on a day like this, what could be better?"

We followed a well-worn path through the trees and down a bank, the air growing cooler as we proceeded. Mike led us over the smooth boulders that lined our side of the lake, then sat to pull off his hiking boots, T-shirt, and empty his pockets into his boots. He gave us a smile, then plunged head-first into the water.

I moved cautiously across the unfamiliar terrain while Ernie forged ahead, ripping off his T-shirt and ditching his boots next to Mike's. He jumped feet-first into the water, then bobbed up immediately and let out a scream before hoisting himself onto the rock.

"*Wow!* There's no getting used to this water, even if you dive in without thinking about it. But damn it feels good to cool off. Come on in."

"I'm scared it's too deep."

"It is, at this spot. I'll check it over there for you." He climbed into a space where three large rocks butted up against one another, leaving a water-filled hole between them. "There's a rock on the bottom here where you can stand, and it's only up to my chest," he said. "Come over here and you can get in."

He climbed out and reached his hand over to help me get to where he stood. I sat on the edge and looked at the area where he said I could stand. He climbed back over the top of the ledge and slid back into the open lake, his face contorting as his body met the water.

I sat for a few minutes, dangling my feet, before I got the nerve to slide in. As I lowered myself into the icy chasm, my feet reached for the rock, and I panicked as they dropped farther than I'd expected. My right foot connected, but my left foot slipped off the edge and into nothingness. The left side of my body slammed against one of the rocks as I grabbed for a holding spot along the smooth, slippery surface. Water rushed over my chin and into one ear, blocking out sound, and I craned my head up with my mouth closed and my nose above the surface. The toes on my right foot were still touching as I pushed myself up to where I could stand, scraping my knee and elbow in the process. I leaned against the shallower side of the hole, breathing rapidly, as my heart pounded.

Now that I realized I wasn't going to drown, I glanced around to make sure no one had witnessed this humiliating event. Ernie and Mike were swimming many yards away, and they were the only people nearby.

I hated not being able to swim. It embarrassed me; I imagined I was the only person over age ten, besides my sister, who'd never learned. Occasionally, I encountered a situation like this one, which filled me with terror. Unlike Anne, who avoided the water, I'd always wallowed around near shore, acting nonchalant, longing to immerse myself and wondering if I would ever learn. I was angry that my parents had not allowed me to play in Mary Ann's pool when I was in the fourth grade, where I could have learned along with the other children. They were always sheltering me from any possible risk, leaving me unable to experience or learn anything new. I'd hated those long, lonely summers, listening to all the other kids in my neighborhood squealing and laughing in play while I lurked around my backyard with Anne, creating elaborate fantasies about a different life.

I was the first one out of the water and back onto the rock, my feet and legs numb from the cold. The scrapes on my elbow and knee were not bleeding, so I hoped no one would notice. Ernie and Mike were right behind me, and we all sat and drip-dried together on the rock. Mike took a joint and a lighter from his boot. We passed it between us, talking, while I watched a nude family swimming on the far side, distant enough so no one could bother them from the road. I guessed this was a cool place, as they felt safe openly swimming naked and we could smoke pot.

Afterwards, we went back to the truck for dry clothes and changed in the bushes.

"I'm on my way into town to meet friends for a beer," Mike told us. "You two are welcome to join me."

"A beer would be great, except I don't have an ID that says I'm old enough to drink." I knew the drinking age in British Columbia was nineteen, and I was still seventeen.

Mike chuckled. "No one will give a shit. It's very laid-back here in Hope. In case you hadn't noticed."

⪻⪻⪼⪼

It was four thirty in the afternoon when we drove back into town and parked next to the Hope Hotel, a two-story building a few blocks from the gas station where we'd been hitchhiking. There were two entrances, one labeled BAR and one labeled LADIES LOUNGE. I wondered if they had the same law here as in Connecticut, where it was illegal for a woman to sit at a bar.

"The only women who sit at bars are prostitutes," my father had explained when I'd asked him about the law. That had made me angry. If a woman wanted to sit at a bar, I'd argued, that was her business. Why should anyone assume she was a prostitute? These were stupid laws made by men to control women. My father had shaken his head in disagreement.

We entered through the door for ladies. The lounge was dark and windowless, with red velour wallpaper and black booths lining the room. In the center of the lounge were a number of plain rectangular tables and chairs in a line. Mike spotted two men he knew already seated and took us over to join them. They were rugged-looking hippies, with weathered faces and untrimmed beards. One man had a braid that hung halfway down his back.

"Bring a round of beers for this table," Mike called over to the waitress, who returned with a tray of drafts. As Ernie reached into his pocket, Mike raised his hand to stop him. "You two are my honored guests, tonight. Your money's no good here, so put it away."

Ernie and I thanked him, stunned by his generosity. A few minutes later, several more people entered the bar, filled the table we were sitting at, and added another table to the row. More beers were bought, and soon I had two in front of me. I finished them, only to have two more appear in their place.

As we drank, more people arrived. We were introduced, and they asked about our trip and how we liked Hope so far.

"It's the people that make this place," one told us. "The countryside is outstanding, but this group of people, we're all like family. If anyone is in need, we all help out. They do the same when it's their turn."

I was impressed.

"Hey, they're here!" a man shouted. The crowd turned toward the door and let out a cheer, clapping and whistling. Two women stood there, laughing and scanning the crowd, and then they rounded the room, exchanging hugs and greetings.

"This is a welcome-home party for them," Mike explained. "They just returned from the mountains, splitting shakes. It's tough work. You use an ax and get blisters on your hands in the first hour. They've been there for ten days, so we knew they'd appreciate seeing everyone. I have nothing but respect for these two. A lot of men wouldn't stick it out that long."

I watched these women with envy, wondering what it must be like to have a whole community welcoming you home. I couldn't imagine heading into the wilderness without a man, but these women radiated confidence. I wondered if living in the country could do this for me.

I heard British accents from several people who mingled with the others like they were all friends.

"They're British, but they seem to know everybody. Do they live here?" I asked Mike.

"No, but they've been in Hope all week, so they've made a lot of friends. They've been traveling all over in a van and said this is their favorite place on the continent." Mike paused. "It's mine, too."

He held up his beer and signaled a toast and we joined him. I had quite a buzz on by now and Ernie had a perpetual smile.

He leaned in toward me. "Can you believe this place?"

I shook my head no.

"This is so cool, I am astonished. These people are already acting like we're one of them, and we just got here."

Hours passed and people began leaving. I wondered where we were going to sleep, but I was too drunk to care.

"Where are you kids staying tonight?" Archie, an older man who was at our table, asked us.

"We gotta tent," Ernie slurred. "Point us toa' woods."

"Forget the tent. I have a cabin with an extra bed. I sleep on the couch anyway. You two can stay in the bedroom."

"We can't throw yaouttaya bed," Ernie tried to tell him.

"I wouldn't ask if I didn't mean it. You kids aren't in any shape to refuse, so shut up and come with me."

I was glad to be in a bed when I awoke in Archie's cabin at dawn. I managed a few shaky steps to stagger to the bathroom, but by the time I made it back to the pillow, I felt faint and was covered in sweat.

The cabin was tiny, with the bedroom barely large enough for the double bed that was pushed into a corner against walls covered in pinewood paneling. I remembered arriving the night before and seeing the bed covered with clothes and newspapers, so I knew Archie was telling the truth about not sleeping here. He had shoved them on the floor. We'd left our packs at the foot of the bed and opened our sleeping bags to pass out.

Through the open door, I could see stacks of dirty dishes and empty beer bottles, and the place smelled of stale cigarettes. My stomach felt queasy.

"How's my little Hawk this morning?" Ernie asked.

I rolled my eyes.

"Feeling like barfing, are we? I can't believe how much we drank last night, and no one would take our money."

"I need toast," I mumbled. "Can you find toast? And water?"

"I'll see what I can scoff up."

❖❖❖❖

It was afternoon by the time I started feeling human. In the other room, Archie sprawled on the couch and Ernie sat in a rocking chair, the two of them smoking cigarettes and reading the paper.

"She's alive!" Archie proclaimed, chuckling, as I entered. "I was starting to wonder."

"Barely." I flopped into an upholstered chair with arms worn through to the padding.

"I've got to go into town and run errands. You know how to cook?" Archie asked me.

"Some stuff."

He chuckled again and stood. "Well, I won't get anything too difficult. You're welcome to stay as long as you like. Clean up a little and cook me a couple of meals in return. That's all I ask. Fair?"

"Sounds like a deal," I replied.

Archie closed the door behind him.

"Do you believe this guy?" Ernie asked. "He said we can stay here however long we want."

"This is an interesting place," I said. "I wouldn't mind staying."

❖❖❖❖

The next few days were filled with chess games at Archie's, while in the evening we became regulars at the Hope Hotel, so it wasn't surprising when we were invited to a house party on Saturday evening.

It was nearly twilight when we reached the salmon bake, a party to celebrate the Chinook salmon run on the Fraser River.

Several of the guys had fished earlier that day. When we arrived, they had three huge salmon roasting over a bed of wood coals, covered with wet corn husks to trap the moisture. A keg of beer was on the back porch, and bluegrass music played on the stereo.

Ernie and I filled paper cups with beer and joined the conversation. They were raving about the fishing conditions. I could hear powerful rushing water and discovered that the river was right behind us.

"Ever eat salmon?" the cook asked as I stared at the steaming grill.

"Only out of a can," I replied. "My entire fish experience has been Mrs. Paul's Fish Sticks and Chicken of the Sea."

He laughed. "Then you've never had salmon. Since this is your first, why don't you start the sampling?" He peeled back the corn husks to expose the soft, pink flesh.

"How do I eat it?"

"Peel a hunk off the bones. That's the way we like to eat it here. Don't be shy. Dig in."

I reached out and, when I realized touching the salmon wouldn't burn my fingers, pulled off a piece for about two mouthfuls. I wasn't expecting much when I took the first bite and was amazed that I barely needed to chew it. The fish nearly dissolved in my mouth with such rich flavor and juiciness, I immediately longed for more.

Meanwhile, the word was out that it was eating time, and the crowd converged on the grill, stripping off pieces and leaving nothing but bones minutes later.

Inside the house, the pace of the party had accelerated. People were dancing to bluegrass. Ernie grabbed my arm and we joined the other dancers, swinging each other around by linking our elbows and stomping our feet. I thought about how much I'd hated square dancing in gym class, but this was fun. Soon I was swinging from one set of arms to another, then a giant circle formed as we all wrapped our arms around each other's waists. The circle began to spin, our feet stomping to the beat, faster and faster, and then a couple jumped into the middle and danced. Other people jumped in and out of the circle until I was pulled in with Ernie. I was laughing so hard I could barely stay erect as Ernie swung me around to the fiddles and guitars wailing on the stereo.

We rejoined the circle and continued spinning until I was out of breath and had to stop. Standing on the sidelines and clapping along with the others, I watched the roomful of happy faces I knew, faces that told me I belonged here in this town so aptly named Hope.

❦ ❦ ❧ ❧

"We can't stay in Archie's cabin forever," Ernie pointed out two days later. "I love it here, too, but pretty soon I have to get back to Ohio."

"Why? What's important in Ohio?"

"I'm enrolled to start school at Ohio State in Cincinnati. Summer's almost over."

"How come you never mentioned that before?"

"I don't know. I guess I didn't expect you to still be around by now, so it didn't seem important. Then I wanted to ignore the possibility that this summer could ever end."

"What would be wrong with staying here? You know, picking apples and working for the Forestry like Mike does?"

"It sounds great." Ernie's tone was flat and sarcastic before resuming his normal voice. "Don't get me wrong. Hope is the greatest. But I have to go to school in September. I took a year off, but my parents already paid."

We sat on the edge of the bed not talking, and Ernie wrapped his arms around me. "I don't want to lose you. I love you."

When I heard those words, staying seemed unimportant. All I cared about was Ernie, and leaving Hope seemed less difficult than staying without him.

"I want you to come back to Ohio with me. I'm not sure how we can work this out, but I want us to stay together, if you want to."

"I want to. And I love you, too. I've loved you since Provincetown."

We kissed like it was our first true kiss to acknowledge our love. Then we held each other.

Ernie spoke softly as I rested in his arms. "We'll come back here next summer. We'll write to Archie, and maybe he can find us a cabin. I've never been as happy as I've been in Hope."

"Okay," I said. "I'll go to Ohio with you, as long as we're together."

We caught a ride outside of Archie's cabin the next morning after exchanging addresses and good-byes. "I've been here for eight years," he told us, "I'm not going anywhere."

Part of my soul got left behind when we crossed the metal bridge over the Fraser River, and I glanced back for one last look.

I'll be back, I promised myself. It was the only way I could bear to leave.

❖❖❖❖

The next time I saw Hope was twelve years later, in a movie. Sylvester Stallone walked over the metal bridge toward the Hope Hotel and proceeded to destroy the town with heavy artillery. In the movie, the town was called Hope, Washington, but I recognized it immediately from that place where the heart stores its most precious memories.

Chapter 21

August 1972
Chagrin Falls, Ohio

It was mid-afternoon when Ernie and I arrived on his parents' street in Ohio. SUGARBUSH LANE—PRIVATE, read the white plaque in black lettering hanging from the signpost. A goose with outstretched wings underscored the name and a split-rail fence decorated each corner of the road. I felt alienated in this manicured, suburban neighborhood.

"Shouldn't you call to say we're coming?" I'd asked earlier, while we were in Michigan. It seemed odd to me that he'd never contacted his parents during our trip, except for one postcard he'd sent from Banff. I called my parents weekly and mailed postcards frequently. I wondered if he was being inconsiderate or if they really didn't care, as he claimed.

I also worried that his one postcard had made no mention of me, and I was nervous about how they would react.

Ernie shrugged it off. "They're not going to say anything. Besides, I don't really care what they think. It'll be fine, you'll see."

His house was a sprawling, mustard-colored, split-level ranch set back from the road across a wide, well-mowed lawn. A flagpole waving the American flag stood prominently at the center. A wave of apprehension swept over me. In our time together, I'd never associated Ernie with a place so conservative.

There was a forest-green Mustang in the driveway, and the garage doors were open. Ernie led me around the house and into the backyard, where his mother stood talking to a neighbor by the split-rail fence.

She looked too young and attractive to be his mother. Mothers were supposed to look like mine, with lots of graying hair and wrinkles. His mother had dark, curly hair, bright blue eyes, and a thin, trim body. Next to her, I felt like a whale, as I was still about fifteen pounds overweight.

"Hi. I'm back." Ernie called to her in a voice like he'd returned from the grocery store. "Who else is around?"

In my family there would have been hugs and embraces, and we would have sat talking for hours. His mother stayed where she stood, talking to him across the lawn, looking from him to me and back again as she spoke.

"Your father's still at work. He should be home about five. Debbie's down in her room."

"Okay. I'm going to go say hi to Debbie." He reached for the screen door as I quietly followed him.

"Aren't you going to introduce me to your friend?" his mother yelled after him.

"Oh. Yeah. Mom, this is Sharon. Sharon, this is my mother."

"Hi," I said, waiting for any sign of disapproval from her, but she simply said hi and continued staring.

He led me through the house to the basement. In the dim light, I could see a bed pushed against one wall and a bureau next to it. A girl younger than me with long, dark hair sat at a card table in tight hip-hugger jeans and a stretch tank top that clung to her body. Across from her was a curly-headed boy about the same age, smoking cigarettes. They stared as we entered, almost smiling.

"Debbie, Steve, how's it going?" Ernie said. "Sharon, this is my sister, Debbie, and her boyfriend, Steve. Guys, this is Sharon."

"Hi. When'd you get back?" Debbie asked, looking me over. I knew I was being evaluated but she showed no expression.

"Five minutes ago. We got a ride right to the end of the street. What's everyone been up to?"

"Stuff. Mom and Dad were wondering when you'd get back. Well, I'm glad you're here. Maybe now they'll get off my case and bug you."

"Are they pissed?"

"I don't know. I think Dad is. But he's always pissed. You know how he is. I don't know what's going on with Mom."

"What do you mean?"

"Hey, I'm not going to tell you everything. Find out for yourself."

"Is she okay?"

Debbie grunted and answered in a sarcastic tone, "How do I know? I try to avoid her."

Ernie reached for the pack of Lucky Strike Menthols that sat on the table between her and Steve.

"Mooch!" Debbie slammed her hand over the cigarette pack before he could get to it. "That's the last in the pack and I'm out of money. Go look in Mom's purse, she probably has more."

He grabbed her wrist with his other hand and began to pry the cigarette pack from her fingers, while she twisted her arm around to free it.

"Ow!" Her tone sounded more like anger than pain. Ernie smiled while they struggled, and finally retrieved the pack.

"Ha, ha, got them anyhow," he teased her. "You go look in Mom's purse."

"You shit."

"Good to be home, sis." He looked at me and motioned with his head for me to follow. "Let's go upstairs. I'll show you my room."

Ernie's room was on the second floor of the split-level, next to his parents' bedroom. He had a set of wagon wheel bunk beds in one corner, and a bookcase and a dresser against two other walls.

"Make yourself at home. I get the bottom bunk." He paused for a moment as he dropped his pack to the floor. "Actually, we can share it most of the time."

He walked over to me and put his arms around me, and we kissed. I closed my eyes and tried to pretend nothing was different from being on the road together, but this all felt weird.

"I can't wait to take a hot shower." I pulled away from him. "And sleep in a real bed, with pillows and sheets."

"I'll show you where the bathroom is, and you can get started. I'll go see if there's any brewskis in the fridge."

Alone in the bathroom, I wallowed in the scent of shampoo, the fluffiness of the shag rug between my toes, the softness of the plush towel I wrapped myself in. I wanted to stay in that luxurious comfort, hiding from the unfamiliar territory that waited for me outside the bathroom door. Hopping in and out of cars with strangers felt far safer to me than the prospect of facing Ernie's family around the dinner table.

❖❖❖❖

"It's about time you got back. I'm getting sick of mowing this lawn." Ernie's father set his briefcase next to the couch, where Ernie and

I sat watching the summer Olympics that were taking place in Munich, Germany. "At least you're home in time for school. I was starting to wonder."

He looked as conservative as I expected for a salesman. His neatly cut, short, brown hair matched his brown-rimmed glasses, and he looked far too young to be my boyfriend's father. I thought he was kind of good-looking, for a straight guy. If his hair was a bit longer, if he got rid of those stupid suits, he would have promise.

"Got back this afternoon. Dad, this is Sharon. She's been traveling with me in Canada. She's going to be staying here for a while."

"Well, we have a lot to talk about, don't we? Like the draft, for one thing. But we can discuss that later."

"What does he mean about the draft?" I asked after his father had left the room.

"This really sucks." Ernie sighed. "My number is ninety-one. Nixon already said they're going to draft to number ninety-five. Can you believe it? And they're saying next year they're going to end the draft, forever. I could be the last person in America to get drafted! How is that for shit luck?"

"Well, you don't have to go. Why did we even come back here? We should leave right away and go live in Hope."

"I don't know." He stared into the hole of his Strohl's beer bottle, then tipped his head back for another drink, only to find it empty. "I'm getting another beer."

❊ ❊ ❊ ❊

A few days after we returned, Ernie's parents asked him to join them in the living room, which was normally reserved for guests. He grabbed my hand to accompany him, and I followed.

We sat on the olive-green brocade couch and I begin fiddling with the tassels on a gold velour pillow propped next to me. Ernie's mother sat quietly across the coffee table from us in shorts and canvas sneakers, her slender legs crossed at the ankles, while Ernie's father, still in his suit, seated himself in a matching chair near Ernie.

"You got a letter from the draft board while you were away." His father handed him an opened envelope. "They're telling you to expect a notice shortly about reporting for duty."

"Aw, man." Ernie yanked the letter out and spread it open, staring at the words. "I'm not going in the Army. I should have stayed in Canada. Aw, shit. What am I going to do?"

"If you stayed in Canada, you might never have been able to come home," his mother pointed out.

"It's better than going in the Army! My life would be over anyway. I couldn't even go to college, so what's the point? What if they send me to Vietnam?"

"I know, I know." His father shifted in his chair to lean toward him. "I've got a solution. While you've been off gallivanting around the world, I've been doing research. They've changed the rules for ROTC. During your first two years, you aren't committed to staying in. You can leave any time, but while you are in, you are considered to be serving your military duty. You would probably only have to join for a year if they end the draft like they are claiming they will."

I couldn't contain my outrage. "ROTC? You want him to join ROTC after they killed those kids at Kent State? It's a half-hour away! How can you ask him to do that?"

"We're not talking about morality here!" Ernie's father shouted back at me, his face turning red. "We're talking about staying alive. We're talking about staying out of the Army and out of Vietnam, about not having to be a fugitive in a foreign country! And—" he paused for effect, thrusting his finger toward me like he was pointing—"still being able to go to college like he wants to."

Ernie slumped into the couch, rereading the letter, then looked as his father. "What would I have to do in ROTC?"

"It's another class. You even get credit. There's no basic training, nothing like that, unless you stay in. The guys who stay past the second year continue on to be officers. They're committed to duty after that, but you wouldn't ever have to go that long."

"Let me think about it."

Ernie stood to leave. His parents nodded in resignation, and I followed him from the room.

When we reached his room and closed the door, I turned to confront him. "How can you even think about such a thing? Practically every college protest was over ROTC. They have no right even having it on campus. If you joined ROTC, it would be like you were supporting the war. Why don't we go back to Canada?"

"But I want to go to college!" He threw his hands in the air and paced across the room, not looking at me. "Why should I have my whole life ruined over this?"

I was too fired up to sit either. "How would going back to Canada ruin your life? I think it would improve your life. *I* want to live close to nature. To hell with this middle-class bullshit!"

He spun around and looked me in the eye. "Maybe you think it's bullshit, but I happen to like living in comfort. I want my own house one day, and a decent, interesting job. I don't want to spend my life picking apples and growing organic bean sprouts. Personally, I don't like to work that hard. I prefer intellectual pursuits."

"I'm not sure working for some corporation is a good use of a decent brain." I wasn't backing down. "I want my life to be spiritual and enlightened. I want to know that what I'm doing isn't being used to hurt people or the environment. I'd love to live in a dome, because I think the energy in a dome would be so much better than four square walls."

Ernie laughed, looking around at the ceiling and walls with his arms outstretched. "Energy? You think a house has energy? Well, there's electricity, that's energy."

"Don't make fun of things you don't understand. Yes, a house has energy. It can be good energy or bad energy, and I can tell you, this house is loaded with bad energy. Your bratty sister hates me; your mother is miserable; your father is oblivious to all of them."

"Why do you think I don't want to stay here? That's why I left all summer." He sighed, and the tension started to diminish. "Look, maybe a dome would be cool, I don't know. I like Canada, too. A lot. We'll go every summer, okay? Whatever you are into is fine. Maybe I don't understand it, but if you're into it, that's cool."

He walked over to me and wrapped his arms around me. I leaned into him, letting him engulf me.

"I love you." He stroked my hair. "That's all I'm really sure about. If you're not with me, nothing else matters. We'll figure it out."

I couldn't imagine not having Ernie in my life. Yet a tiny thought was poking at me: How could I get him to want the same things in life I wanted? Was it even possible?

⟪⟨⟩⟫

Early one evening about a week later, Ernie and I were in his room when there was a knock on the door.

"It's your mother. I need to talk to you."

He unlocked it and she sauntered in with a drink in her hand. I could tell she was buzzed. I had noticed she always had a drink with her in the evening. At first, I thought it was cool that she liked to party, until I realized she was sloshing them down alone. She wasn't drinking to have fun.

"What's up, Mom?" Ernie acted casual despite her odd behavior.

"We need to talk." She closed the door behind her and leaned on his dresser. "I know you are planning to have Sharon live with you while you go to school. I won't allow it."

"What does it matter?" Ernie sounded upset.

"If Sharon goes with you, you're going to spend all your time screwing instead of studying. You'll flunk out." She took a gulp.

I stayed silent.

"You can't stop her from going."

"No, I can't. But I can stop you. I can tell your father not to pay for school, and he'll listen to me." She wrapped her arms around herself, the drink still sitting in her hand as she steadied herself against the wall. "I'm giving you a choice. I'll give you five hundred dollars and you and Sharon can take off and get married. Or I can use the money to pay your tuition, and Sharon can go home to Connecticut while you go to college." She looked over at me.

I said nothing. I had no interest in running off to get married, and I was certain Ernie didn't either.

"That's not fair," he argued.

"Then take the five hundred dollars and go make it on your own. Go to Canada, if you want." She swung her arm out, pointing north.

"This is absurd. I don't want to take off and get married. I came home to go to school."

"Never mind," I interrupted. "I'll leave. Go to college." I had no intention of leaving, but I figured we could fake it, and they'd never know. We'd keep it a secret.

"Your father is in the family room," she said. "He wants to talk to you."

Ernie left, but his mother stayed and closed the door again. She turned toward me, took another gulp to finish her drink, then stared at it as she rattled the ice cubes. I remained sitting on the bed, wondering what was coming, twiddling my hair between my thumb and forefinger.

She looked up and stared at me, unblinking. "You'll never be happy with him. He's a perfectionist, like his father. He'll make you miserable, the way his father has made me miserable. I was young and in love like you are, once."

I looked at the floor, intimidated by her brutal honesty.

"I was only eighteen when Ernie was born, a few months older than you. Look at us. Is this what you want your life to be?" She put her glass on the dresser top. "We don't even have sex anymore. I lie in my bed awake at night listening to the two of you, next to a man who won't even touch me. Get out now while you can. You have no idea what a favor I'm doing you. Maybe one day you'll appreciate this." She retrieved her glass and left the room.

I felt as if the wind had been knocked out of me. I wondered how many drinks she'd needed to talk about this. I tried to squelch the ideas she'd planted with logic. After all, Ernie wasn't conservative like his father. And I wasn't like her. It was a different world from twenty years ago. We had no intention of getting married. Well, maybe way off in the future. Besides, if Ernie didn't touch me for even a day, I'd know there was a problem.

I'd begun to feel better by the time he returned. I ignored the odd, nagging sensation deep in my gut. I didn't even notice when it grew wider and larger each day—not until I finally decided it was a better idea for me to return to Connecticut to finish my last year of high school while Ernie went to college.

Chapter 22

July 1973
Candor, New York

I took a deep breath, inhaling the sweet scent of meadow grass and wildflowers, noticing a faint hint of the dairy barn I had passed a while back. These were the aromas of my new home, the home I would soon see at the top of the dirt road I was climbing, a commune named Hubbard Hill.

I plodded along the steep, rutted road, sweating in the July heat under my jeans and tank top. Tenya, my nine-month-old Irish setter, trotted ahead of me on her leash, weaving from one side of the road to the other on her skinny legs, stopping to sniff at curiosities that eluded me.

I stopped to adjust the weight of my backpack, full of the belongings I expected to need living in the country, as it was digging into my shoulder blades. Pulling on the straps, I shifted the frame higher and pulled the waistband tighter before continuing.

Around each bend of the road I expected to see the log cabin, which I understood to be the first building I'd reach, but instead there was more road. A horse fly buzzed around my head, hovering near enough to annoy me until I shook my braid at it.

I stopped again to catch my breath. There wasn't a house or a barn in sight, just rolling, distant hills, patches of trees, and forests beyond the meadows. What had begun as a dream a year ago in Hope, British Columbia, was becoming reality. I'd fantasized many times while reading the classifieds in *Mother Earth News Magazine*, where people and communes advertised in an attempt to find compatible new homes or new members, but it wasn't until I'd broken up with Ernie that I'd pursued the opportunity. After spending nearly all of my senior year in high school in a long-distance relationship with him, I came to realize we'd never agree on what we wanted in life. Once we were over and I'd graduated high school, I was free to seek the commune life with similarly minded people.

I'd answered a classified ad by Hubbard Hill seeking new members and received a letter back from Jodi, describing the commune and inviting me to visit. I'd been particularly pleased that she indicated men and women were treated as equals. She'd explained that each person built their own yurt to live anywhere on the one hundred and eighty acres of hills, fields, and forests, while the community house was a log cabin used for cooking and meals. The members were vegetarians, like I'd become that winter, and supported themselves by making crafts. She also wrote that they had no electricity or plumbing.

Even though I was excited, I was also apprehensive. What if they didn't like me, or they thought I knew too little about living off the land? I wanted to live on a commune that respected the earth, with members who lived in harmony with it and each other. Hubbard Hill portrayed that ideal to me in Jodi's letter.

The first sign that I was nearly there was the vegetable garden, a sprawling mass of tangled vines, giant squash leaves, and rows of bean poles. It was enclosed in chicken wire, with a gate framed from wood scraps.

Not long after, the green-and-red checkerboard roof of the log cabin came into view. It stood perched on cement block pillars, a large window facing downhill toward me, with two smaller windows on either side. My heart raced even faster than it was already from the climb.

Several dogs rushed forward to greet us, yelping and barking, and Tenya dove behind me, wrapping her leash around my legs, forcing me to stop and step out of it. At the same moment, the screen door popped open and out walked a smiling man in a T-shirt and bellbottom jeans with long, dark hair in a ponytail and a full beard. My heart still pounded, and I was afraid I might make a stumbling fool of myself during the introductions. Would they see through me to my complete ignorance?

"Hi, I'm Sharon. Did you get my letter that I was coming?" I'd written to tell them I'd be arriving on July 15th.

"Sure did. We've been waiting for you. Welcome to Hubbard Hill. I'm Mike."

My first impression of him was his kind face and transparent warmth; he was the kind of emissary who could put anyone at ease. I relaxed a bit.

"Don't let the dogs scare you," he said. "They just like to make a lot of noise. Come on in and meet the others. I just finished making dinner. Are you hungry?"

"Yes, I am." I was lying; I didn't know if I could eat in my current state of anxiousness. But I was pleased that a man had done the cooking. Mike held the door and Tenya scooted ahead. Another Irish setter rose from the floor, and the two began the doggy dance of sniffing around one another.

The inside of the cabin was dark and funky, with bark-covered log walls, a plywood floor, cabinets made of vertical wood that matched the logs, and a mass of old furniture.

Two men and a woman sitting at a table made from a huge telephone wire spool in front of the picture window greeted me with a chorus of hellos. I realized they'd had a view of me as I approached the cabin.

"Have a seat," said one of the men, nodding toward an empty antique chair at the table. "How did you get here? Didn't you have a ride?"

"My parents drove me, but they were afraid to drive up the hill." I removed my pack and sat in the chair. "They said they were worried about getting stuck, but I think they were afraid of who might be here."

They all laughed.

"That's quite a walk. Have any trouble finding the place?" Mike asked.

"No, the directions were great. I followed the map."

"Everyone introduce themselves," he said. "I have to get the Mexican pan bread out of the oven."

"Mike does most of the cooking here," explained a thin, wiry man with chin-length, kinky, dark hair, a short beard, wired-rimmed glasses, a narrow face, and a protruding nose. "I'm Peter, the only original member still living here. Bonnie was one of the originals, too, but she's moved on."

"Yeah, I live in Ithaca now," said the woman. Her curly dark hair formed waves around her shoulders. "That's my Irish setter who's making friends with yours. Nice to meet you."

"Well, I live here." The next guy was a well-tanned, muscular man wearing only red shorts, with a lot of bushy, long, dark hair in a ponytail and a thick beard. His mouth was lopsided as he forced out his words. "I'm John. I like to work in the garden . . . and I'm . . . building barns right now with a crew . . . I've been here since . . . last September. Welcome to Hubbard Hill." He gave me an enthusiastic grin.

"Where's Jodi?" I asked. "She's the one who wrote to me."

"She went to Florida for a while," Peter replied. "We're not sure how long she'll be gone, but hopefully she'll be back soon."

A heavy clay bowl filled with salad sat in the middle of the table. John stood and got plates and silverware for everyone. The others already had glasses of water and mugs of herbal tea.

"You want some water?" Mike asked from the kitchen area, where shelves were stocked with canned goods, jars, and dishware, while pots and pans hung from nails above the propane gas stove. A counter divided the kitchen area from the rest of the cabin.

"Yes, please," I replied.

He reached under the counter, uncovered a five-gallon metal milk can, and ladled out some water into a glass for me. "We have to haul the water in these milk cans since we don't have a pump for our well," he told me.

"The well is one hundred and twenty feet deep," Peter said. "You can't prime a pump that deep by hand, you need electricity, which we don't have. It costs too much to get the electricity here, because they charge you for every pole they install, and it's a half-mile uphill. We can't afford it."

"How about a generator?" I asked.

"We've talked about a generator," he said. "But there's the issue of the noise and the smell. They run off gasoline, and they're loud. People thought it would spoil the atmosphere."

"Where do you get your water?"

"In the winter, there're streams that run," Peter said. "It's clean, because we're the highest point on this hill. But this time of year, they're dried up, so we fill them from the faucet in the farmer's barn at the bottom of the hill. He's been good about letting us do that."

Mike placed a cheese-covered pie dish in the middle of the table. He sliced it into pie-shaped pieces and took a slice before handing the spatula to Peter. The insides resembled hamburger, but Mike said it was made from black beans, corn meal, onions, and eggs.

Just then, another man came in, gray clay speckling his brown hair and beard. He sat across the table from me in the last chair as Bonnie passed me the spatula to serve myself some dinner.

"Hi, I'm Don," he said to me with a smile. "I heard you arrive, but I was in the middle of throwing a pot that I wanted to finish. I have a potter's wheel in the shed, but I'm getting ready to build a new yurt that's going to be my workshop."

"How long have you been making pottery?" I asked, dishing pan bread onto my plate.

"I started doing it as a hobby when I was at Cornell and enjoyed it. When I moved here a year and a half ago, I started again." Don dished salad onto his plate. "First I was going to the studio at Cornell to work, but now that my wheel is here, I accumulate my work and then haul it there to be fired."

"That must be a pain."

"It is. I'm planning to build a kiln here once we have the money. Hopefully before winter."

"Great dinner, Mike," Bonnie said, taking a breath between gulps.

"Another good one . . . Mike," John said.

"Mexican pan bread is one of our favorites," Peter told me.

The conversation stopped as everyone ate. I had never eaten a meatless entree before, and I found it delicious. As a vegetarian living with my parents, I ate the same as them but skipped the meat.

Peter addressed the group after a while. "Should we ask Sharon to take a dish week now that she's here?"

There was laughter.

"That would sure make me happy," Don said, "because I'm supposed to be next."

"Dish week is the only rule we have here," Peter explained. "Nobody tells anyone what to do with their time, except for dish week." Peter had a grin on his face now, and it spread to the other members at the table. "Because there's no running water, you can't do the dishes every day. You have to haul the water, pour it into those dishpans over there, and heat them on the stove. With all these people eating three meals a day, baking bread, and canning, we make a bunch of messy dishes. Everyone takes turns getting a dish week, and your dish week ends whenever you finish on Sunday. The only rule about when you do them is we can't run out of dishes. Most of the time, that means about every two days."

"It gets good . . . and stuck on," John added.

"It helps if you bribe Mike not to cook anything that takes too many pans," Peter said.

"I'll take the next dish week," I told them, eager to be accepted.

"All right, Sharon!" John responded, nodding his head in my direction.

"That's okay," Don said. "I'll take this week and you can go next. It's probably not fair to throw you right into dish week the day you arrive."

I thanked him, relieved.

When dinner ended, Peter took me on a tour of the yurts. I followed him across a field along a well-worn path.

"Yurts are originally from Mongolia," he explained. "The nomads make them out of yak hides, rolling them up to take with them. Ours of course are stationary, but the tax inspector called them tent frames, so they aren't taxed. Another reason we keep building them."

"What are they made out of?" I asked as he showed me Don's yurt, the first we encountered.

"There's a latticework of wood that forms the frame. A cable between the walls and the roof holds the whole thing together. Over that we put insulation, tar paper, roofing shingles, and sometimes burlap to cover the fiberglass." He pointed out the different parts of Don's yurt before continuing. "We've experimented with a few different materials, but we keep trying new things to see what works. We may find ways to build them cheaper, or with recycled stuff. You can cut any size or shape doors and windows. But there's always a skylight at the peak of the roof that we cover with old windows or plastic."

We arrived at Peter's yurt. He swung open his diamond-shaped plywood door and attached the latch on it to a hook on the wall to hold it open. Inside it seemed huge—big enough for a raised double bed on a wooden platform, a dresser, many shelves, and a long workbench built into one area. There was a small tin wood stove on four legs for heat, with the pipe vented out the side of the yurt.

He pulled out a few pieces of the silver jewelry he'd made and showed me new designs he was trying. "Most jewelers hate to file, but I smoke a joint and sit here filing for hours. That way I can make some bizarre shapes. People buy hand-crafted items because they want something unique and artistic."

He showed me the other yurts before we headed back to the cabin. When we reached it, Bonnie was getting ready to leave, piling her Irish setter into her car. Mike had finished the dishes and was lighting the gas lamps hanging from the ceiling beams that ran off a tank of propane fed through tubes. They burned nearly as bright as electric bulbs.

Peter pointed out the flashlights for trips to the outhouse below the cabin to the right.

"Pee outside anywhere you want," he told me. "Everyone does. There's lime in the outhouse. It doesn't smell as long as you dump at least a cup or more of lime on after you take a shit. You can sleep in any of the yurts you want, or in the loft. There are mattresses on both ends. When we first moved here, everyone slept in the cabin because it was the first building we built."

"I'll sleep in the loft for now," I said, thinking how awkward any other arrangement would be.

The cabin loft was divided into two sides, with a wooden catwalk connecting the two and a ladder for access. At bedtime, I carried Tenya up the ladder, then unrolled my sleeping bag onto a mattress. We lay down together and I stroked her fur while my head buzzed with the myriad possibilities of living here and getting to know these new people.

Chapter 23

July 1973
Hubbard Hill

By Wednesday, I was settling into my surroundings. Since I loved baking bread, which I'd taught myself to do using *The Tassajara Bread Book*, I decided to try it out at Hubbard Hill.

In my first three days, I discovered that life at Hubbard Hill revolved around preparing food. Since there was no refrigeration, everything was cooked daily from scratch. This process took hours, since all the grains, beans, and legumes were dried and needed soaking and pre-cooking, and some were used in every meal. The bread-baking process took almost five hours, including activating the yeast, punching down the dough and letting it rise again, forming loaves, and baking, and the bread ran out every two to three days.

I searched through the grain closet for my ingredients. Tins marked with masking tape and black ink contained food purchased in bulk from the Ithaca Food Co-op: bulgur, red lentils, soybeans, wheat, oat and rye flour, dried apricots, raisins, dates, corn meal, split peas, dried milk, sesame seeds, and brown rice were some of the staples.

After warming water in a kettle, I combined it with yeast in a large bowl, then added honey, dry milk, and whole-wheat flour. Once I mixed it, I placed it in the oven with the door open and turned the temperature on low. Too hot and the yeast would die. Too cool and the yeast would not activate.

Next, I took a walk to the garden to see what was ready. Lettuce, spinach, and pole beans were fully grown. I picked some of each for dinner. In the weeks that followed, summer squash would become abundant, along with tomatoes, cucumbers, eggplant, onions, peppers, and okra. No two dinners were ever the same.

By early evening, Mike and John had returned from work and Peter was back from buying jewelry supplies. Don had been throwing pottery much of the day.

My first bread came out of the oven and the yeasty scent filled the cabin. The guys circled around, slicing off large, steaming chunks and smothering it in butter and globs of honey.

"Wow, this is incredible," Mike said with his usual sincerity and a big smile. "I think we found ourselves a new bread baker."

"Good . . . stuff," John agreed in between chews, his mouth full. Within minutes the first loaf was gone.

"We would have been back sooner, but we stopped off at the lake," Mike said.

"Shit, you guys went to Empire Lake without us?" Peter protested. "Hey, how about tomorrow we all meet there after work? We could bring dinner and eat there. I could sure use a shower by now. And Sharon can get to see the lake."

"Empire Lake is where we go to shower this time of year," Mike explained, cutting another slice of bread. "It's run by SUNY Binghamton, the state college, so they have great facilities for all the students. Plus this beautiful lake in the middle of the woods that no one even knows is there."

"And the best part is," Peter said, "it's mostly all us locals from the communes in the area. The students only go there on weekends. And no one has to wear clothes. I mean, you can if you want to. But they don't care if there's a bunch of stark-naked hippies running around. It's truly clothing optional."

"Sounds cool," I lied. I wasn't sure which worried me more: the prospect of making a fool of myself in the water by not being able to swim, or getting naked for the first time in front of all my male commune partners. Nudity with my lover was fine, but this was different.

As I thought about it, I realized that this was about trust. Not just getting naked at the lake but also living with a group of people. There had to be trust that they wouldn't hurt me or humiliate me—that they would be there for me, and I would learn to be there for them.

When the weekend arrived, we were out of bread again, so I baked a batch of six loaves after breakfast. John was working in the garden, Peter and Don popped in and out of the cabin for food while they were working on pottery and jewelry, but by noon, I hadn't seen Mike all day. When Peter came in for lunch, he explained that Mike was in his yurt, tripping.

I was attracted to Mike, and curious about him too. I wondered if I should walk out to his yurt and knock on the door . . . or would that be presumptuous?

Instead, I went for a hike that would lead me past his yurt. I followed a path along the edge of the tree line that looked out across an open field to distant blue green hills.

When I came to a V-shaped pine grove, there stood Mike's yurt, plopped among the trees like a Hobbit house, a large blue eye painted on the front door that stared at approaching visitors. I inhaled the sweet scent of pine needles that covered the ground as I slowed my gait, making sure I wouldn't pass too quickly by his large, open window.

"Hello there," he called out to me.

Looking in, I saw Mike sitting on his bed. "How's it going?" I called back.

"Really good. Would you like to come in?"

My tactic had worked!

I walked over to the entrance and entered past the eye. Mike lowered himself onto the floor, saving a piece of rug so I could sit across from him. He usually wore his hair in a ponytail but today he'd left it loose and flowing over his shoulders in shiny, mahogany waves that reminded me of Jesus Christ. Mike radiated kindness and sincerity. He was always praising my smallest contributions and going out of his way to put me at ease.

He explained that he had taken three hits of acid, an amount I considered extreme, yet he spoke quietly and smiled, behaving normally. We traded stories on our backgrounds. He told me about his life, starting with Catholic school in his South Philly Italian neighborhood. After graduation, he moved to New York City because movies were his passion.

"I won third place in the National Kodak Teenage Film Awards for an animated film I created. My brother shrinks into this toy person who has to find his way off the bed and ends up getting stepped on. I was nineteen and totally naïve, so when this movie studio in New York called me and wanted to hire me, I was thrilled."

"Wow. You must have freaked." I was in awe. I had never met anyone involved in movies.

"I did." His face turned sad. "I went to New York as an idealistic kid expecting to make movies, because that was all I ever wanted to do. They wanted some gopher they could hire cheap to do their dirty work. Their studio made soft porn. After wasting two years working for those assholes, I realized that dream wasn't going to happen. I hung around New York a couple of more years, hoping for a break, until I finally capitulated. One day I saw an ad for Hubbard Hill in the Village. So here I am, where there isn't even electricity, never mind a movie projector."

"Do you miss all that?"

"Not the bullshit. But I miss watching movies on the big screen. I like to sit close, second or third row, so there's nothing between me and the screen. I get lost in them. Have you ever felt that way?"

He looked into my eyes and I was drawn to the intensity of his gaze. *George Harrison eyes*, I thought, noticing how Mike's thick eyebrows arched the way George's did. He'd been my favorite Beatle when I was ten; I'd been in love with his big brown eyes.

"Yeah, when I saw *Romeo and Juliet* in eighth grade," I said. "I saw it twice, but I could have watched it a hundred times. And it was Shakespeare. I'm amazed I knew what they were saying."

"Franco Zefferelli. That was a beautiful film. But I think all the guys went to see Olivia Hussey's tit."

We giggled together a little, and then Mike couldn't stop laughing, which caused me to laugh even harder, until we were both wiping tears from our eyes. Soon he was crawling around the room on his hands and knees, pulling out artifacts to show me.

"Take a look at this." He opened a huge book and, shifting closer, showed me a series of photos of a person running, then walking, then jumping; another of a horse trotting and breaking into a gallop.

"Muybridge studied motion using cameras in the 1800s, before film. See how each photo is one shift in movement from the one before it? This is what animators study. When you are creating an animated character on film, the model must be moved in tiny increments, to give it the appearance of being alive. The real masters make the motion look fluid and flawless."

He reached under his bed and slid out a box. In it lay a wrinkled, tangerine-colored rubber creature over a foot tall, with short, mangled arms and a hunched back. He lifted it out and stood it on the floor, smiling like a proud father. "I built this guy. He's a special effects model."

He handed it to me to examine, explaining how it was constructed with multi-rotational joints that gave it jaw movements, facial expressions, fingers, and knuckles, so it could bend, twist, dip, and stretch. He explained the process I took for granted—the five-minute sequence that took weeks to create, the dedication it took an animator to fashion an imagined living being out of ball bearings and liquid latex to breathe life into it.

We spent the rest of the afternoon talking and laughing, sitting close together, and learning about each other but never quite touching, except for the occasional brush of the arm.

❖ ❖ ❖ ❖

"Sunday morning, time for Communion," John announced to the rest of us sitting around the table in the cabin as he stood above us. "Now stick out your tongue . . . and Father John will administer . . . the sacrament."

"AHHHH." Peter stretched out his tongue in mock reverence as John placed the tiny white LSD tablet in Peter's mouth. Peter swallowed and took a gulp of tea, looking around at the rest of us with a grin reminiscent of a little boy who's just hit the teacher with a spit ball.

"You forgot to say Amen," John chastised Peter.

"What do I know about this? I'm Jewish!" Peter hunched his shoulders and laughed.

John walked over to Don and held another tablet above his head, reciting a phrase that I guessed was in Latin, which brought more giggles from all of us. I could see John was enjoying this.

Peter shook his head. "I can't believe you know all this stuff. Imagine that. Hubbard Hill has its own priest! We've had a lot of different people here, but this is a first."

"Almost priest," John said as he made the sign of the cross over Don. "I dropped out before . . . completing the vows. Say Amen . . . Don."

"Amen!" Don yelled out like he was at a Baptist revival meeting. John chuckled and placed the tablet on Don's tongue.

"None for me, thanks," Mike replied when John turned to him. "I had my share yesterday. Today's my day of rest."

"Sharon," John turned to me. "Are you going to . . . to join us?"

Two years before, I had quit tripping and sworn I'd never do it again. I was torn between wanting to participate and being afraid of the drug. Yet by watching Mike the day before, I could tell this wasn't very strong LSD. Perhaps a little wouldn't hurt.

"I don't want to take a whole one," I said. "Give me a quarter."

"A quarter?" John looked stunned. "You won't even feel . . . a quarter. I already took . . . two."

Mike interrupted. "If she wants to do a quarter, that's her choice. Let her do a quarter."

"How strong do you think it is?" I asked Mike.

"Not strong at all. But do whatever you feel like. Half probably wouldn't bother you."

"Okay. I'll do half."

John broke the tablet in two and I stuck out my tongue while I muttered Amen, taking pleasure in the dig at the Catholic Church.

"I'll take the other half," Peter offered.

The reason for tripping was because Hubbard Hill had been asked to help raise a roof on a yurt someone was building, and according to their tradition, they always tripped when they raised a yurt roof. However, they'd been asked because the people building the yurt didn't know how to assemble the roof.

By the time we drove to the construction site in the woods, Peter, John, and Don could barely speak two words without breaking into hysterics. The yurt owner looked concerned.

Peter leaned over to him and said in a low voice, "We're all tripping."

The yurt owner folded his arms and shook his head.

"Sorry," Peter said solemnly. Then the fits of laughter began again.

"But Mike's okay," Peter added, seemingly as an afterthought. "He's seen it done. He can get you through it."

The yurt owner, looking relieved, led us over to the rest of the crew.

I was still coherent, feeling a little high and enjoying the beauty of the day. Several other hippies stood around the yurt waiting for direction. Mike walked over to a pile of lumber and selected a pair of boards.

"I see you already nailed together the one-by-twos. You have fifty pairs?" he asked, pulling the set he was holding apart to examine the nail placement.

"Yes, I do," the yurt owner replied.

"Good. Let's get started. We're going to need some poles for bracing. You have any scraps around?"

I watched Mike demonstrate how to make braces for balancing the roof as others copied him. He stationed us around the interior perimeter of the yurt walls. He had the others raise a pair of boards and rest them on the braces we were holding, opening them, scissor-like, and then raising the next pair and nesting the tops together until the fourth set was raised. He nailed the end of the first set to the end of the fourth set, and the nail between the two boards straddled the wire that held the walls together.

I recognized the pattern and knew what should happen next. *This is easy*, I realized. Don, Peter, and John tried to keep from giggling while holding the support braces, while Mike hammered the sets together and others carried new pairs of lumber over. There was confusion as a couple of new people tried to maneuver the roof lattice into place, until I explained it to them. The next thing I knew, I was telling them how to lay the following set of boards and how far over to place them to connect them, and where the wire belonged.

We progressed smoothly around the circle. Mike smiled at me as he hammered, silently letting me take the lead.

Finally, the circle was completed, the support braces were removed, and the roof leaned into itself, leaving a three-foot opening in the center for the skylight. Peter, Don, John, and Mike hoisted the yurt owner until he could grab the opening. They stepped away as he hung there, swinging from his new roof, as we all cheered. We formed a circle beneath the dangling yurt owner with his other friends, wrapping our arms around each other. I felt incredible energy flowing through me, this mass of human good vibes, as we gazed at the yurt owner's triumphant face.

❖ ❖ ❖ ❖

Afterward, we drove to Empire Lake. This was my second trip, and this time I felt comfortable taking off my clothes; in fact, I barely noticed that we were all naked.

When I stepped into the water, it felt like silk caressing my body, cool and inviting. Mike suggested I lean back and try to float, assuring me he would stand next to me and catch me if I sank. I knew the hardest part was to relax and trust the water to support me. I stretched out my arms, slid back, and closed my eyes. The water seemed to buoy me in a cradle. I was floating, as if I had been floating forever!

I opened my eyes and looked at Mike, completely unafraid. He was smiling at me, waiting in case I should need him. I knew he understood, because he hadn't learned to swim until he was nineteen.

After a few moments, my feet began to sink, so I stood.

"I knew you could do it," he told me. "If you can float, you can swim on your back. You start to move your arms as you're floating and pull yourself through the water." He leaned back and demonstrated.

I was touched by his effort to help me. No one had ever tried to teach me to swim except my father, once, when I was eight, which ended with my sister accidentally dropping me underwater when she reached to fix her slipping bathing suit strap.

When Mike stood again, I leaned into the water, followed his instruction, and felt myself moving backwards. I was swimming!

"Damn it," I heard Don yell nearby. "I stepped on a nail."

Mike and I ran from the water and joined the others coming on shore. Peter stooped and looked at the bottom of Don's foot.

"The nail's rusty. We better get you to a doctor right away for a tetanus shot. This could get serious. There's that doctor who has his office at his house in the center of Candor."

We gathered our things and rushed for the parking lot, piling into John's red Opal station wagon. Mike and I slid in the back next to Peter, crushed against each other. Mike reached over and took my hand in his as we smiled at each other, oblivious to Don's pain.

When we reached the doctor's office, John, Don, and Peter got out.

"We'll wait here," Mike told them, and I didn't disagree. When the others disappeared inside, he leaned over and kissed me, and I felt a rush of excitement pour over me. Mike was different from any man I had ever known. Besides being my friend, we shared the same ideals, the same vision; we wanted the same kind of lifestyle. As we kissed, I knew this was the beginning of a good relationship.

When we arrived at the cabin later, four people were standing outside, next to a car. They looked like a family—a short-haired man in his early thirties, a woman about the same age, and two little blond children, a boy and a girl.

"Who's this?" Don asked, but no one knew.

"Is this Hubbard Hill?" the man asked as we climbed out of the Opal.

"Yes it is," Peter answered. "How can we help you?"

"I'm Helen," the woman said, stepping forward. "I wrote to you and said I would be coming. I'm here to see about joining the commune. These are my children, Todd and Amy. And this is Tim. He's a friend from Ithaca who came with me to look around."

"Welcome," John said. "We just came back . . . from swimming. Come on in."

Mike was still holding my hand. He looked at me and whispered, "Want to come out to my yurt?"

"Okay," I whispered back, not caring about Helen.

"See you guys later," he said, and there were smiles from the rest of the Hubbards as we walked off to Mike's yurt.

❋ Chapter 24

July 1973
Hubbard Hill

My first round of dishes for my dish week was two days after Helen arrived. I had two large enamel pans of water steaming on the counter, one bubbling with dish soap, the other accumulating a film from rinsing all the cups and glasses. Silverware, spatulas, cooking spoons, and chopping knives soaked in the wash water while I placed stacks of plates and bowls on top of them. Three frying pans, a wok, and two glass casserole pans were next.

Throughout my ordeal, Helen sat at the table talking with me while Todd played outside. Amy stood by her mother, periodically lifting her shirt as though asking to nurse. Finally, Helen scooped her onto her lap and Amy reached for her mother's milk.

"They recommend you nurse children until at least age two or three for good health," Helen said. "In fact, it's better if you let them give it up when they're ready. In other cultures, women nurse until their children are seven or eight."

"Are you going to nurse Amy that long?" I scrubbed a plate and stacked it in the rinse water.

"I don't think it should be up to me. She'll know when it's time. Neither of us are ready to quit yet. She only just turned two. Back in Ossining, people thought I was a pervert. That's how sick that society is, suggesting a perfectly natural act between mother and child is deviant. I'm glad to be out of there. I've been dreaming about this since Amy was born. Now, here I am!" She gave me a big smile and shook her short brown hair out of her eyes as she cradled Amy.

The benefits of nursing babies bored me. I figured if I had one someday, far in the future, I would probably nurse mine, since it was gaining in popularity, especially among hippies—but in the meantime, I had no interest. Helen looked matronly to me and was older than the rest of us. I wondered how she and her children would fit in, and if she had other communes she was considering.

"Why did you pick Hubbard Hill?" I asked.

"I think because it's near Ithaca. I went to school at Cornell. I was happy then, and I haven't been since." Amy stopped nursing and looked at me. As Helen started to lift her from her lap, she pulled up Helen's shirt and began again. "It was my fault for marrying Chuck. I let myself get trapped into that female stereotype. After all, every woman I knew was getting married, and I figured Chuck would make a perfect husband." She paused for a moment, and then laughed. "Actually, he is a perfect husband. There's nothing wrong with Chuck, it's me that wants out. I feel like there's no *me* anymore. I'm just Chuck's wife and Todd and Amy's mother. The world is moving on while I'm playing house in Westchester. It's pathetic."

Amy slid from her mother's lap and stood between her legs, gaping at me. I added more soap to the wash water and twirled it around, hoping it would make more bubbles, but it felt too cold. I put the wash pan back on the stove to reheat with the silverware still in it, then heard an unfamiliar female voice outside the door, speaking to Todd in a southern drawl.

"And who might you be? What are you holding in your hand? . . . Let me see . . . Oh! You have a toad! Well, it looks like it's dead to me. How long have you been holding that poor thing?"

A girl about my age with long blond hair almost to her waist burst through the screen door of the cabin and gave Helen and me a puzzled look.

"Who are y'all, and where is everyone?"

"I'm Sharon." I smiled, wiping my hands on the dishtowel, as I headed toward her. "Are you Jodi?"

"That's me. You're the woman with the Irish setter that I wrote to, right?"

"Yep. I made it here." As I reached her, I put out my arms to hug her, and she responded by hugging me back. "They're going to be thrilled you are back."

"Well I sure missed them, too! Where are they?"

"John and Mike are off building barns. Peter drove to Ithaca, and Don went into town to do laundry."

"Shit. My whole drive back from Florida I kept imagining running into the cabin and finding everyone waiting for me. Well, I guess I'll have to wait a bit longer." She surveyed the cabin as I went back to the rinse pan to shift dishes to the drying rack. "I see they've got you doing dish week. Didn't take them long to palm that one off, did it?"

I laughed. "Oh, I don't mind. I offered to go next to be useful. I've been baking a lot of bread, too. Are you hungry?"

"Oh! Fresh-baked bread! Oh God, how I've missed that. It is so good to be back home."

Throughout this conversation, Helen sat silently, watching the two of us. Amy was leaning against her mother, yanking on her shirt again.

"And who are you?" Jodi finally asked.

"I'm Helen. I arrived Sunday."

"Are these your children? Because one of them has been holding a toad so long the poor thing died, and he still won't put it down." She stood facing Helen in her chair as Amy crawled into her lap again.

"Well, he's curious, that's all." Helen cuddled Amy. "I'm sure he didn't mean to hurt it. This is how children learn. He's too young to understand about dying yet."

Jodi didn't move. "Well, I think the toad was too young to understand about dying either, but he does now. I don't think he should still be carrying it around. Shouldn't you say something to him?"

"I don't want him to develop a hang-up about this. This is his first experience with death. I think it's important for adults not to lay our negative feelings on our children. They should form their own judgments."

Jodi stared at Helen for a moment, then turned away, smirking. She walked over to the kitchen table, sat, and lit a cigarette.

Even though I didn't know her yet, I could tell Jodi disliked Helen. I had already noticed that when she talked, I knew what she was feeling by the way she said it. As I came to know her better, I would become fascinated by the musical quality of her voice and the way joy, anger, or bitchiness rolled off her lips without remorse.

It was one of the things I came to love about her.

❖❖➤➤

It started with the sneakers. They were the ugliest shoes I'd ever seen, blue with large ivory colored plastic designs shaped like the emblems of a Mercury sedan on each side and across the toe. Several pair appeared at a church rummage sale in Candor one morning, selling for a dollar each despite being brand-new. They fit me, so I added them to my bag along with a plaid wool shirt and a snowflake-laden ski sweater.

The ugliness of the sneakers made them almost cool, and I carried them proudly into the cabin and laid them on the table to show off my bargain. As I was bragging about their cost to John and Mike, Jodi walked in and interrupted me with a shriek.

"I can't believe you bought those," she said through gasps of laughter as she held her hand to her face, pretending to stifle herself. I felt insulted until I noticed her other hand frantically pointing at her feet. Leaning over the table I saw she was wearing an identical pair of sneakers. I broke into laughter with her and donned mine, then we danced like can-can girls with our arms around each other's waists, kicking our feet in the air.

From that moment on, Jodi and I discovered how much we had in common. We'd been born exactly one month apart to the day. We both loved Leon Russell, chocolate milkshakes, shooting pool, and Dr. Bronner's peppermint soap. We both believed women should be treated like equals to men. Jodi boasted that women could do anything they could do, which gave me the guts to agree with her. We were both eighteen, the youngest of the adults in the group, while the men ranged in age from twenty-four to twenty-eight, with Helen the oldest at thirty-one.

Jodi and I began doing errands together, like grocery shopping, collecting the co-op food pickup on Saturdays, and hauling water.

When we drove to Candor to do laundry, we'd sneak off to the drug store for a milkshake during the wash cycle. Two more quarters wouldn't be missed when you had several loads washing.

At the drugstore, a teenage boy a couple of years younger than us made our milkshake. Fifty cents was the cost of whipped milk and chocolate syrup, but he often threw in double scoops of vanilla ice cream without charging us extra.

With two straws and two spoons, we sat across the table from each other, sharing our treat.

"Can you imagine what the guys would say if they saw us eating this?" Jodi giggled.

I licked my lips. "It sure isn't health food. You know what their problem is? They're all too serious."

"Well, that's guys for you. They don't know how to have fun. Especially Don. He must be the most serious of the bunch." She took another mouthful of ice cream before continuing, "And he thinks he's the only one who does anything important. Like cooking dinner every night doesn't matter. How would he have time to do his pottery if everyone else wasn't working in the garden or running to the food co-op? He's free to create while the rest of us do the dirty work, then acts all high and mighty because he's making money." She waved her spoon in the air as she made her point. "And we have to feel guilty for spending fifty cents on a milkshake."

"I do feel guilty," I admitted. "I know it's stupid, but I do."

"I know. I do too. But it sucks, doesn't it? I mean, it's supposed to be that we're all equal, that we all contribute what we're good at and who makes the money shouldn't matter. But it still does. Because that's Don's ego. He has to be *the man*. He says he believes women are just as good as men, but he doesn't act like it."

"You and Don are such a weird couple. It's almost like you aren't a couple sometimes."

Jodi nodded as she sucked on her straw. "Sometimes I wish we weren't a couple. But I love him. I don't know what I see in the man, and God knows, he doesn't deserve how I feel about him. But I'm not going to let him walk on me. I am as stubborn, if not more stubborn, than he is." She leaned back in her chair and smiled at me. "Of course, Michael is such a sweetheart, he would never act the way Don does. I love that you're with Michael now. He needed someone, and he deserves to be happy. But mostly I'm glad you're here to keep *me* company. It is *so* good to have a woman here I can relate to."

✿ Chapter 25

August 1973
Hubbard Hill

When we built yurts, we constructed the octagonal floor first, forming a twenty-foot-diameter frame with four-by-four wooden beams and then covering them with sheets of plywood. We built the floor upside-down to insulate the bottom, since it would be impossible to crawl underneath it later. Then it had to be turned over. A floor flipping required neighboring communes to help, since seven of us couldn't handle the weight.

Don had driven to Owl Creek commune, seventeen miles away in Spencer, a couple of days earlier to ask for assistance, since we had no phone and neither did they. Several people had agreed to help.

When the day arrived, a carload of Owl Creek members joined us at the construction site near a huge oak tree alongside our road. Don had picked this spot for his new yurt, as he could easily drive in to load pottery into his car to take to craft fairs.

This was my first floor flipping, so I didn't know the logistics yet. I noticed he'd attached a set of two-by-four beams on opposite ends of the floor that each pivoted from a nail. I wondered why, but I figured I'd find out soon enough.

He directed most of us to line up along the downhill edge of the floor, then explained that we were going to raise it on end and have it land on the other side. I stood at one end, figuring there would be less weight there for me to support.

"We're going to walk it upright hand over hand," Don instructed, standing on the uphill side. "Me, John, and Jim will stand on this side and hold it so it doesn't flip up and land on anyone. Once we get it vertical, Mike and Peter will run over here to help us catch it and lower it. Then we'll all lift it onto the base and rest it on the footings. And be careful. If it falls, someone could be crushed."

We looked around at one another and nodded, acknowledging that we were prepared.

"Everyone ready? Let's do it!" Don called out.

Those of us on the lower side began walking the floor upward, but the higher it got, the more the weight resisted moving. My arms grew fatigued as I stretched them above my head as high as I could reach, pushing against the floor as it moved in jolts. Then the beam that was attached to my end swung down and knocked into my upper thigh.

"Ow!" I cried out, wincing.

Everyone turned to see what happened.

"Grab the beam!" Don yelled to me. "You need to hold onto the beam."

I let go of the floor and cupped my hands together, placing them under the end of the beam, pushing upward with everyone else. Suddenly, it became apparent why the beams were nailed near the top. The center of gravity had now risen to a point that those of us on the downhill side could no longer extend their arms any higher, but we had to remain in place to prevent it from falling back onto us while those on the uphill side dug their heels into the ground, straining to keep the bottom down. Within moments, the entire forward momentum of the floor was depending on the two attached beams, and I was holding one.

My arms trembled from the strain as the weight began to force apart my locked fingers. I braced the beam against my thighs and my arms against my torso, using my whole body to support it, but I was losing control.

"I can't hold it!" I yelled. "It's going to fall!"

"Hang on!" Don shouted. "Don't drop it! We almost have it! Walk slowly this way."

He wants me to walk? Every muscle in my body was quivering from strain, and I wondered if I could stand any longer, let alone walk.

"Move!" Don sounded angry. "If you don't move, it's not going to get over the top."

You shit! I wanted to scream. *You saw me standing over here, you knew this would happen. How could you?*

Rage finally drove my body to move, allowing my spent muscles to flex a moment more. I wanted to shove the whole damn floor on top of Don as I felt the weight release from me, and the floor reached the halfway point and stood on end. For a moment, I hoped he wouldn't catch it in time, that it would crash to the ground and shatter into pieces.

As it passed the tipping point, the floor accelerated, but the men on the uphill side had it under control and seconds later, it was safely on the ground. My arms collapsed into limp appendages.

Jodi walked over to me from her spot in the middle and muttered, "That bastard. He did it on purpose. He knew exactly what he was doing to you. Well, you showed him, didn't you?"

I felt ready to burst into tears.

"Okay, now we're going to lift it onto the footings," Don called out as everyone spread out around the circumference. I knew I was useless to lift any weight, so I positioned myself next to Jim, a muscular biker from Owl Creek, and faked it.

The floor slipped into place around the separate platform Don had built to support the weight of his potter's wheel. There was cheering and hooting from the crowd, but I felt beaten. At any second, someone's life could have ended because I wasn't strong enough. Everyone knew I was a fraud, especially Don.

Mike walked over to me and smiled, his brown eyes soothing me with kindness. "You did a great job, babe."

⪡ ⪡ ⪢ ⪢

Later that afternoon, Jodi, Michelle (one of the day's helpers), and I arrived back at the cabin after taking a walk to view the progress on the yurt Jodi was building in the woods. Jodi put on the kettle for tea and we began discussing the floor flipping, which led us to a debate about Don's motives and character.

"I don't see why Don would have done that on purpose," Michelle said. "What would be the point?"

"The point," Jodi replied as the three of us settled around the table, "would be to prove that women are inferior to men. That is always his point. A woman could never know as much or do as much as he does." She lit a cigarette and placed the pack and her lighter on the table in front of her.

"Don definitely thinks he's superior to us," I agreed. "You can see it in the way he acts. He never notices what anyone else does around here."

"Unless, of course, it's Peter, only because Peter's a better craftsman than he is, and it drives him nuts," Jodi added.

"I guess he has a pretty big ego," Michelle admitted. "But I figured that's just his personality."

"Big ego isn't the word for it," Jodi said. "I'm surprised his ego can be contained in his body."

We all giggled.

"You'd think he was the only one around here who did anything," I said. "Look how Mike cooks almost every night for the rest of us, and John is constantly out there weeding the garden. All Don does is work on his yurt."

"Potter's studio," Jodi emphasized, "not merely a yurt. And he …"

A sudden shuffling noise came from the ceiling. Jodi froze. Someone was moving around in the loft directly above us. We stared at one another with wide eyes, then Jodi mouthed the words, "Who's up there?"

Michelle and I shook our heads to show we didn't know, but already I was starting to feel sick. Who would be staying silent while we had this conversation, listening to every word?

Heavy footsteps clomped across the ceiling as we all stared up at the catwalk. In the shadows above our heads, I could see it was Don, but I couldn't make out the expression on his face before I turned away. I felt my heart pounding. Jodi's face flushed and she slapped her hand against her cheek, closing her eyes. He stepped slowly down each rung, as if he enjoyed knowing we must be suffering, and when he reached the bottom, he stood facing us, his face stern and his brow wrinkled. When he looked at me, I dropped my eyes to the floor.

Jodi stood up and spoke. "I'm not going to tell you we didn't mean it, because that would be lying," she said. "But it was wrong of us to talk about you behind your back. We should have had the guts to tell you to your face. That would have been the fair thing to do."

Don stood speechless, his expression unchanged.

"If you have something to say to us," she continued, "you should say it. I'm sure we deserve whatever it is you are thinking right now."

Don looked at Michelle for a moment, then over to me, and I felt my face burning. Finally, his eyes rested on Jodi. "I think enough has been said already." He turned and left the cabin.

"Oh my God." Jodi slid down into her chair. "I can't believe this happened. He will never forgive me. And I don't blame him."

She grabbed her cigarette pack to pull one out, then realized one was already burning in the ashtray and picked it up to inhale. "What am I going to do? He must hate me."

"God, Jodi, I don't know," I said. "I feel so bad."

"Maybe we should each go and apologize individually," Michelle suggested. She hesitated for a moment before continuing. "But maybe it will make him think. I mean, everything we were saying had truth to it. Maybe he needed to hear that."

The tea kettle boiled, and I got up, poured the three of us a cup each, and brought them back to the table.

"I don't know. Maybe. Of course, it probably doesn't matter, because Don is never going to speak to me again." Jodi mashed the end of her cigarette into the ash tray. "Why do we have to love men? I wish I was a lesbian. Women are so much easier to love."

"I know what you mean," I said. "Even Mike drives me nuts sometimes, and he's a sweetheart."

Jodi nodded, then stood up and picked up her cigarettes and lighter. "I think I better try to have a talk with Don. I'll see you two later."

By dinnertime, Don and Jodi were sitting together by the cabin window, smiling and talking as though nothing had happened, happier than I had seen either of them for the last several days.

❦ ❦ ❧ ❧

The Ithaca Woman's Center was on the second floor of an old two-story house downtown, a few blocks from Cornell University. They had potluck suppers every Monday night, followed by an informal discussion group. Jodi and I were thrilled when we learned of this and began attending. None of the guys volunteered to watch Helen's children, so Helen couldn't join us, which gave Jodi and me an excuse to venture alone into Ithaca for the evening. We enjoyed it so much we made it our weekly ritual, always bringing a vegetarian dish from our garden.

The majority of women attending were students or in their mid-twenties, but a few were older. Dinner was held in a room encircled with donated couches and upholstered chairs. Two metal folding tables were set up to hold the food. When the seats ran out, women sat on the floor or brought in folding chairs from the office.

After dinner, a woman from the center led a discussion on the topic of the week. Whoever showed up was encouraged to voice their opinion and share their thoughts with the women in the group. The only rule was consideration of others' opinions. We all agreed we were there to learn and share, not to argue or prove we were right. That was what men did.

One evening, we discussed sexual preferences. Two women in the group said they were exploring bisexuality because of the desire to have an emotional closeness with their sexual partners. "I have never been able to find that with a man," an attractive woman with long blond hair admitted. "Unfortunately, with my female lover I feel like something is missing, so I don't think I will be able to give men up completely."

"Have you told her?" another woman sitting on the floor asked.

"No. I don't want to hurt her feelings."

There were a few sighs in the room.

"But isn't that doing the same thing a man would do? Isn't that the same as using someone?" the same woman asked.

"I don't think so, because I really care for her." She looked around, as though searching for empathy. "I mean, I love her, even. It's just that sexually I'm not totally satisfied. I still want a penis."

"It sounds like you're saying you're not gay," Jodi replied.

"No, I guess I'm not," she answered.

"I've found I prefer women," the second bisexual woman told us, "because they don't treat you as sex objects. Women remember you are a person first. But being bisexual is not the same as being gay. I still like sex with men sometimes."

"We all have choices," the group leader added. "That's the most important part to understand."

"I don't know if it's really a choice," Jodi said. "I love a lot of women, but I don't want to have sex with them. I couldn't imagine giving up sex with men. This doesn't feel like something I made a choice about, it just is. In fact, if I could make a choice, I would probably choose women, too."

"Well, I've been married for ten years," another woman spoke up, "and I am very happy with my husband. Our sex life is fine for me."

"I wanted to mention to everyone," the group leader told us as we came to a close, "to make sure you pick up the surveys about sexuality on the desk on the way out. A woman named Shere Hite is doing a study and she needs input from lots of different women. Fill them out and bring them back next week."

Jodi and I took the multiple-page survey and spent hours filling in the information, reading our answers aloud to each other, sharing details of our sexual fantasies, experiences, likes, and dislikes, before returning them to the center. Three years later, we'd learn that we'd participated in the Hite Report, the most famous and extensive study ever done on female sexuality.

✦✦✦✦

On a separate occasion, we discussed women and the law. A few people there were students from Cornell Law School.

"If you want to change sexism in our society, you have to legislate it," one law student explained. "Men aren't going to give up control voluntarily. The only way for women to gain equality in this country is to become a feminist lawyer. Law schools are under pressure to accept women now. It's the first step on the long road to change. If you can take a case to court, you can set precedents. If enough women become lawyers, we can affect the judicial process. Eventually, we can run for office and make the laws ourselves."

That night on the way home, Jodi and I were excited by the concept of becoming feminist lawyers and changing the world.

"I've been thinking of finishing high school," she said. "I only have a year left. If I hadn't dropped out and married that creepy ex-husband of mine, I could be enrolling in college right now. But at least I can get started. Can you see me going to Candor High? I wonder how long it would take me to get to law school?"

"Maybe I could start community college," I said. "Except I have no money for tuition. I wonder what it costs? I would need a job first, but no one is hiring around here."

✦✦✦✦

While the weekly sessions at the Women's Center were exposing me to people with new ideas, I had also begun reading hordes of literature on the condition of women. *Ms. Magazine* had been on the market for a few months when we sent in our subscription.

While any other expense would have been subject to scrutiny and justification to the group, the men seemed to know better than to question our spending money on *Ms*.

The Hubbard Hill bookshelves were stacked with paperbacks left from former members and visitors, and I began devouring them—Betty Friedan's *The Feminine Mystique*, Kate Millett's *Sexual Politics*, and a 686-page collection of writings entitled *Woman in Sexist Society: Studies in Power and Powerlessness*, edited by Vivian Gornick and Barbara K. Moran. This last book contained essays, plays, research, and interviews of women ranging from scholars to prostitutes to activists. There were essays on the portrayal of women in advertising, in fiction, in magazines; articles about influences during childhood, about hopelessness, depression, and repression. Whatever book I read, with each page I turned, I found myself growing both surprised and angry. It was as if I were viewing my life for the first time with the curtains parted to let in the light.

Moments from my past began to leap into my mind with stark clarity as I read *Prostitution: A Quartet for Female Voices*. One voice was Kate Millet.

"Somehow, every indignity the female suffers ultimately comes to be symbolized in a sexuality that is her responsibility, her shame . . . It can be summarized in one four-letter word. And the word is not *fuck*, it's *cunt*. Our self-contempt originates in this: in knowing we are cunt. That is what we are supposed to be about— our essence, our offense."

I remembered Jack in Venice, grinning as he told me the news about Bob having the clap, eager to let me know that the man I loved was disgusted with me. Now my humiliation was fading, my anger growing. I wanted to find Bob, wherever he was, tell him it could have been him that gave me the clap, and demand to know what right he had to blame and criticize me when I knew he'd slept with others.

My anger took me back to those guys in Boston, holding down my arms and tearing at my clothes, saying to each other, "She's been asking for it all night, now she's going to get it." Only instead of wanting to cry from helplessness, I wanted to spit in their faces.

Later, I read Elaine Showalter in *Women Writers and the Double Standard*: "Women were created to be dependent on men: their education and training must prepare them to find and keep husbands."

Even though she was writing about women in the Victorian age, I didn't see much difference in my own life.

I could hear my mother reiterating that college was a waste of money for girls, since they only went to find husbands. "It's a good thing we didn't have boys," I recalled her saying. "I don't know how we could have afforded to educate them." I wanted to call my mother and tell her she hadn't been fair, that I deserved to go to college as much as any boy I knew.

I thought about Ed in Venice, stroking my hair and telling me, "You're so sweet, someone will always take care of you." Now I understood the anger I'd felt when he spoke, only it was more than anger—I was screaming inside! I wished he were there next to me so I could tear his hair out when he forced himself on me afterwards, so I could shriek at him, "I am not going to be sweet so some man will take care of me! My body belongs to me, not you or some other man! I will take care of myself!"

I wanted to be strong and tough and able to push back against anyone who tried to push me around.

I'd spent too much of my life playing the female role they'd all expected, trying to follow rules made by men to control me or hurt me if I strayed into their territory—men who had made sure I knew my place and had been quick to belittle me if I deviated.

Now I felt proud I'd held that beam on Don's yurt floor, pushing with my whole body and no one else's help—that the floor and the lives of the people around me had counted on my strength. Because now I understood that I wasn't a fraud, that women could be strong and powerful, as much or even more so than men. That all those women in Cornell Law School and other law schools throughout the country would one day be making the laws and changing the world.

Somewhere, somehow, I would be part of that change too. I knew there must be many more challenges I was capable of vanquishing that I knew nothing about yet.

 # Chapter 26

October 1973
Hubbard Hill

"Spiro Agnew resigned!" Jodi shouted, running from the cabin toward Mike and me, as we stepped from the Volvo. The back bumper had a sticker with the dome of the White House on it and the words HONK IF YOU THINK HE'S GUILTY, meaning Nixon. Vice President Agnew was no better in our opinion, particularly because he'd blamed the demonstrators at Kent State for the violence on the day four of them were killed by the National Guard while protesting the invasion of Cambodia. He was now being investigated for tax evasion, and it was a joy to know he would not succeed Nixon.

Ever since he and Nixon won the election the previous fall, I'd given up hoping for change. My eighteenth birthday had fallen right before the presidential election in 1972. I was thrilled to register to vote in the first election where eighteen- to twenty-year-olds could vote for the president, hoping to elect the one man I believed would save us: George McGovern.

I was devastated as I watched the results tally up on my television screen on Election Day. McGovern lost by a landslide. The only state he won was Massachusetts, spurring a flood of bumper stickers that read, DON'T BLAME ME, I'M FROM MASSACHUSETTS."

Now, nearly a year later, between the Watergate investigation and Spiro's tax evasion, my outlook was improving.

"This calls for a celebration," Mike said as we walked into the cabin. "Let's see. We can't smoke dope, or we all go to jail for life. Let's have a cup of tea."

We joined Jodi in the cabin, where she was doing homework with the radio on.

Mike was referring to the new drug law that had gone into effect in New York State on September 1st, giving New York the toughest drug law in the country. For possessing even relatively small amounts of pot, or any amount of LSD, pills, or other drugs, you were automatically sentenced to life without parole. Hubbard Hill members had all agreed that no drugs of any kind would be kept in the cabin. Each of us was responsible for not endangering other commune members if we chose to keep drugs in our yurt.

Mike, Jodi, Helen, and I had decided to quit drugs. None of us cared that much about getting high, so it didn't seem worth the risk. Don and Peter indulged in smoking pot occasionally in their own yurts. Only John seemed reckless about following the rule.

❦❦❦❦

The next day, while Jodi was in school, having enrolled for her senior year at Candor High, I heard a vehicle approaching the cabin from the woods and stop outside. Peter and John walked in, kicking mud off their boots as they entered.

"We got the Jeep running," John announced. "She's all set for a . . . wood run."

The previous year's woodpiles were almost gone, but we had a few logs from the nearby woods that had been cut and needed splitting. Getting the big ones required the Jeep, which was only used as a workhorse for hauling wood and left sitting the rest of the year.

"Can you teach me to split wood?" I asked Peter. He beckoned with his finger and I followed him outside to watch him split a log.

"Ahhhh!" Peter shouted before landing the ax partially on the edge of the upright log, forcing it to split directly in half and fall to the ground in two pieces. He stopped and took a breath, exhaling visible vapor in the cool autumn air.

"If you scream, it adds force to your motion," Peter explained. "That's why they yell in karate. Before you start, I want to go over a couple of things."

I stood at an angle to him and focused on his instruction.

"First, always wear heavy shoes like those, so you have protection in case you miss." He pointed to the thick leather work boots I was wearing. "Next, keep your feet spread apart, so if you miss, the ax hits the dirt and not your foot. Then bend your knees slightly so you don't lean too far forward." Peter shifted his feet apart and bounced on his knees to demonstrate as I mimicked him. "Otherwise, you could lose your balance from the momentum of the ax."

He lifted a log onto the huge stump he was using.

"So you place the wood up on a level base like this, standing it on end. Make sure there are no knots where you plan on splitting it, because the knots strengthen the log in that spot." He turned the log and pointed out a knot part way around the side before returning it to the original position. "Lift the ax over one shoulder with both hands. Don't let it fall backwards. You always want it under control. Then let it drop with a scream. Aim it so you get part of the ax on the edge, but most of it in the middle."

I stepped away as he lifted the ax and took a swing, splitting the log in two.

"Here, Sharon, give it a try." He placed a smaller log on the stump, stood the ax upright, and stepped away.

I leaned over the ax, wrapping my hands around the rough, weathered handle, which reached my navel, and I lifted it slightly, awed by the weight that would help give me the momentum to blast logs apart. I planted my feet apart and rocked back and forth to make sure I felt steady. Lifting the ax over my left shoulder, I slowly dropped it in a practice swing to gauge where it would fall. After adjusting my stance, I raised the ax, inhaled, and felt the full power of my body as I let out a roar, plunging the blade into the log. It split easily into two parts, and the blade stuck into the stump below.

Peter nodded and smiled his approval.

I eased the blade out of the stump by wiggling it back and forth.

"You don't need any more help from me," Peter said. "There's the wood. Have fun."

I moved on to bigger logs, stripping off clothing as I progressed, until I was working in a sleeveless tank top and jeans. "Wood warms you twice," Mike liked to say.

As instructed, I piled the bark separately for kindling, and the split pieces began to grow into a pile. I was surprised how satisfying chopping wood felt and proud of my new skill.

❈ ❈ ❈ ❈

That weekend, Kirsten and Gary from Ithaca joined us to help cut trees. Helen needed to watch her children. The rest of us piled into the Jeep and rattled along our grassy road into a thicker part of the woods. It was overcast and the air was crisp, but our mood was upbeat.

I liked Kirsten. She believed in women's rights, like Jodi and me, and was usually up for anything. She was from Holland and had been living with Gary for a couple of years. However, she couldn't get a permanent visa, so every few months she had to leave the US and go back to Holland. Often Gary went with her, but other times he couldn't get a visa to stay there long enough. Today, as always, she was smiling and cheerful, eager to help out.

The men took turns felling dead trees and slicing them into logs, trying to outdo each other as they sawed through larger and larger trunks. Jodi, Kirsten, and I each cut smaller trees. We had two chain saws running all the time, filling the woods with saw dust, fumes, and roaring motors. Whoever wasn't running a chain saw was loading the logs onto the Jeep.

John cut the largest tree that day, and Mike helped slice it. Gary and Don started showing off by lifting a huge log onto the Jeep between the two of them. Kirsten winked at Jodi and me, nodding toward the next log, and we smiled back at her in agreement. The three of us headed over to pick it up.

"You women can't lift that," Don said. "You're crazy."

"Oh, you think we cannot do this, you say?" Kirsten taunted him. "I am glad you said that, because now I am mad. And when I am mad, I am strong!"

"Me too!" I agreed.

"Let's show these men what we can do once and for all," Jodi said.

John agreed with Don. "I don't think they can . . . move that. Never mind get it on . . . the Jeep."

I looked at the log. It was absurdly large, about two and a half feet long and maybe a foot and a half in diameter. We positioned ourselves around it and looked into each other's eyes. I could see the determination on Jodi and Kirsten's faces as our eyes spoke to one another.

"Sisters, we *can* do this," Kirsten said. "Together, we can."

I thought of the stance for chopping wood—the foot placement, the bent knees, the strength that came from a spot deep in my core. I called on that strength and felt it rise. A moment later, the three of us had that log off the ground, our faces nearly purple, and we were taking baby steps to the Jeep.

I loved the sound of the log landing on the metal floor when we dropped it there. Our work done, we broke into victorious smiles and threw our arms around each other.

Don, John, and Gary looked at us with new respect on their faces. I got a kick out of that, but I didn't need that from them. I already had all the respect I needed from Jodi and Kirsten—the same respect I had for each of them.

⊰⊰⊱⊱

One night in late October, I was dozing off in bed next to Mike when I was startled by the sound of a vehicle bucking and revving, getting louder as it got closer to our yurt. Mike leaped out of bed and ran for the window.

"What is it?" I called to him. The only vehicle that ever drove through the field was the occasional tractor from the farmer downhill during haying season, but not at eleven o'clock at night.

"Jesus, it's a bust!" Mike screamed. "They're coming this way."

I jumped from the bed and grabbed my boots, carrying them in one hand, as Mike pulled me frantically by the other. We ran outside, branches and rocks jabbing my tender, socked feet, and dove into the pine forest that surrounded Mike's yurt.

Mike threw himself on the ground and motioned for me to do the same. Thankfully, both of us were in our long johns. I heard the motor roar as the headlights zoomed past in the field. In the distance, we heard it stop, and then car doors slammed. My heart was pounding. What would happen if they found us? We didn't have any drugs in our yurt, but did that matter if they were at the commune? And stupid John had those marijuana plants growing in his yurt greenhouse in full view of the field behind him. Now that the farmer below hated John, maybe he'd turned us in.

The farmer hadn't always hated John. For the first two years of Hubbard Hill's existence, they'd had a good relationship with him. In the summer, when our creeks went dry, we'd filled our milk pails with water from the faucet in his barn, and he'd let us take a gallon of milk once a week at cost, as long as we used clean plastic containers when we dipped it into the vat.

One day, however, he caught John sneaking extra milk using a glass jar. He dropped it in the vat. Fortunately, it didn't break, or the farmer would have lost an entire truckload of milk. But it was obvious John was cheating him and endangering his livelihood. As a result, both our milk and our water rights had been cut off. Now we had to drive into town to a friend's house and use their hose for our water.

The farmer still owned a legal right of way through our property to his back acreage, so it was possible he had seen John's plants. Both Mike and I had been appalled when we'd discovered them, but since he was abiding by the rules and keeping them in his own yurt, we felt we shouldn't complain.

Lying there in the icy air without a jacket or shoes made me wonder if I should have complained.

I strained to listen for footsteps or voices. After a while, the car drove by again in the direction of the cabin.

Convinced that no one was stalking us in the woods, we returned to our yurt.

Back in bed, the relaxation I'd felt earlier eluded me. The door to the yurt pushed open and Tenya crept inside and settled near the stove. I rose and hooked the latch. It depressed me to think we needed locked doors now.

The next morning, we discovered that it had been John and Mark driving to John's yurt after an evening of getting wasted in the Ithaca bars, smoking too much dope, and tripping. I would have felt relieved if I wasn't so pissed off at John for endangering us.

❖ ❖ ❖ ❖

The first snow of the season fell overnight in early November, the day before my nineteenth birthday. All I could see through our yurt window was a mass of white with gray, distant shadows under an overcast sky. The stove had burned out and the air on my face felt icy. I didn't want to move from our warm bed.

Mike leapt out of bed, scrunched newspaper into balls, and threw them into the stove with some kindling and a match to get a quick flash of heat into the yurt. Then he dove back under the covers, where we cuddled together.

"Winter is here," he murmured. "From now on, it will get colder and colder. Wait 'til we have to chop away the frozen shit in the outhouse because it gets too high."

I cringed.

Once the yurt was warmer, I forced myself out of bed and into my clothes. I shook my boots upside down before putting them on—a habit I'd developed after discovering that field mice had been hiding acorns in them. Then Mike, Tenya, and I walked the path to the cabin, making fresh footprints alongside other paw prints.

A muffled silence surrounded us. I felt as if my senses were sharpened, and I could trust my gut to steer me correctly.

I'd been reading up on spirituality. Some declared we were in a new age, and lots of books were being published on this topic. I'd read *Be Here Now*, by Baba Ram Dass, and consulted the *I*

Ching, the ancient Chinese *Book of Changes* regularly; I kept three copper pennies in a leather pouch and used them for divination; and I wrapped my book in silk to protect the vibrations. I had devoured all three of Carlos Castaneda's books, and fell asleep at night trying to fly in my dreams, as he had done, to a different plane of consciousness.

This particular Sunday, Hubbard Hill had company. Mark and Bonnie had come from Ithaca, as had Helen's friend Tim. Mark and John had gone off together, but the rest of us sat around the table drinking tea.

"I bought twenty acres in Tompkin's County," Bonnie announced as she wrapped her hands around her mug. "I got it for twenty thousand dollars, which is a good price there. And it's close enough to Ithaca that I can commute to work if I have to."

I felt an immediate twinge of envy. Bonnie had a job as a social worker, so she had been able to put aside money while living in the tiny A-frame house she and Mark rented. I thought about how I'd love to own my own land and not have to tolerate certain people.

"Ever since I left Hubbard Hill, I've missed having land," she told us. "It's what I've been dreaming about."

"That's fabulous," Jodi said. "If you need help when you get started, come get us. You know we'll all come up and help you build."

Tim paced around the table, waiting for the right moment to break into the conversation.

"I've got news, too," he finally announced. "I haven't told Helen yet, so this is news to her as well."

Helen's smile turned to concern as she stared at him.

"I'm on my way to Alaska. I'm going to go work on the pipeline." Helen gasped.

"They're paying big bucks to anyone with oil rigging experience," Tim explained, "and I've done that before."

Alaska, I thought to myself. *True wilderness.* "They hire women there?" I joked, knowing that the pipeline would be the ultimate male environment.

"Actually," Tim said, "they do hire women in the camps as cooks. They get paid well, too. Plus, all your room and board is included, so there's nothing to spend it on."

"When are you leaving?" Helen asked, her voice cracking.

"Tuesday."

Helen looked away. Tim seemed nervous. I had never been sure of what their relationship was. Of course, she was still married to Chuck. Lately, Tim hadn't been coming around as much as when she'd first moved to Hubbard Hill, and now he was telling her good-bye.

About that time, John and Mark burst through the cabin door, laughing and acting silly, obviously wasted. John walked over to the antique desk that leaned against the front cabin wall, reached into his pocket, pulled out a baggy, slipped it under the desk cover, and closed the cover again.

"I hope you aren't planning on leaving that there," I said to John. We still had a rule about no drugs in the cabin.

"Naw. I'll take it . . . later." It was as if he only half heard me. He and Mark walked over to the bread box and began slicing bread and cheese, giggling.

That evening after the others had left, Mike and I returned to the cabin to check on John's drugs. I opened the desk cover and saw the baggy still there. Not only was there pot, there were also several tiny purple barrel-shaped pills that were likely LSD.

"Here's a guaranteed life sentence right in our cabin." I showed Mike the baggy. "John left it here, like I thought he would."

Mike shook his head. "That asshole. He's out of control. He's going to get us all busted. I'm sick of his bullshit."

I shoved the drugs into my pocket to dump in the woods and faced Mike. "I had a gut feeling today that it's time for a change. Bonnie is so lucky to have her own land. I would love that too, but of course, there's the issue of money."

Mike smirked. "It would be such a relief not to live with assholes, but we'll never have that kind of money."

"But what if we could?" I was excited by my new idea. "What if you and I went to Alaska, too, and worked in the oil fields? I could cook in a camp and you could work on the pipeline. We'd save all our money, and after a year we'd have enough to buy our own land."

Mike rested his elbow on his other fist and pulled at this beard. "How would we get there?"

"I was thinking about that, too. We would have to get a crummy job first and save enough to buy a car. Then we could drive and camp."

Mike's expression looked dubious. "There's no place to work around here. Besides, if we were working, we would have to pool all our money with Hubbard Hill."

"I know. I think the only way we can do it is to leave. There're jobs around Hartford, and I know the neighborhoods. We could get a cheap apartment and be ready to drive north by late spring, in time for the good weather for getting to Alaska."

Mike stood quietly, contemplating, looking at the floor. He had been at Hubbard Hill for over two years. After Peter, he had the second-longest seniority, and he was a stabilizing influence. I knew Mike's leaving would be a blow to the commune. And no one would be more hurt than Jodi, whom we both loved dearly.

"What about Jodi?" He looked at me through almost weepy eyes.

I felt sick to my stomach when I thought about hurting her. "I know. She's the only reason I'm not sure about this. Oh God. I wish we could take her with us, but she needs to finish high school. If she leaves now, she may never get it done. I will miss her as much as anyone I've ever loved."

Mike wrapped his arms around me. I buried my face in his soft flannel shirt and cried, because I knew he agreed we needed to do this, and despite my excitement, all I could feel was sadness.

❀ Chapter 27

November 1973
Hartford, Connecticut

I hated being in the city again. The first night, the square walls were closing in around me. Mike and I hung prints from a Botticelli art book he owned, and I tried to focus on *The Birth of Venus* instead of the sirens outside my window. I longed to hear the sound of leaves rustling near my door as I drifted to sleep, to feel the wind blowing through the cracks of our yurt, to savor the sweet scent of wood smoke drifting from the wood stove. Instead, I gritted my teeth and listened to the clanging radiators in our third-floor apartment while sweat poured off my body.

"I need to open a window. I can't breathe," I whined to Mike, rising from my sleeping bag on the floor to shove open the heavy wooden sash. I inhaled the cold air into my lungs, hoping for relief. It smelt slightly of garbage, car exhaust, and asphalt.

Already I regretted our move. Had Hubbard Hill really been as bad as I thought? If it was, why did I miss it?

I reminded myself that this was temporary. Mike and I would work hard and save money as fast as we could to leave for Alaska in the spring. Of course, we would have to pay Mike's mother back first for the money she'd loaned us to get us started in Hartford.

I heard a scratching noise in the wall, followed by scurrying. I remembered the hole I had noticed in the wall of the closet and jumped up to shut the closet door, worried that a rat might slip into our room. I shuddered. The radiator clanged—one, two, three times—then hissed before clanging three more times.

I lay on the hard floor, my bones already sore on the spots that rubbed against the wood. I closed my eyes and tried to picture Jodi laughing, but all I could see was her tear-streaked face when we told her we were leaving. I leaned into my pillow and wept silently, wondering if all this would be worth it.

To furnish our apartment, we bought a refurbished mattress and my parents donated a card table and two chairs from their basement. In our living room, we added four sofa cushions we found on an abandoned couch and used them as chairs, leaning one on the wall and sitting on the other. We placed a lamp on a cardboard box next to our bed and saved another three boxes to store our clothes.

I'd had to find a new home for Tenya because I couldn't stand to think of her cooped up like us. It wasn't fair that she should suffer. After placing a classified ad in our local newspaper, I interviewed prospective owners from my parents' phone, insisting that they have acreage for her to roam in if they were going to adopt her. I settled on a family with two little girls, and she wagged her tail and trotted after them as she headed to their car.

One more part of my life was gone. I was taking on a monastic future, stripped of joy, devoted only to work and frugality.

It took me about a week to find a job as an inventory control clerk. I had experience from working part time during high school for a furniture store. It took Mike another week to find a job as a janitor in a factory not far from where I worked.

We celebrated by opening a bank account and depositing all but the minimum amount of money we needed for groceries, bus fare, and rent.

Two days later, a letter from Jodi arrived.

She had finished building her new yurt, moved in most of her belongings, lit a fire in the wood stove, and walked to the cabin for a cigarette. When she returned to her yurt, there had been nothing but smoldering ashes. Her months of labor, her clothes, her photo albums, her favorite books—all had been destroyed.

I broke into tears as I read the news to Mike, stunned by the thought that Jodi could have been inside if she had started her fire and gone to bed.

Mike shook his head slowly and moaned. "Poor Jodi." His lip trembled as he looked into my eyes, and we wrapped our arms around each other, as though our hugging could somehow comfort her.

"Yurts are built like a perfect bonfire," Mike said. "All the wood's stacked inward to reach a peak. We're probably lucky this never happened before. Thank God nothing happened to Jodi."

I continued on through the letter and discovered that the farmer down the hill had shot and killed John's dog for chasing cows, which was legal in Tioga County. Tenya had been John's dog's constant companion. More tears stained my face, but I was grateful Tenya was safely in her new home.

I was almost afraid to read on, but at last there was happy news. "Mike, she's coming to visit us! She'll be here after school gets out at Christmas!"

I checked the calendar. That was about seventeen days, depending on when she actually arrived. Too long. But I would have to live with it. After all Jodi had been through, I certainly had no right to complain.

❦❦❧❧

The day Jodi was to arrive, Mike and I prepared a vegetarian feast. I'd baked bread on Saturday, and Mike had soaked black beans for his sweet and sour vegetable curry. Now it was Sunday evening, and I chopped pickles while Mike shelled peanuts. We had splurged to buy pineapple and coconut. Mike began sautéing the carrots while the other ingredients—chopped onions, broccoli, raisins, honey, curry powder, and the cooked black beans—sat on the counter, waiting to be added.

After checking that the brown rice was steaming, I wandered into the living room.

Our living room was simple, and I liked it that way. Since we had only two kitchen chairs for our card table, we'd moved it into the living room and folded the legs, resting the corners on piles of books. That way the three of us could eat while sitting on pillows on the floor. I'd covered the table in an Indian bedspread and placed two bulky candles on either side of a bowl of apples and oranges.

Our Christmas tree stood in the center of the room. It had no lights or colored glass balls like my parents' tree. Instead, we'd strung rows of popcorn and cut out delicate snowflakes from folded white paper. The top of the tree was decorated with a star made of aluminum foil folded over a cardboard one.

The tree was my favorite thing in the apartment, partly because of Christmas, but mostly because it reminded me of the pine forest that had surrounded our yurt at Hubbard Hill. The more natural our tree looked, the less guilty I felt about it being killed.

Mike and I had debated the ethics of getting a tree—of destroying nature in the name of a Christian holiday. Eventually, our longing to bring a tiny bit of the woods into our home had won out over ethics, as we rationalized that the tree had already been cut.

By six o'clock, I was worried about Jodi. It had been dark for two hours and she was hitchhiking alone. In her bulky down jacket, with her hair tucked into her wool knit hat, at least no one would realize she was a woman. I had hitched alone many times at night, but it was different sitting here worrying about her than it was when I was on the road myself. I wanted her safely at my door, knowing she had survived those random odds of danger.

About eight o'clock, the buzzer rang, and we dove for the door and raced down the stairs to greet her. We met on the second-floor landing, and I screamed with joy and threw my arms around her.

Jodi broke into tears and buried her face in my hair for a moment, then kissed Mike on the lips while the three of us held each other.

Mike took her knapsack as we led her upstairs.

"My God, it's fucking freezing out there," she said as we climbed. "I was starting to wonder if I'd ever get here. Y'all moved way the hell too far away, you know that? And what's with all this ice?"

"That's Hartford," Mike explained. "I think I prefer the three feet of snow at Hubbard Hill. This stuff's a pain in the ass."

"Well, I had a hell of a time getting rides," she said. "Do you know I started out at one o'clock this afternoon? Not much Christmas spirit out there on the highway."

"Well, at least you made it. Dinner is waiting for you. How 'bout a cup of peppermint tea?" Mike grinned.

"I'd *love* it."

Mike put her things in the living room, where she would sleep while she stayed with us. Then he ladled out the food, and we settled on the floor around the table and ate.

"I really miss your cooking," Jodi told Mike. "John's doing a lot of the cooking now, but it's not the same. He doesn't have your touch. This is absolutely delicious." She paused. "I miss you both so much!"

Having her there filled me with bittersweet euphoria. I thought I might cry, but I gave her a soulful smile as her eyes started to tear again. She reached into her pocket, pulled out her cigarettes, and lit one. "Anyhow, Don and I finally broke up. I wanted to tell you in person, instead of in a letter."

A smirk stretched across her face and she raised her eyebrows at us, as if saying, *What do you think?*

"We all knew that was coming," I told her. "It's got to be for the best. You were so unhappy with him recently."

"He never deserved you," Mike said. "You're so much more of a sincere person than he is. I don't dislike Don, but let's face it. He's shallow."

Jodi giggled, as though soothed by our comments. "You know, I don't see why I didn't end it a long time ago instead of letting it drag on. When my yurt burned down, it made me think about my life. I was so depressed. I couldn't stand it, between losing my yurt and you guys leaving."

Mike reached over and rested his hand on Jodi's arm.

"And, of course, he has his brand-new, perfect yurt, with his kiln, which he used to fire pottery for Christmas. Him and that damned kiln. I'm glad he has it for the benefit of Hubbard Hill, but now work is all he cares about. I certainly didn't get any sympathy from him with all I was going through. I really need to be with a kind, decent person who respects me. Meanwhile, I'm perfectly capable of getting along by myself."

I knelt over and hugged her again. "Is it hard being there with him around?"

"Oh shit, no. In fact, I'm better off now, because I don't need to worry all the time about what he's thinking. And I'm at school a lot, and I have a couple of pretty good friends there now."

"Do you think you'll ever build another yurt?" I asked.

"Oh no!" she shouted, putting down her fork and shaking her head. "No more yurts for me! I moved into the loft of the cabin and I am staying there. It gives me the creeps every time I think about those smoldering ashes. I was only gone long enough to have one cigarette!"

Mike nodded. "We couldn't believe it when we read it. Thank God you went to the cabin. At least you weren't hurt."

We finished our dinner and talked on into the night. After a while, Mike brought out his guitar and his new book of Paul Simon songs, and the three of us sat around singing "Lincoln Duncan," "The Boxer," and "America."

It was in the early-morning hours when we finally retired. It seemed like a waste sacrificing this precious time to sleep, but I knew Jodi was exhausted after her trek.

The next morning was Christmas Eve. We gathered by our tree to exchange gifts. Ours to Jodi and hers to us were all books, a gift we each used every day. Jodi's gift to me was a square book called *Seed* by Harmony Books, the first half printed on brown grocery bag–type paper symbolizing the earth, with green lettering for plants. The second half was filled with black-and-white cards to punch out along the dotted lines. They contained pictures of holy men, goddesses, tarot cards, Jesus, Sufi symbols, babies being born, people dying, prayers, and incantations. Jodi, Mike, and I spent an hour punching them all out into a deck. These images became part of my daily ritual of reflection. The first half of the book contained quotes, verse, poetry, and comments relating to the cards. I came to cherish these as one of my most important possessions.

By afternoon, Jodi had to leave to get back to Hubbard Hill for Christmas Day. She'd committed to being home and felt the need to help hold together what was left. We held each other and I tried not to cry, knowing it would be awhile before we saw each other again.

"Despite everything, I still really love it there." She mounted her pack on her back. "Come back and visit on your way to Alaska."

Chapter 28

Spring 1974
Bike Trip

*D*oes it make sense to drive to Alaska when gas prices have qua-
drupled in a few short months and the federal government has
ordered gas stations to close on Sundays to discourage long-distance
driving? I wondered.

My parents were aware of my plans for Alaska, and my
mother, who had become accustomed to my wanderlust but always
prayed I would get over it, called me one evening in late February.

"I just watched a long newsreel on Alaska tonight on Walter
Cronkite," she told me. "They had cameras there interviewing
people right on the streets of Anchorage. There are so many people
unemployed, all gone there to work on the pipeline thinking there
would be jobs because of the gas crisis. Now they're living out on
the street. They said only people with oil experience found jobs,
and all these others are stranded there."

"If we can't make any money, there isn't any point in going,
is there?" I acknowledged, not letting on how much this upset me,

since all our future land-buying plans revolved around making money in Alaska.

"No, I would think not." Her voice sounded hopeful.

I no longer found the need to argue with my mother, and she seemed to be avoiding that as well. We talked for a while longer, but I was preoccupied with her bad news.

Afterward, I walked into our bedroom, where Mike sat on the mattress leaning against the wall and reading, his wavy, dark hair hanging loosely around his shoulders, his face deep in concentration. I flopped beside him on the bed.

"I'm starting to think we'll never get our own land." I filled him in on the Walter Cronkite segment. "If we don't go to Alaska, what do we do?"

Mike closed his book and tugged at his beard.

"Well, baby, I certainly don't want to pour all our money into getting to Alaska so we can do the same thing we're doing now." He paused in thought before continuing. "You know, Hubbard Hill isn't the only commune in the world. Maybe we could find someplace we like better, where everyone has their act together."

Leaning over the pile of magazines next to the bed, I pulled out the latest issue of *Mother Earth News* and flipped to the classifieds in the back.

"This is how I found Hubbard Hill," I told him. "There're always interesting places in here. Maybe I should start writing to some of them." I scanned a few of the ads.

"Here's one that sounds good. 'Ten-acre farm in Hudson River Valley with large house, barn, and good, fertile soil, looking for new members willing to commit time and energy to bringing together a communal household based on farm living.' What do you think?"

I picked up a ballpoint pen and circled the advertisement.

"Sounds interesting," Mike said. "How will we get there?"

"Well, if we aren't going to Alaska, it doesn't make sense to spend money on a car, does it? I suppose we'll have to hitchhike."

"I have a better idea," he countered. "We could bike."

"Bike? As in bicycles? I don't know. I got that three-speed while I was in high school and barely made it up hills."

"Yeah, but you're in a lot better shape now. Look at you." Mike nodded his head in my direction. "You walk two miles to work every day. You were chopping wood and hauling water at Hubbard Hill. You're much stronger than you were in high school. Besides, I've been reading about the new ten-speed bikes built intentionally for long distance traveling. They're called touring bikes. They're made for hills."

"Touring bikes, huh?"

It was a warm Saturday morning in early May when Mike and I attached all our gear to our two-month-old Motobécane Gran Touring bicycles. The weather had been getting warmer for the last few weeks, and we wanted to start biking before the heat of summer set in. We'd given our notice at work, and I'd visited my parents to say good-bye.

We packed spare tire tubes, a patch kit, a portable tool kit with Allen wrenches and tire irons, a hand pump that attached to the bike frame, and canteens. We each had two panniers—the equivalent of saddlebags for bikes—one strapped between the handlebars and the other hanging over the carrying rack on the back.

On top of the carrying racks, we strapped sleeping bags and mats. Mike carried the tent and a tiny gas cook stove just like the one Ernie and I had used two summers earlier when we'd hitchhiked across Canada, and a small glass jar of gasoline for fuel.

Each of us carried clothing, food, dishware, rain ponchos, soap, and maps. I also packed the meditation cards Jodi had given me at Christmas, a deck of playing cards, a book, and the letters from the four communes we intended to visit as we searched for a new home. All these items I wrapped in plastic inside our panniers, in case of rain.

We had been training for eight weeks, ever since we purchased the bikes. We rode between ten and fifteen miles every day after work, and over thirty miles daily on the weekends. I thought I was in great shape, able to pace myself on the hills around Hartford's suburbs.

I'd mapped out our route the day before we planned to leave, picking roads I had never traveled where there were long stretches between towns, since we planned to camp in the woods at night. Our first destination was Copake Falls, New York, a few miles outside of northwestern Connecticut, about seventy miles away.

After following the Farmington Valley from Hartford, our route turned toward Burlington. A gentle uphill stretch loomed ahead of me, and I paced myself into it with ease. As I rounded the next bend, I saw it was now steep enough to warrant an additional lane for slow traffic. Full of optimism, I cranked into a lower gear and felt the pressure of the climb ease off as my pace slowed. Mike pushed on ahead, advancing farther, before giving in to the gear drop. I waited too long to downshift the next time and felt the gear grab with a jerk when I forced it in under pressure; I had to stand on my pedals to continue.

With each turn of the road, I expected it to level off, but instead it climbed farther upward. I tried to shift yet again, only to discover I was in my lowest gear and had to stop. I dismounted, walked awhile, got back on and pedaled some more, walked again, rode, walked. This continued for nearly an hour, until at last, the

steepness decreased and I could ride. Mike stopped several times—
to offer encouragement and to keep from getting too far ahead—
but my confidence was damaged, and I was no longer convinced I
was prepared for this trip.

When we finally reached the top, we stopped to rest.

"That was brutal," I said. "I hope we don't get many more
hills like this."

He nodded. "I had a hard time too. It wasn't just you. But we
made it. After this, it should be easier."

"I hope so."

As we started downhill, I experienced a sense of exhilaration
as I accelerated, but suddenly my bike began to shimmy rapidly
from side to side. I squeezed the brakes hard to slow down, but
the oscillation grew worse as the road grew steeper. I was terrified.
Mike pulled over and I flew past him, clenching my brakes, my
hands feeling like they would explode as I tried to stop. I threw my
whole body into steadying the bike, squeezing my elbows against
my sides, gripping my knees together around the frame, and trying
to pull the handlebars straight in a desperate fight for control. At
last the bike responded, and I brought it to a stop. Mike caught up
and jumped off his bike. From the look on his face, I knew how
close I'd come to disaster.

I collapsed into the grass next to the road, shaking, feeling
sick to my stomach, and broke into a cold sweat. Mike joined me
and wrapped me in his arms against his chest.

"God, baby, I thought I was going to lose you just then. That
was scary."

His body was comforting, and I started to calm down. After
a few minutes, I could breathe normally and was able to continue.

Unfortunately, the joy of whooshing down hills was gone
forever. Instead, each downhill experience brought with it

anxiety, causing me to slow my speed more than was necessary instead of gaining enough speed near the bottom to accelerate up the next hill.

Throughout the day, the drudgery of the first hill repeated itself as we crawled toward our destination.

When dusk approached, we watched for a wooded spot where we could camp as we approached Litchfield, our goal for that day. We spotted a high point on the side of the road where we would be hidden and dragged our bikes over the ridge and into the woods. Mike picked out a level spot and we assembled the pup tent, then dug a trench around it for water to run off since it looked like rain.

While I unloaded our gear into the tent, Mike rode off to fill our collapsible gallon water jug in town so we could cook. By the time he came back, it was nearly dark. In our frying pan, we cooked instant rice, canned beans, and vegetables, then melted cheese on top. We needed our flashlight to finish. I was so exhausted I barely noticed eating.

A fine mist was falling as we washed the dishes with water heated on the stove. Fatigued and damp, we crawled into the tent and fell asleep. Several times during the night, I awoke from the sound of rain pounding through the trees above us. Fortunately, we were protected from a direct onslaught by the dense foliage.

I felt like everything had worked against me that day to make the trip harder. I hoped I would wake up to sunshine.

◈◈◈◈

Morning arrived without an end to the rain. The tent wasn't big enough to sit erect, so after Mike mixed powdered milk with water to pour on our granola, we ate it while leaning on our elbows. With one shower curtain draped over the top of the tent and another on the floor, we were staying dry, but little patches of water were beginning to seep through along the edges.

By midday, the rain hadn't slowed. We read, played cards, and read some more. My body ached from being in the same position too long, and whichever way I turned didn't seem to help. Whenever I had to pee, I knocked into the walls of the tent as I slipped on shoes and a rain poncho, and when I unzipped the sopping wet doors, water poured through onto the floor. Once back inside, I felt wetter and colder than before, with no way to get dry or warm. I dreaded the minutes that crawled by as I huddled inside my sleeping bag; it was as though the hands on my watch were stuck in sludge.

The rain continued into the evening. Rather than go outside again to cook, we agreed to eat cheese and whole wheat bread for dinner. It was surprising we could agree on anything by evening. I was increasingly irritable and arguing with Mike over everything. When he moved and knocked into the tent, I screamed at him for getting more water inside. When we played cards, I quit after losing two straight hands of gin rummy and refused to count my points. Later, after I bitched at him for something else, he yelled that I was being an asshole, so I punched the tent over his head and made water fall on his hair. He glared at me like he might reach out and choke me. I felt like a caged animal that needed to escape.

When night came, neither of us could sleep. After hours of tossing and turning, I shoved my face into my inflatable pillow and screamed, pounding my fists into the ground and kicking my feet, until I was relieved by tears. Finally, the tension in my body subsided, and I fell asleep.

❦❦❧❧

In the morning there were patches of sunshine. I pulled open the zipper and dove outside, thrilled to be mobile again. Unfortunately, I knew this meant another dreadful day of hills, although only about half as many as the first day.

We reached Copake Falls, a town in the flat Hudson Valley, late that afternoon, ending the day with easy pedaling.

The commune was on forty acres, with a large, white farmhouse in need of repair and a two-story barn. A woman about my age introduced herself as Lisa when we arrived, and showed us around. When she explained that they faced a five hundred–dollar rental payment each month, Mike and I exchanged dubious looks. Hubbard Hill had a one hundred and fifty–dollar land payment each month, and we'd had trouble meeting that at times. The house used oil heat as well. Lisa shared that their only income was from food stamps, unemployment, and one person's full-time job in town.

At dinner, we joined two other men who were visiting for the first time, along with four commune members. We ate the casserole made from mushrooms that Mike and I helped Lisa harvest in the field that afternoon.

"Did she tell you this place is haunted?" one of the visitors asked me. "I just found out this morning. That was *after* I saw the ghost last night."

"I won't sleep in this house," Lisa admitted. "I've got my room over the barn. You're welcome to sleep there too, if you want." She nodded to us. "There's an extra mattress."

"It was so real, it totally freaked me out," the guy continued. "I was in that room at the top of the stairs, reading. When I looked up, this little girl was standing in the doorway. I was surprised because I didn't think there were any children here. Then she turned around and left. This morning I asked Jim who the little girl was. That's when he told me about the ghost. I was in her room."

"Other people have seen her, too," Lisa said. "She was murdered in this house. About twenty years ago, a mother was living here with her two small children. She couldn't afford to feed them, and they were starving to death, so she killed them both and committed suicide. No one has lived here since until us. The local people won't come near this place."

"I probably would never have believed it if I hadn't seen her myself," the newcomer said.

We slept over the barn that night and left early the next morning.

For the next three days, thick, gray rainclouds taunted us, sometimes dropping a light drizzle, always reminding me of our first night in the tent. With my body beaten and exhausted at the end of each day, I could not endure more discomfort, so I convinced Mike to stay at motels. They were cheap in the Catskills in early May, as tourist season didn't start until Memorial Day.

As if the physical challenge wasn't tough enough, I was also discouraged by my inability to enjoy the scenery. When I began the trip, I'd imagined that biking would be an opportunity to feel close to nature. Instead, my focus went no farther than the blacktop a few hundred yards ahead, the width of the shoulder that sometimes disappeared, or the ominous look of the sky. At the end of the day, I couldn't recall any fields, forests, villages, or towns we'd passed. At night, I closed my eyes and felt like I was still moving. The road haunted my twilight minutes between wakefulness and dreams, taunting me with yellow, pulsing lines and making me jolt awake as I felt I was falling off the edge of the pavement.

Each morning, I dragged my body out of bed again, ate my granola, washed my plate and spoon in the bathroom sink, showered, and stuffed the leftover bars of motel soap into my bike panniers. My body and my mind felt numb. I kept expecting it to get easier, but each day I dreaded it more.

Aside from my shoulders aching from hunching over my handlebars, aside from my hands sweating inside the leather gloves I wore to prevent blisters, aside from the cramps that randomly shot through my calves, thighs, and knees, the part I hated most was that I felt like a failure. I had taken on this bike trip with enthusiasm, spent time and money preparing for it, and now I wondered why the hell I was doing it. And this wasn't a passing thought. This was a reverberating theme that flowed through my aching muscles every minute of every hour. Each crank of the pedals drilled this deeper into my consciousness. I had time, lots of time, to review every failure in my life, with this being the pinnacle of them all.

Not trying harder to go to college was my first failure, and I blamed my parents over and over, anger seething, as I recalled the way my mother agreed to let me drop all my college prep courses in my sophomore year of high school when the material got tough. I'd begged them to let me try the courses even though college wasn't in their plans.

"I didn't think you'd be able to do this," she'd told me when I suggested dropping the classes, and those words had stung me, reinforcing my fear that I was not as good as the rest of those kids with brighter minds and richer parents. *It wasn't fair,* I argued back with her in my mind as my legs punched the pedals. *I could have done it, if only you'd believed in me, if only you had found me the help I needed to keep going. Instead you encouraged me to quit, and I've quit everything since that wasn't easy.* I'd quit living at home, I'd quit school, I'd quit boyfriends and Hubbard Hill, and now, most of all, I was desperate to quit this stupid bike trip!

Tears were streaming down my face when I reached the bottom of the latest hill somewhere near Howe Caverns. I jumped off my bike, threw it on the side of the road, and started walking, sobbing and angry. Mike turned to look back and stopped before turning around to bike back to me.

"I'm not doing this anymore!" I screamed. "I'm finished! I refuse to pedal up one more fucking hill! I hate your stupid idea! I'm sorry I ever agreed to this!"

Mike set his bike down and walked over to me, his eyes sympathetic. He tried to put his arms around me, but I knocked them away.

"It's no good. You can't just hug me and make it all better. I'm taking my stuff and hitchhiking."

"What about your bike?"

"To hell with my bike! I hope someone takes it. I don't want to ever see it again. I'm leaving it in the ditch."

I paced around on the pavement, angry still, but my tears had stopped.

"Look," Mike said, "why don't we just sit here for a while and take a break? Let's think about this before rushing into anything."

"Think? All I do is think. I want to stop thinking."

I started to cry again, and this time I let him comfort me. Mike kept me stable, I knew that. He was the level-headed person I needed in my life, the one who could get me to stop and reconsider before impulsively blundering into my next decision.

I agreed to sit, and we rested on the grass for a while. I talked about the thoughts I'd been having about my parents and how they'd screwed up my life.

"Parents are assholes," Mike agreed. "They have no idea how much they can mess up a child's life. That's why I'm never having children. They don't do it on purpose, though. I think they just don't know any better."

"Well, my parents kept me locked away from the world with a long list of rules to force me to become just like them. And I hated it. I had to get out of there."

"And you did," Mike pointed out. "You got out, and now you're your own person. You put yourself down too much. I know you are capable of a lot more than you think. Give yourself a break. This bike trip is tough, but you're doing it. It's tough for me, too. Sometimes I wonder if I can keep on going, then I look at how far we've come." He looked me straight in the eye, raising his eyebrow. "We've ridden almost two hundred miles! That's an accomplishment I'm proud of. And I'm proud of you." He pulled me against his shoulder and stroked my hair. "Look at the faces of the people we meet in the little stores we stop at. They all smile and ask about our trip and treat us with respect. We're doing something they can't do, and they know that."

I sniffed, wiped my eyes, and sat up straight. "I know you're right. And we're probably only another day from the next commune. I guess I can get that far, at least."

"Look, why don't we stop early today?" he suggested. "We've been making good time, doing over thirty-five miles a day. So what if we only do twenty? We'll stop, eat dinner in a restaurant instead of cooking in our room, relax, and read. Maybe even have a drink."

"Okay. I know I can make it to the next motel with a restaurant."

In our motel room, I watched soap operas and game shows, mindless dribble that I found amusing, allowing my brain to unwind. Our afternoon off from biking was like an afternoon off from my whole lifestyle. In the restaurant, I ordered a Manhattan from the cocktail menu because it sounded sophisticated, and I soon felt drunk. Since the only vegetarian item offered was iceberg lettuce and tomato salad, I said what the hell and ordered chicken cacciatore with pasta and sauce. I hadn't eaten meat in over a year, but instead of feeling repulsed and guilty I ate ravenously, wolfing the chicken down to the bones and wishing I had more. It felt good to abandon all my principles for a few hours; it was as if they had become a burden from which I needed a reprieve.

Later that evening, I opened my Carlos Castaneda book and immersed myself in his story. He spoke of a power deep within our navels that could be summoned to perform incredible feats, both spiritual and physical. As I considered how this could apply in my life, it occurred to me that I could use this power he described to overcome my biking trials—that I could turn this journey into a spiritual one, much like monks I had read about elsewhere who had endured hardship to reach greater enlightenment. I pulled out my meditation cards and delved into them, searching for inspiration. I encountered a Buddhist chant I had used previously for meditating, *OM Mani Padmi Hum*. Repeating it sent a feeling of tranquility throughout my body.

In the morning, I added additional words for my personal power-invoking chant: *OM Mani Padmi Hum, Use the Power, Sat Nam*.

When Mike and I set out on our bikes, I repeated the chant in time to my cycling. It was the perfect rhythm for pedaling, and instead of constantly changing my speed I kept the same, steady pace. When it started getting too difficult to pedal, I downshifted and maintained the pace to my chant. When my thoughts began to drift, I pulled them back using the chant, maintaining serenity while gazing at the road in front of me, rather than getting discouraged by worrying over what lay ahead. I was experiencing the ability to *Be Here Now*, breathing in . . . out . . . in . . . out . . . *Use the Power . . . Sat . . . Nam . . .*

Instead of feeling beaten, I felt fresh and energized. I no longer cared about how far we needed to go, what the curve ahead would bring, or if I would even reach it. I eased past Mike on a difficult hill, and never needed to stop. When we took a break, Mike shook his head in disbelief, and I explained what was happening. It was as if the books I'd been reading over the last couple of years about reaching a spiritual state of being were suddenly alive to me, like I was no longer reading theory but instead experiencing a shift in consciousness.

My mind was now clear of negative thoughts. I felt calmer. Instead of my thoughts controlling me, I was in control of them. The trip was only torturous if I allowed it to be. I could shape my experience to be positive. I didn't have to quit or fail like I'd done in the past. This energy inside of me had been waiting to begin anew. Now I understood I could control this power to pace myself through my journey.

That's when I realized I needed to let go of my anger at my parents for the ways I felt they'd failed me. Regardless of the past, they weren't in control anymore. What happened from now on was my responsibility, and if I wanted something to be different, only I could change it. My parents' vision of my value as a woman had been limited by what they'd been taught during an earlier time, but my view was exploding with possibilities, thanks to the women leading our liberation. I had become a strong woman with the ability to navigate these hills and valleys, and I could shut out the voices in my head that told me I wasn't capable.

Summoning my confidence, I got back on my bike and rode toward the hill I would climb to my next destination.

🌸 Epilogue

For most of us, the line between the destinations in our lives is seldom a straight one. That's how it was for me. The strength and vision I recognized during my bike trip at times grew foggy, and at other times buoyed me through to success.

Mike and I never found another commune. Instead, we rented a house near Hubbard Hill until our relationship broke down and we went our separate ways. At that point, I returned to Connecticut, and I have lived here since.

The next few years brought a marriage, a child, and a divorce, followed by a job reviewing medical claims, and then I finally began taking college courses at night.

In 1980, at the age of twenty-five, I enrolled full time in a technical school and, after completing, entered the world of technology as a computer programmer. I suspect my first boss hired me because I was a woman, as he had outstanding sexual discrimination complaints (now called gender discrimination) filed against him with the company. Those complaints helped to open a door for me, as well as the woman hired soon after me, on the previously all-male team. As the woman from Cornell Law School had pointed out to us at the Ithaca Women's Center in 1973, men aren't going to give up control voluntarily. It was cases that were tried in the '70s that set the precedents to strengthen those laws to where ordinary working women in companies across the country could access them for their grievances and be taken seriously.

While still in technical school, I sought the help of a therapist. I was suffering from depression brought on by a difficult relationship, along with struggling to survive while living alone on unemployment and hoping my car would hold together until I had a job.

My therapist suggested that my state of mind was the result of more than just this relationship and circumstance. "Each hurt triggers the unresolved feelings from a prior pain," she told me. For her to begin to help me, she explained, I needed to face my past.

"How do you confront your feelings?" she asked me.

"I write."

I went home to my apartment and began handwriting pages on a pad of lined paper, detailing the memories that were still vivid in my mind. In between coding programs and studying for tests, I wrote pieces that would morph into a book over time. I began to heal through writing, and to learn better ways of handling relationships through my therapy.

By 1992, I had experienced enough success in the technology industry to start a consulting business. With that came my first personal computer. A writer friend read my ramblings from 1980 and convinced me to transfer them to the computer and continue writing. That was the beginning of years of drafts, writing workshops, conferences, classes, and a writer's group.

By 2000, technology had shifted to the internet and my career had shifted to project management. Eventually, I became a deputy director for state government, managing a technology area in the male-dominated field. During those years, my career became more demanding, and I put the draft of this book aside. I retired in 2017. After retirement, I finally picked it up again and completed it.

For many years, I kept quiet about who I was at the time of this memoir. I feared that exposing my life would hurt my career or diminish my credibility in the workplace—or, worse, have a negative impact on my children when they were teenagers. As I read other memoirs, however, it struck me that I did not think less of the authors who wrote them. Instead, by sharing their stories, those writers had exposed their humanity and their struggles, and grown stronger in my eyes. I came to understand that by sharing my story, others might make sense of their own struggles and triumphs and be less likely to judge themselves or others harshly. Our lives are all laced with setbacks and mistakes, even tragedy, and at other times breakthroughs and joy. We all cope as best we can with what we have and hope to grow in the process.

Whatever path you take, it will change you. My evenings at the Ithaca Women's Center and the awareness I garnered from reading feminist writers and activists changed me. Books set me on a path to dive into a field I knew nothing about, where I knew of no female role models, and gave me the strength to push forward. I'd been taught to believe women should live limited lives, that we should follow the rules men had put in place for us—advice I thankfully ignored. My mother had preached that a woman didn't need an education, that she couldn't have a family and a career, which was one of the reasons I'd left home in the first place. I'd dreaded my future. The women's movement changed that for many of us. Like other women of my generation, I stumbled through the unmarked trails of marriage and family along with a career and responsibility seldom available to women in prior decades.

At times I still hear young professional women saying they are not feminists. They don't believe in "women's lib." They seem to be unaware that the only reason they have such myriad career options is because of those women who walked the feminist path so they could have choices. For those of us who straddled that change and witnessed the before and after, there is no denying the gifts handed down from those feminists who enlightened and educated us, who stood for change and helped create the culture shift that is still in progress.

Many of the people I've written about here have reentered my life over the years, often in random and unexpected ways. Some continue to be activists in one form or another, advocating for climate protection, peace, and human rights, including women's rights. Some have passed on. One of the reasons I continued to write this story over time was the desire to preserve these people as I remembered them, when youth, freedom of expression, and unlimited possibilities converged like nuclear fusion.

I think of the individuals from this time as my first tribe. They all played a role in taking me from my sheltered youth and transporting me to a larger world as a stronger and more resilient person. I am grateful for their place in my life, even the ones whose lessons were painful. I have forgiven the past hurts imposed upon me, and forgiven myself for the pain I imposed upon others, particularly my parents. We were young and had years of learning ahead of us.

I still have much to learn and more to experience. The challenges, like life, keep changing, but I know I am better equipped to handle them now than I have ever been. And on most days, if you asked me, I would tell you I am happy.

Acknowledgments

This book is an accumulation of years of work and input from instructors, workshop coordinators and attendees, a writer's group, and friends and family who shared their knowledge and support along my writing journey. It would be impossible to name every person who was there to lift me up along the way, so I apologize in advance for those I missed below.

First, I would like to thank Brooke Warner—coach, teacher, cheerleader, and publisher. She literally changed my life by enabling me to transition from an endless work-in-progress, bordering on volumes, to a completed book. By believing in my work, she inspired me to finally bring this out into the world.

I am endlessly impressed by the professional team at She Writes Press, including Samantha Strom, my project manager, for her quick responses to my questions as she moves my book through the publishing phases; Krissa Lagos, my editor, whose attention to detail goes far beyond my capabilities; and Julie Metz for her stunning cover design.

I thank my publicist Crystal Patriarche at BookSparks along with Tabitha Bailey and her team for their wide reaching effort and support of this book.

Karen Cwirka came along just when I needed her, providing in-depth reading and input at a critical moment that helped me reach the finish line. I will be forever grateful.

Without Laura Denino reading parts of my scribbled first draft and convincing me to type those pages onto my first computer and keep writing, this book would still be a pile of yellowing pages stuffed into a file cabinet. Thank you.

For several years, I participated in a writer's group that kept me moving forward with twice-monthly deadlines for submitting and reviewing work. A number of members came and went but Sandra Karakoosh, Karen Biernat, Lisa Calhoun, and Susan Omilian were there through most of it. These women read through chapter upon lengthy chapter, providing feedback and commenting on the evolution of my story as we pulled each other along. Thank you for being my readers and keeping me motivated. I learned from all of you.

Marcia Olsson, Nancy Teed, Maria Matarazzo, Claudia Traskos, Amanda LaPlant, Pauline Kendall, Mary Meggie, Pam Civiello, and Anne Hughes Smith were each my early and later readers. They offered support, feedback, and encouragement, despite their busy lives. Many thanks to all of you.

I am indebted to the consistency and dedication of Tammy Delatorre, a talented writer who runs online writing sessions multiple days a week. These forced me to sit at the computer and keep on a schedule even when distractions were overwhelming. I am glad to know you are still there as I move forward with my new work.

Going back, I must thank my seventh grade English teacher, Jerry Hilliard, who believed in my work enough that he submitted a poem of mine to the *Hartford Courant*; they published it, gifting me with my first opportunity to see my words in print.

I attended a number of writing conferences and workshops to learn craft and stay inspired. Those that had the greatest impact on me were the International Women's Writing Guild Summer Writers Conference and the Iowa Summer Writing Festival, which I would highly recommend to others. There were many individual workshops or instructors from other conferences that stand out in my experiences as well—Linda Joy Myers, Katha Pollit, Cynthia Huntington, and Amy Ferris, to name a few.

For the women I met at the Ithaca Women's Center so many years ago, whose names I cannot recall, who imparted their wisdom, shared their experiences, and taught me to believe it was possible for women to change the world if we supported one another, I thank you for changing my world.

Most of all, I want to thank my husband, Richard, who has provided his endless support for my work. He has cooked lunches and dinners while I typed, and entertained himself on vacations while I sat in a quiet room with a laptop. When I traveled to conferences or spent evenings in writing groups, he never complained about his extra responsibilities, even when our children were small. He gave me the freedom I have always needed to be myself while loving me unconditionally, and even promised not to read my book until I was done so I would not feel constrained by imagining his reaction. He is the love of my life.

About the Author

photo © Karen St. Denis-Piazza Photography

Sharon Dukett has been a computer programmer, deputy director in state government, cocktail waitress, and project manager (PMP certified), and she has designed and embroidered handmade clothing. She travels extensively, using loyalty points and avoiding tourist traps. When she is home, she and her husband live in central Connecticut in a house he built that overlooks the Connecticut River—the house where they raised their family. When not writing or blogging, she is reading, skiing, biking, golfing, spending time with family and friends, creating clutter, and committing to more activities than she probably should. She loves reading memoir from a variety of backgrounds—to learn how others feel, experience life, and deal with their struggles. *No Rules* is her debut memoir.

www.sharondukett.com

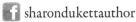 sharondukettauthor

 @travelsed

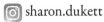 sharon.dukett

Suggested Discussion
Questions for Readers

1. What aspects of the author's story do you most relate to?

2. How is the era the author describes different from the one you experienced as an older teenager? How might this story be different if it happened today?

3. How did your life as a teenager compare with that of the author's? What might you have done in her situation, knowing your future was limited?

4. Reading this story, did you believe the author was being honest? Were there points where you thought she over-shared or you wish she'd filled in the gaps more completely?

5. What was your reaction to Sharon's decisions throughout this story? Did you find any of them disturbing? Compelling? How might you have handled yourself at her age?

6. What other characters in the story are the most memorable and why?

7. Was there something you found especially surprising about this story, or about a particular scene?

8. How does Sharon shape the events in her life? When does she give that control to others? Does that work in her favor, or against her?

9. What do you think the author's life would have been like if she had not left home when she chose to?

10. Did you have preconceived opinions about this era and the people who lived it before reading the book? Did the book affect those opinions?

11. Was there a time in your life when you questioned religion? Did you experience events, as the author did, that strengthened, weakened, or changed those beliefs?

12. Is there a lesson you can take away from this story? What did you find yourself thinking about at the end?

SELECTED TITLES FROM SHE WRITES PRESS

She Writes Press is an independent publishing company founded to serve women writers everywhere. Visit us at www.shewritespress.com.

Hippie Chick: Coming of Age in the '60s by Ilene English. $16.95, 978-1631525865. After sixteen-year-old Ilene English, the youngest of six, finds her mother dead in the bathroom, she flies alone from New Jersey to San Francisco, embarking upon a journey that takes her through the earliest days of the counterculture, psychedelics, and free love, on into single parenthood, and eventually to a place of fully owning her own strengths and abilities.

Home Free: Adventures of a Child of the Sixties by Rifka Kreiter. $16.95, 978-1631521768. A memoir of a young woman's passionate quest for liberation—one that leads her out of the darkness of a fraught childhood and through Manhattan nightclubs, broken love affairs, and virtually all the political and spiritual movements of the sixties.

You Can't Buy Love Like That: Growing Up Gay in the Sixties by Carol E. Anderson. $16.95, 978-1631523144. A young lesbian girl grows beyond fear to fearlessness as she comes of age in the '60s amid religious, social, and legal barriers.

All the Ghosts Dance Free: A Memoir by Terry Cameron Baldwin. $16.95, 978-1-63152-822-4. A poetic memoir that explores the legacy of alcoholism and teen suicide in one woman's life—and her efforts to create an authentic existence in the face of that legacy.

Not a Poster Child: Living Well with a Disability—A Memoir by Francine Falk-Allen. $16.95, 978-1631523915. Francine Falk-Allen was only three years old when she contracted polio and temporarily lost the ability to stand and walk. Here, she tells the story of how a toddler learned grown-up lessons too soon; a schoolgirl tried her best to be a "normie," on into young adulthood; and a woman finally found her balance, physically and spiritually.

Times They Were A-Changing: Women Remember the '60s & '70s edited by Kate Farrell, Amber Lea Starfire, and Linda Joy Myers. $16.95, 978-1-938314-04-9. Forty-eight powerful stories and poems detailing the breakthrough moments experienced by women during the '60s and '70s.

CPSIA information can be obtained
at www.ICGtesting.com
Printed in the USA
JSHW031228121122
33006JS00004B/16

9 781631 528569